Victorian Engravings

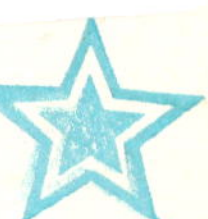

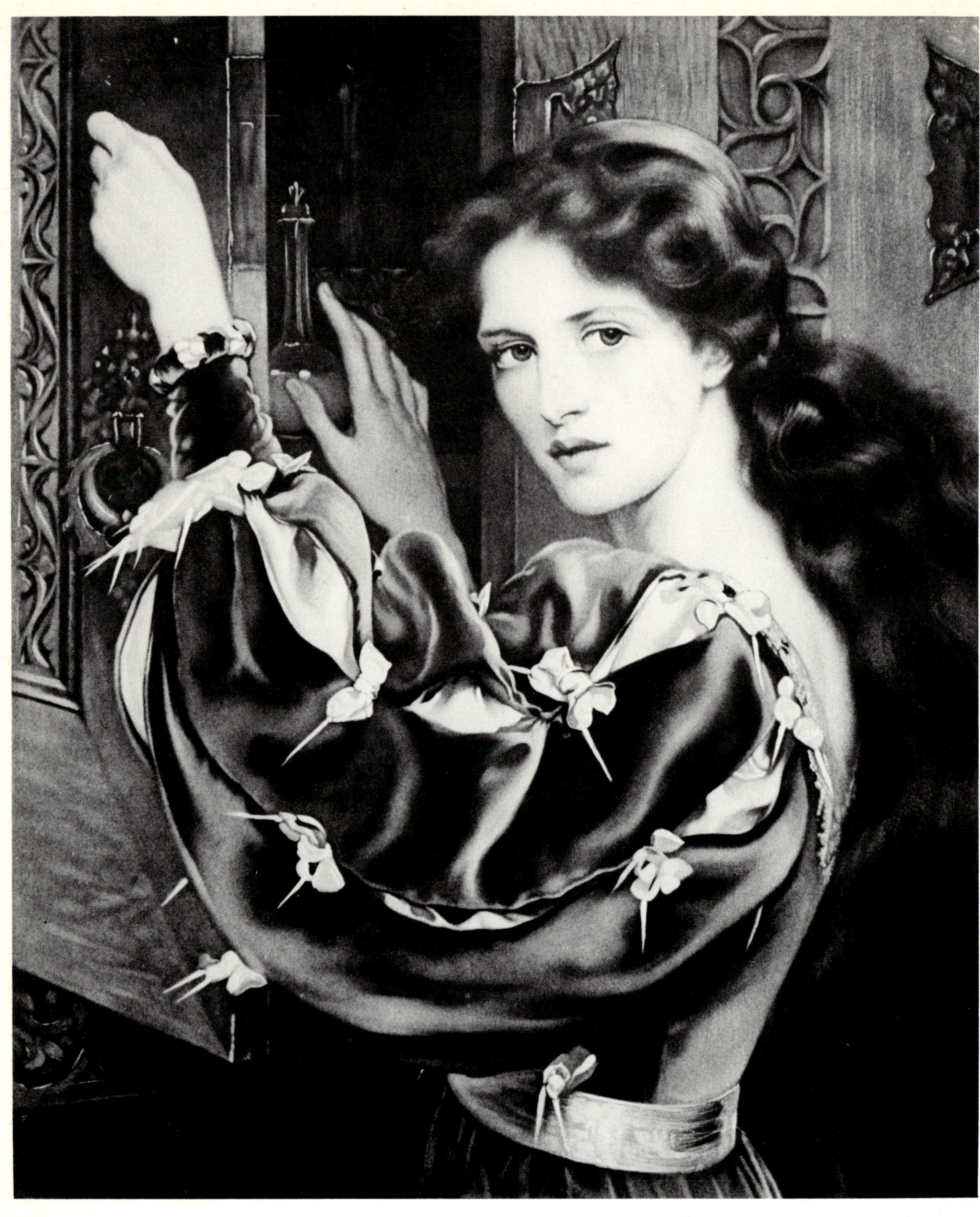

Thomas G. Appleton *The Love Philtre* mezzotint
After the painting by William Wontner, published by Henry Graves in 1895 and declared to the
Printsellers' Association

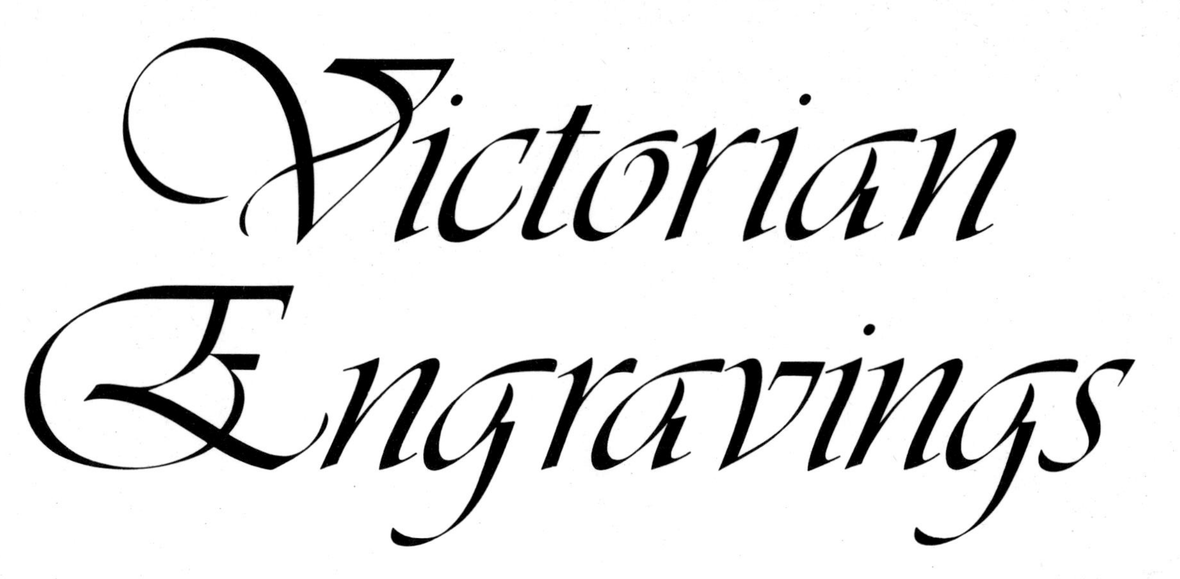

Victorian Engravings

RODNEY K. ENGEN

edited by Hilary Beck

ACADEMY EDITIONS · LONDON/ST. MARTIN'S · NEW YORK

Acknowledgments:
The author wishes to acknowledge his debt to Mr. William Plomer and the staff of Thos. Agnew and Sons; Mr. Frank Dickinson and the staff of the Department of Prints and Drawings and the Library, Victoria and Albert Museum; The Witt Photographic Library; and the assistance of Richard Wells in the preparation of this book. The exhibition catalogue *Victorian Engravings*, H.M.S.O. 1973, by Hilary Beck was also helpful.
I also record my grateful thanks to The Victoria and Albert Museum for permission to photograph many of the works produced here.

First published in Great Britain in 1975 by
Academy Editions 7 Holland Street London W8

SBN cloth 85670 225 0
SBN paper 85670 220 X

Copyright © Academy Editions 1975. All rights reserved

First published in the U.S.A. in 1975 by St Martin's Press Inc.
175 Fifth Avenue New York N.Y. 10010

Library of Congress Catalog Card Number 74-83428

Printed and bound in Great Britain at
Burgess & Son (Abingdon) Ltd.

Introduction

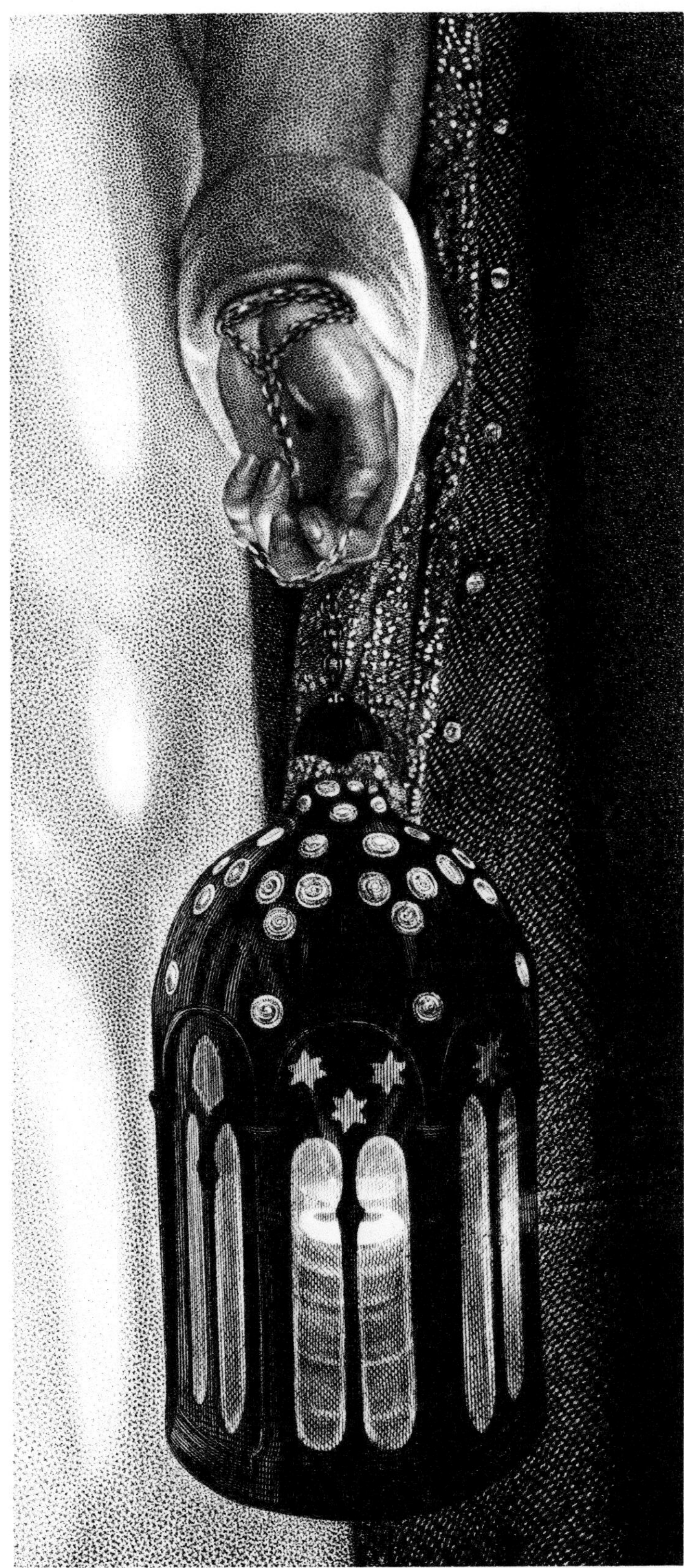

William Henry Simmons   *The Light of the World* (detail)
line and stipple engraving

Walls without pictures are like houses without windows; for pictures are loopholes of escape to the mind, leading it to other scenes and spheres, as it were through the frame of an exquisite picture, where the fancy for the moment may revel, refreshed and delighted. Pictures are consolers of loneliness; they are a sweet flattery to the imagination; they are a relief to the jaded mind; they are windows to the imprisoned thought; they are Books; they are Histories and Sermons. They make up for the want of many other enjoyments to those whose life is passed amidst the smoke and din, the bustle and noise of an over-crowded city.

(Gilbert, from *Catalogue of Engravings*, Frost & Reed Ltd.)

Victorian reproductive prints, whether engraved, etched or lithographed, mirrored a prosperous, nationalistic people who were eager to decorate their homes and clothe their families according to the latest fashions. Apart from the trappings of surburban life, they wanted to conform to the manners and morals of the times. Victorian prints carried Victorian attitudes to every corner of the Empire. As a mass medium, the first of its kind, these engravings fulfilled a social rather than an artistic function. The print industry boomed in response to this social need, and its huge financial success had little to do with a love of art. Engravers during this period were condemned to work for the satisfaction of the publishers and the public, and abandon the fine traditions of their craft.

The wide range of subjects engraved provide a fascinating documentary of Victorian life and times. Domestic pets, women's fashions, public transport, seaside resorts and country churchyards describe a people who believed in moral rectitude, military heroism, patriotism and 'the common man'. The rising demand for illustrated periodicals such as *The Graphic*, *The Illustrated London News* and *The Keepsake* was evidence of growing literacy and a desire to know about current affairs. The Byronic mood of the early annuals, with their wood and steel engravings of Victorian femininity, gave way to a demand for large scale engravings less frivolous in character, which could hang above the mantelpiece with an air of prestige and sobriety.

Britain's prosperity grew with the size of her Empire. The population doubled in fifty years, and the rapid steam-powered industries and rising standard of living created a prosperous middle class. The printing industry did much to bring a common idealism to the lowliest of homes and foster an interest in literature, history and art. Regarding prints, George Baxter (1804–1867), pioneer colour printer and engraver, wrote:

While their artistic beauty may procure for them a place in the Royal Palaces throughout Europe, the prices at which they are retailed introduced them to the humblest cottages.

(C. T. Lewis, *George Baxter*, 1908)

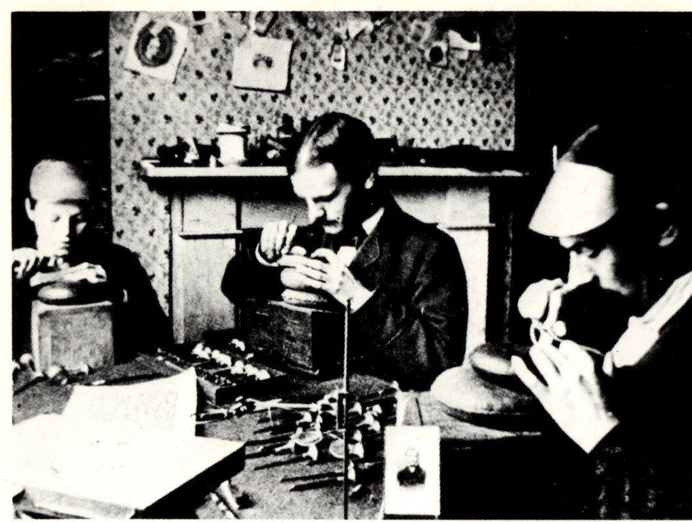

A master wood engraver's studio with apprentices, 1885
(*Victorian Snapshots*, 1939; photograph by Paul Martin)

The first criterion for engraving a work was its human interest. Just as Dickens, Trollope or Thackeray revived the narrative literary tradition of Defoe and Fielding, painters and engravers gave pictorial shape to the present and to the events of history. Engraved biblical stories and historical portraits hung in churches and offices providing familiar images and moral guidelines. One wonders how many mothers saw their own sons going off to the city in the print of *The Departure (Second Class)*, 1857, after Abraham Solomon. The public could easily identify with subjects drawn from contemporary life, and this guaranteed their immediate popularity.

Prints also influenced the development of a popular political opinion. Engraved portraits of national heroes like the Duke of Wellington, or the Prime Ministers Palmerston and Disraeli, and especially Queen Victoria, were revered. Prints depicting military achievements such as *Fight for the Standard*, 1861, after Richard Ansdell, and *In Memoriam* after Sir J. N. Paton (painted in 1858) reminded people of the sacrifices made for national honour at Waterloo, in the Crimea, or during the Indian Mutiny. Less idealised prints about war were prepared by on-the-spot wood engravers – the forerunners of press photographers. These reporters were also hired to record events such as the opening of Parliament or the Great Exhibition of 1851. These topical prints stemmed from the eighteenth century tradition of political comment in the engravings of Hogarth, Rowlandson and Gillray, but had lost the element of satire.

Prints provided an ideal outlet for the teachings of Church of England and the numerous evangelical movements and missionary societies. Considerable fortunes were made by painters and engravers who were commissioned by religious societies, or who adopted religious themes. Allegorical scenes such as *The Pursuit of Pleasure (A Vision of Human Life)*, 1864, after Sir J. N. Paton graphically reminded sinners of the temptations of worldly pleasure and the consequent vengeance of God. George Baxter stopped designing and printing popular genre subjects in order to engrave exclusively for missionary societies. Many artists and engravers including J. J. Tissot contributed to illustrated editions of the Bible. A set of such engravings by the Dalziel Brothers was published in 1881.

The Victorian neo-classicism of Lord Leighton, Poynter, Lawrence Alma-Tadema and Albert Moore, depicting statuesque beauty in luxurious and elaborate 'antique' settings, seemed to reflect the elite opulence and hauteur of the upper classes at the height of the Empire. Limited editions of engravings after these artists were published, as the Academicians believed that large editions would cheapen their work. As President of the Royal Academy, Lord Leighton presumably approved of art for the masses, providing it was not his own. Soon the grand classical motifs were adopted by advertising firms to give products an aura of nobility, strength and beauty associated with the classical past, such as engravings of Greek maidens awarding laurel leaves to an athlete representing cocoa. Classical fashions had come over from Paris during the Napoleonic wars and continued to influence the English through magazines such as *The Keepsake* and *Vanity Fair*, and *Women's World* which was edited by Oscar Wilde.

The production and sale of prints was a lucrative business which grew with the public demand. In the early 1820s individual engravers would spend years on one plate, working with only one or two apprentices, but the engravers' studios evolved into large 'factories', employing numerous apprentices who each practised a special skill and thus increased the speed and volume of production. Master engravers' apprentices worked for four or five years, often twelve hours a day, perfecting each

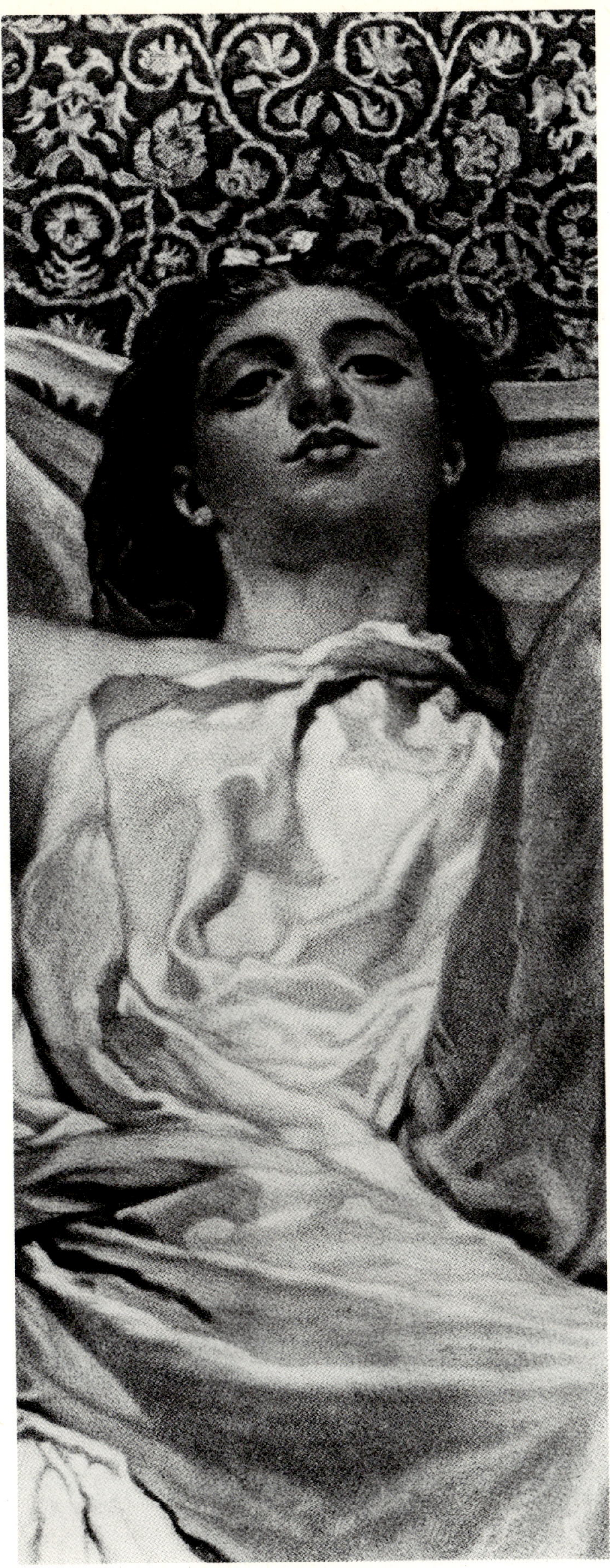

aspect of their craft until they became proficient in one particular skill. The 'facsimile man' copied the artist's design on to the plate and the 'tint man' was responsible for applying colour to the plate before printing. Other tasks included 'grounding' a plate for mezzotint, grinding the ink, etching or engraving a plate, and the final hand-colouring of the print if it had not been printed in colour by the 'tint man'. It was normal for a young artist to begin his career in an engraver's workshop. Both J. M. W. Turner and Thomas Girton began their artistic lives in hand-colouring sporting prints.

The engraver's studio was often a single room, in which a row of engravers were seated along a fixed bench which ran the length of the room. Each would have before him an eye-glass stand, a row of gravers, a gas lamp, a clear glass globe filled with water to direct and magnify the light for night work, and a leather sand-filled bag to steady the block. In the nineteenth century engravers lost much of their former esteem due to the influence of commerce, and were often reduced to employing deaf and dumb or unskilled labourers. Hilary Beck describes the prejudice against the increase of stipple engraving as the curious result of a change in shoe fashion which caused unemployed buckle-punchers to seek work as 'dotters', punching stippled backgrounds onto copper plates. However, engravers using apprentices and assistants on various projects simultaneously could acquire large fortunes. One engraver claimed to have amassed £20,000 solely through the work of others. When Walter Crane worked for W. J. Linton his tasks encompassed medical dissection diagrams, biblical pictures and the drawing of iron bedsteads for mail order catalogues. He subsequently illustrated Christina Rossetti's *Goblin Market*.

During the first half of the nineteenth century aspiring engravers had emulated the grand masters of their art – John Gilbert, John Leech, William Sharp, James Henry Watt – but the increasing pressure from new commercial techniques forced them to abandon these aspirations and turn to mixed methods. Good line-engraving created an exquisite system of dots and dashes, but this brilliance was lost when engravers were required to rival that new and uncompromisingly accurate invention, the photograph.

The publishers' requirements were at odds with those of the art critic, as John Ruskin makes clear:

> . . . so in lace, a certain delightfulness is given by the texture of meshed lines. Similarly, on any surface of metal, the object of the engraver is, or ought to be, to cover it with lovely lines, forming a lacework, and including a variety of spaces, delicious to the eye . . . so an engraver is to cover it with pleasant lines, whether they mean anything or not. That they should mean something, and a good deal of something, is indeed desirable afterwards; but first we must be ornamental.

The influence of photography caused those 'spaces delicious to the eye' to close up and the lines to loose their rhythm and become dull and lifeless. It is not surprising therefore that engraving fell into disrepute and that the Royal Academicians would not, indeed could not, make any effort to rescue the art from its demise. In spite of the illustrious examples set by David Lucas's mezzotints after Constable and J. M. W. Turner's collaboration with Charles Turner on the *Liber Studiorum*, 1806, engraving remained beyond the pale of the Royal Academy. In the mid 1850s, with the help of Royal patronage, the titles of Associate Engraver and Academician Engraver were introduced and Samuel Cousins was the first to receive these honours. In 1928 engravers were finally awarded full R.A. status, along with painters, sculptors and architects.

The popularity of Victorian prints was in no way affected by the attitude of the Royal Academy. On the contrary, it was the huge success of engraving that stigmatized it. Queen Victoria and Prince Albert set the Royal seal on this success by making their own drawings and etchings with the help of Sir Edwin Landseer. They also allowed, and possibly encouraged, numerous engravings of themselves, their children, their dogs and their life at Balmoral to be distributed among their subjects.

The distribution of prints was given great impetus by the establishment of the Art Unions, the first of which was formed in London in 1836. The Unions organized lotteries which offered paintings and prints as prizes, and they commissioned well-known painters and engravers to produce these works. They championed and shaped a uniform attitude to the arts, and claimed to be improving public taste. In this they failed, but they did not fail to accumulate public money. The sums of over £50,000 caused the government to intervene in an effort to stop this thinly disguised form of gambling, but the Art Unions were declared legal in 1844 and continued their influence until the end of the century.

The Printsellers' Association, founded in 1847 to register and control the publication of fine art prints, was another strong influence behind the boom in the print industry. By giving monetary values to prints, and particularly to proofs, they encouraged speculation. Members included publishers, printsellers, artists, and engravers, who paid a fee and a certain number of prints to the Association for registration and the use of the Association Stamp. All dealers had access to the Association Lists in which prices and edition numbers were published. This Association survived until just before the first World War.

Changes in technical methods dealt a serious blow to the small engraving firms. Wood engravers could not compete for the market in large prints for obvious reasons, and in the production of small prints they had to compete with the engravers of the small steel plates which produced a finer and more fashionable result and larger editions. Woodcut and wood engraving was the traditional and ideal method of book illustration, as the block and type-

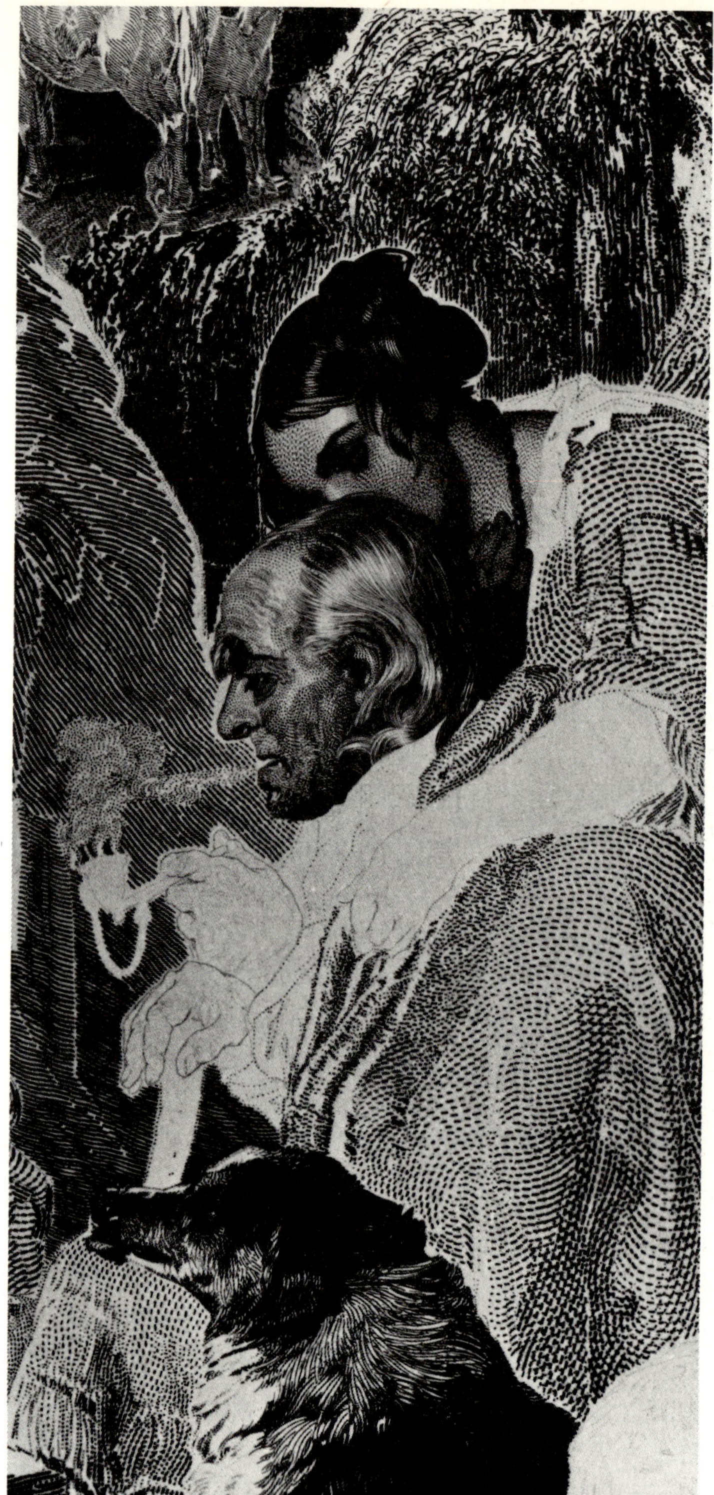

J. H. Watt *The Highland Drovers* (detail) etched state

face could be printed together in a platen press. Wood engraving remained popular into the 1880s for this purpose, and was used, for example, in Moxon's edition of the *Poems of Tennyson*, 1857, and William Morris's Kelmscott *Chaucer*, 1894.

George Baxter increased the popularity of coloured wood engravings when he introduced his patent printing method. A 'key' impression in a neutral tone served as a

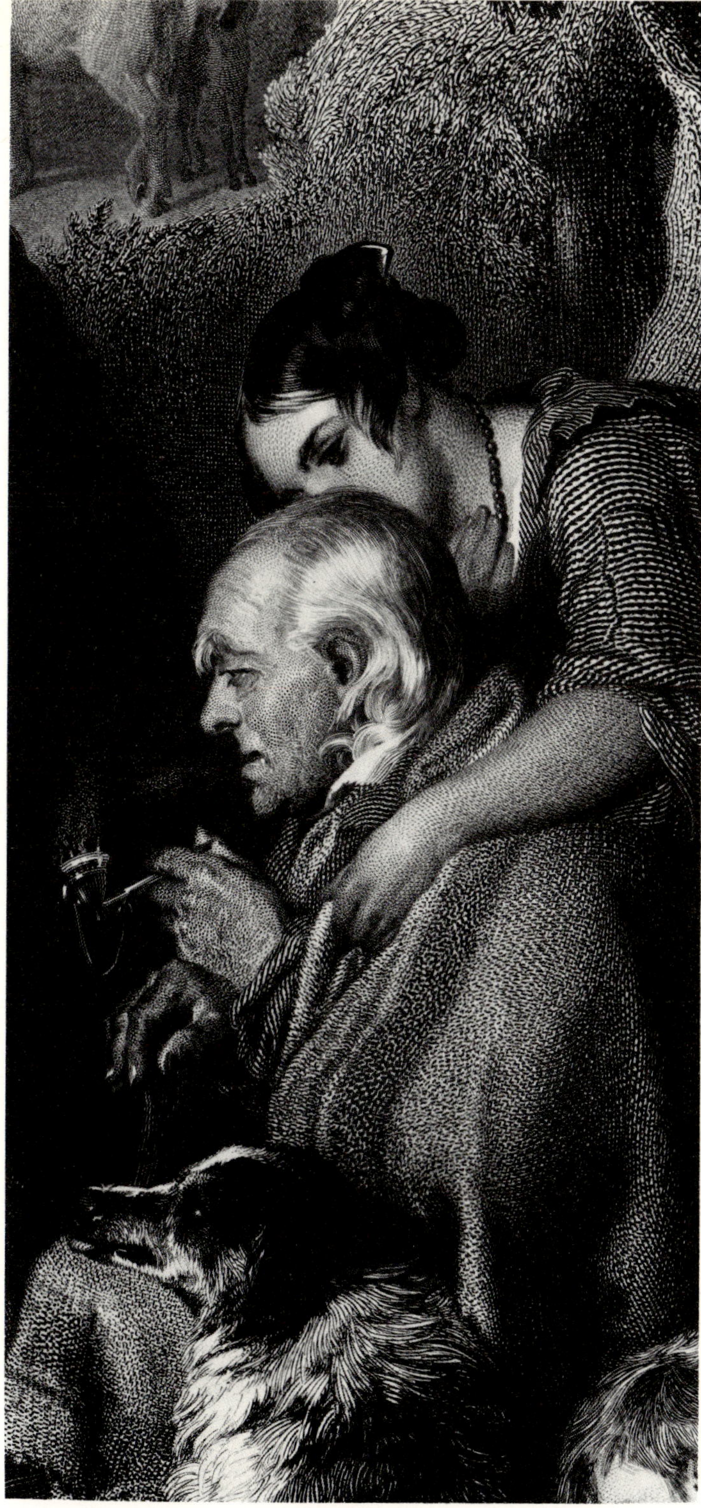

J. H. Watt *The Highland Drovers* (detail) engraved state
The print in the mixed style was published in 1838 after the
painting by Sir Edwin Landseer

guide on to which oil-based colours were applied in a
succession of fifteen to twenty individual blocks. The
skill of overlapping the blocks to create fine gradations
of colour produced prints like *The First Lesson*. J. M.
Kronheim later used eight to sixteen zinc and copper
plates, individually coloured with stippled flesh tones, as
a variation on Baxter's method. Edmund Evans used
subtle pastel colours for the children's books by Kate

Greenaway and Walter Crane in the 1870s, and introduced an unprecedented sophistication into colour
printing.

The use of lithography for fine art printing was
limited during the first half of the nineteenth century for
two reasons. Firstly, it was considered too facile for fine
art printing and suitable only for commercial purposes,
and secondly, there was always the danger of the stone
breaking, a danger which increased with the size of the
print. However, lithography could reproduce an original
drawing exactly, and it utilised a platen press. These
two characteristics were to be exploited in the search for
cheaper, faster and more accurate methods of reproduction. They had to find a way of applying the litho-
graphic techniques to steel plates so that large editions
could be printed. This was achieved by the use of
chemicals instead of wax and water and the use of
photography in transfering the subject. Hence the
development of photo-lithography which, with the addition of colour, became chromo-lithography. Chromo-
lithography was a sophisticated development from the
lithotints introduced by Charles Hullmandel and T. S.
Boys in the 1830s, and appeared in such works as Owen
Jones's *Grammar of Ornament*. The work of Henry Fox
Talbot on photo-lithography meant that designs could
be enlarged or reduced, and this added another dimension to print production.

The soft steel plate had been first introduced by
Thomas Lupton in 1822. Steel drastically altered the
quality of engraving but increased the quantity of prints.
It was not suitable for the interpretation of landscape,
but people were no longer interested in landscape as they
were now living in cities; they wanted interiors,
portraits of themselves and their animals, and above all
pictures of topical interest. Steel was suitable for subjects
such as these. The rich tone and dazzling highlights of
copper plate engraving degenerated into uniform, grey
tones and harsh machine-like lines. In fact it was often
necessary to use machines on steel-faced plates, as they
were so hard to work.

Etching had traditionally been the quickest method
of working on metal for the fluidity of an etched line
allowed more freedom than that of line engraving or
mezzotint. It was customary for a Victorian engraver to
etch in his preliminary design before engraving or mezzo-
tinting. They frequently used acid on top of the finished
mezzotint in order to add rich, dark tones, which often
proved an unhappy combination. Large reproductive
prints produced by etching alone were not common
until they were popularised by foreign etchers such as
Emile Boilvin and L. Lowenstam, who copied the works
of Burne-Jones and Sir L. Alma-Tadema. There were
fine English etchers like Herbert Dicksee, but etching was
always the shorthand of painters and was a creative
rather than an interpretative medium. The school of
painters-etchers at the turn of the century is evidence of

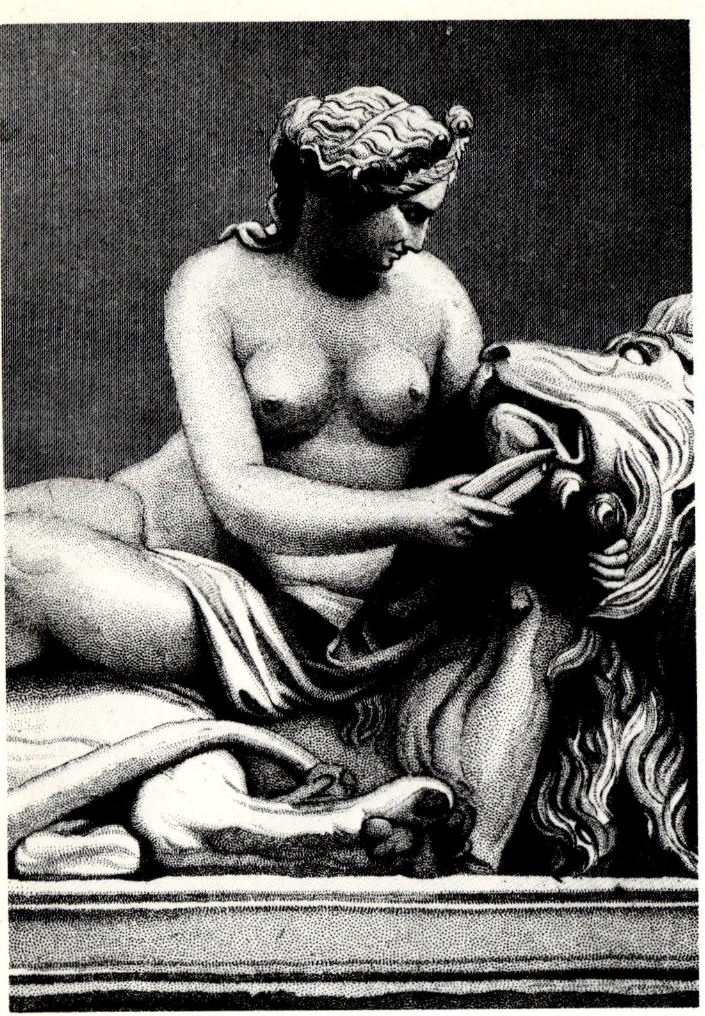

this affinity. James McNeill Whistler and J. J. Tissot belonged to this group and did a lot to unite English and French painting.

Mezzotint was the only method which involved working from dark to light. The plate was first roughened or 'grounded' with a rocker so that it would print black, then the roughness was scraped away to produce greys and whites. The soft tonal effects were ideal for imitating painting. As imitation was the essence of much Victorian engraving, this method was used as a base onto which line engraving and etching were added.

Copyright was a major factor in print selling. A painter's reputation was often decided by the popularity of the engraving rather than the success of the painting, and the copyright of a 'salable' painting was often a better investment than the painting itself. A publisher might acquire a copyright, publish a successful edition of prints and then resell the copyright to another firm at a higher price. Sir John Everett Millais sold his painting of a boy blowing bubbles to a dealer. The dealer then sold it to A. F. Pears Ltd., the soap manufacturer, who had it engraved as an advertisement with a bar of soap in the foreground, much to the chagrin of the artist. Nevertheless the advertisement did as much to boost the popularity of Millais as it did to sell the soap.

Much legal wrangling surrounded the transference of copyrights. A famous precedent was set when Henry Wallis's painting *The Death of Chatterton* (1859) was sold and engraved for *The National Magazine*. A copy was made by another artist who boldly exhibited it at the Academy. Wallis contested this, but the court ruled that once a work had been engraved there could be no further control on its copyright. Copyright values were manipulated in much the same way as stocks and shares. In 1873 Lord Leighton's painting *Moretta* was engraved by Samuel Cousins R.A. for £750 and published by Lucas and Sons. Their sales amounted to £20. William Agnew bought six dozen artist's proofs and sold them all in six weeks. In six months the prints were selling at five times their original price. Gambling with prints was further complicated by the variety of proofs available, which ranged from signed proofs on vellum through India proofs to lettered proofs, and all had different values. This practice led to absurd excesses. In the case of Holman Hunt's *Shadow of Death,* a total of 4,110 proofs were offered for sale. In order to counteract these abuses, Lord Leighton and many of his fellow Academicians were in favour of limiting the number of prints. Some artists, Burne-Jones for example, had the plates destroyed after only 250 or 300 prints had been taken.

Victorian engravings might lack the wit and satire of the eighteenth century and the sophisticated cynicism of the twentieth; their motives may seem transparent and their idealism naive, but they expose the real history of an age with unprecedented candour.

Lion in Love line and stipple engraving
From a daguerrotype by Beard after the statue by Guillaume Geefs (shown at the Exhibition of 1851; now in Brussels)

The Engravings

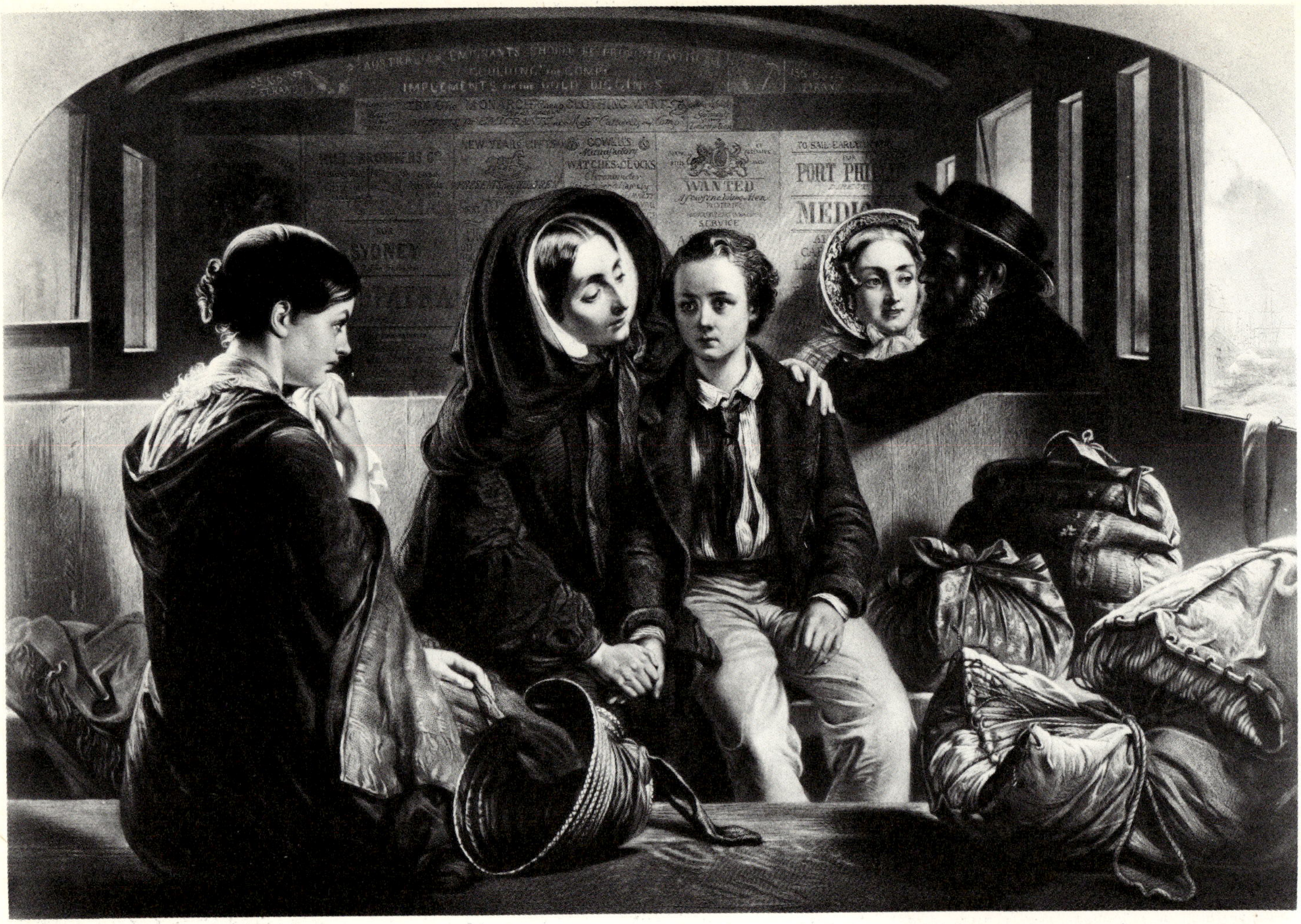

William Henry Simmons (1811–1882)   *The Departure (Second Class)*   mixed mezzotint

After the painting by Abraham Solomon (1824–1862). The painting was exhibited at the Royal Academy in 1854 with the subtitle 'Thus part we, rich in sorrow, parting poor', alongside its companion *The Return (First Class)*. It was published by Gambart and Co. in 1857, and declared in an edition of 225 pairs to the Printsellers' Association. Simmons was one of the most popular engravers of his day, with over 175 plates declared to the Printsellers' Association (1894), including works after Landseer, Millais, Frith, Paton and Tissot.

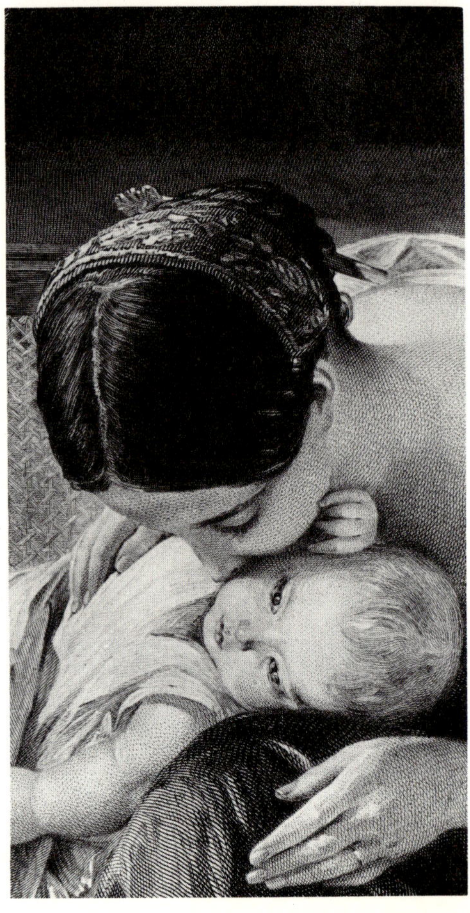

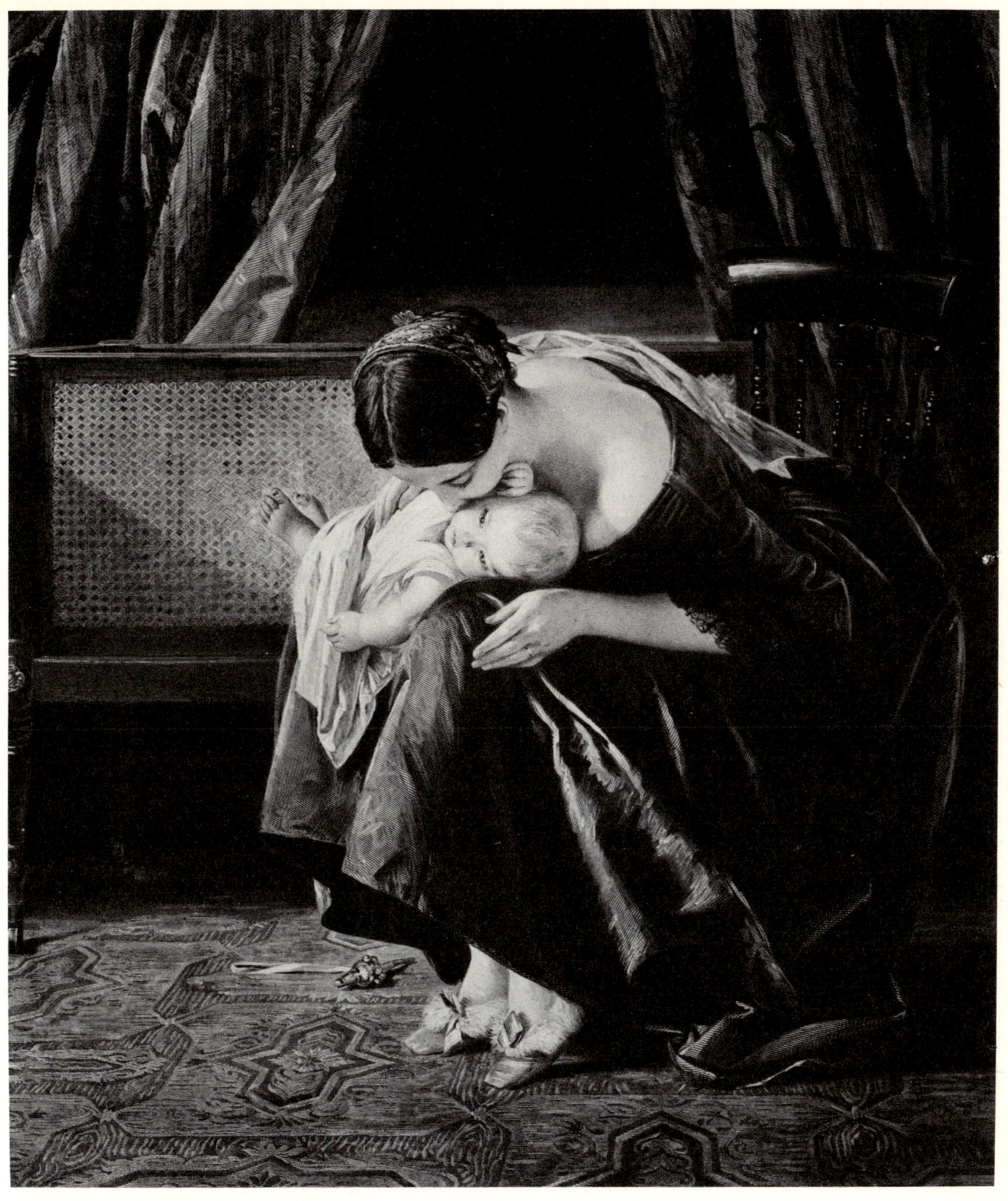

John Henry Robinson R.A. (1798–1871) *Mother and Child* (with detail opposite) line engraving
After the painting by Charles Robert Leslie R.A. (1794–1859). Published in 1853 by J. Hogarth. Robinson was admitted to
the Royal Academy in 1867 and became well known for engraved portraits after G. Richmond R.A. and his book illustrations.
His crisp style, with sharp lines following the forms of objects, recalls the techniques of seventeenth and eighteenth century
master line engravers.

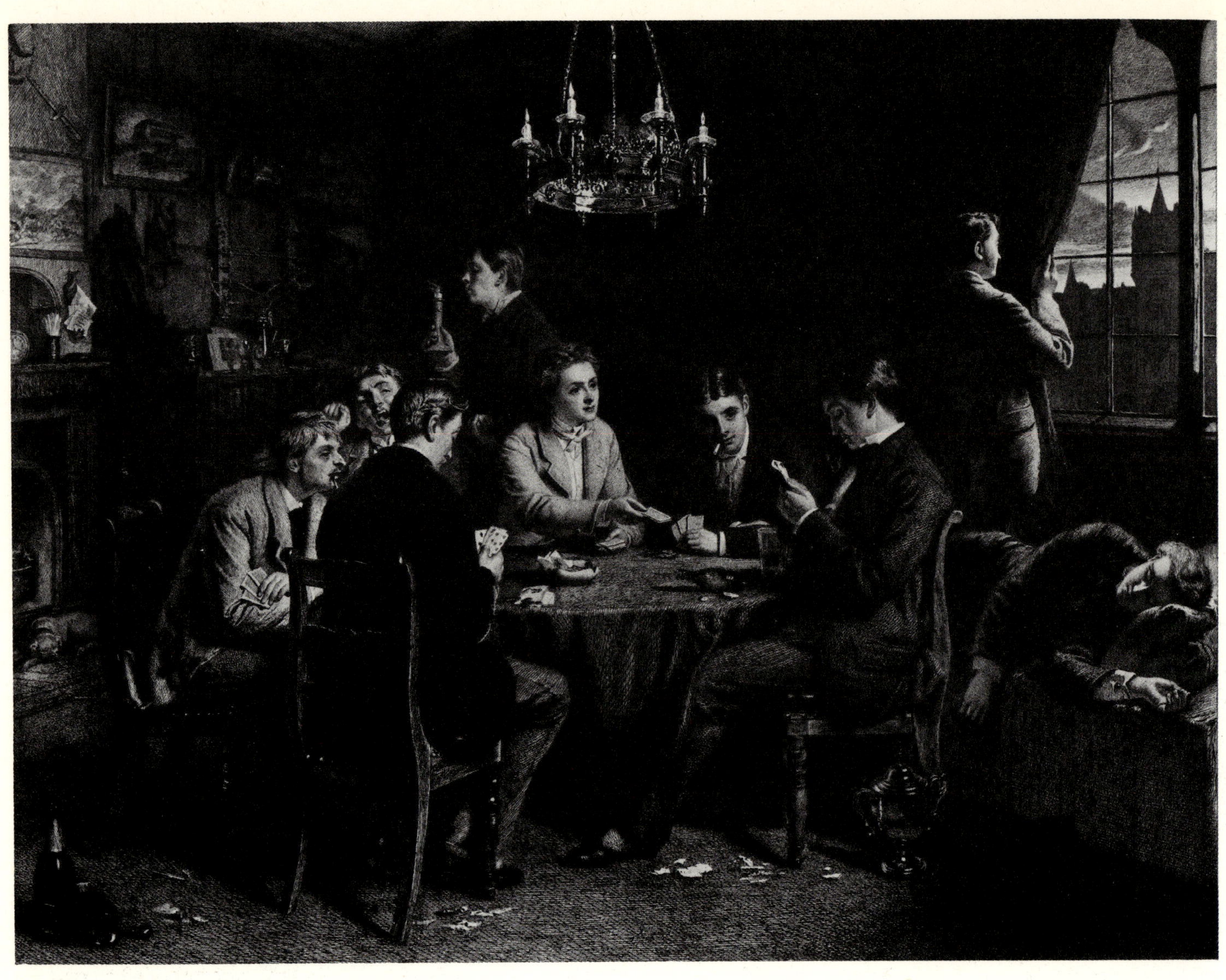

The Road to Ruin: College

Leopold Joseph Flameng (1831–1911)   *The Road to Ruin* etchings (PAGES, 14, 15, 16, 17)
After a series of five paintings painted in 1877 by William Powell Frith R.A. (1819–1909), published for the Art Union of London in 1882. Over 15,000 photogravure prints were also produced after the series, including the fifth painting entitled *The End*. Flameng was a Belgian etcher and engraver who created prints after G. F. Watts, Fildes, F. Sandys and J. Collier.

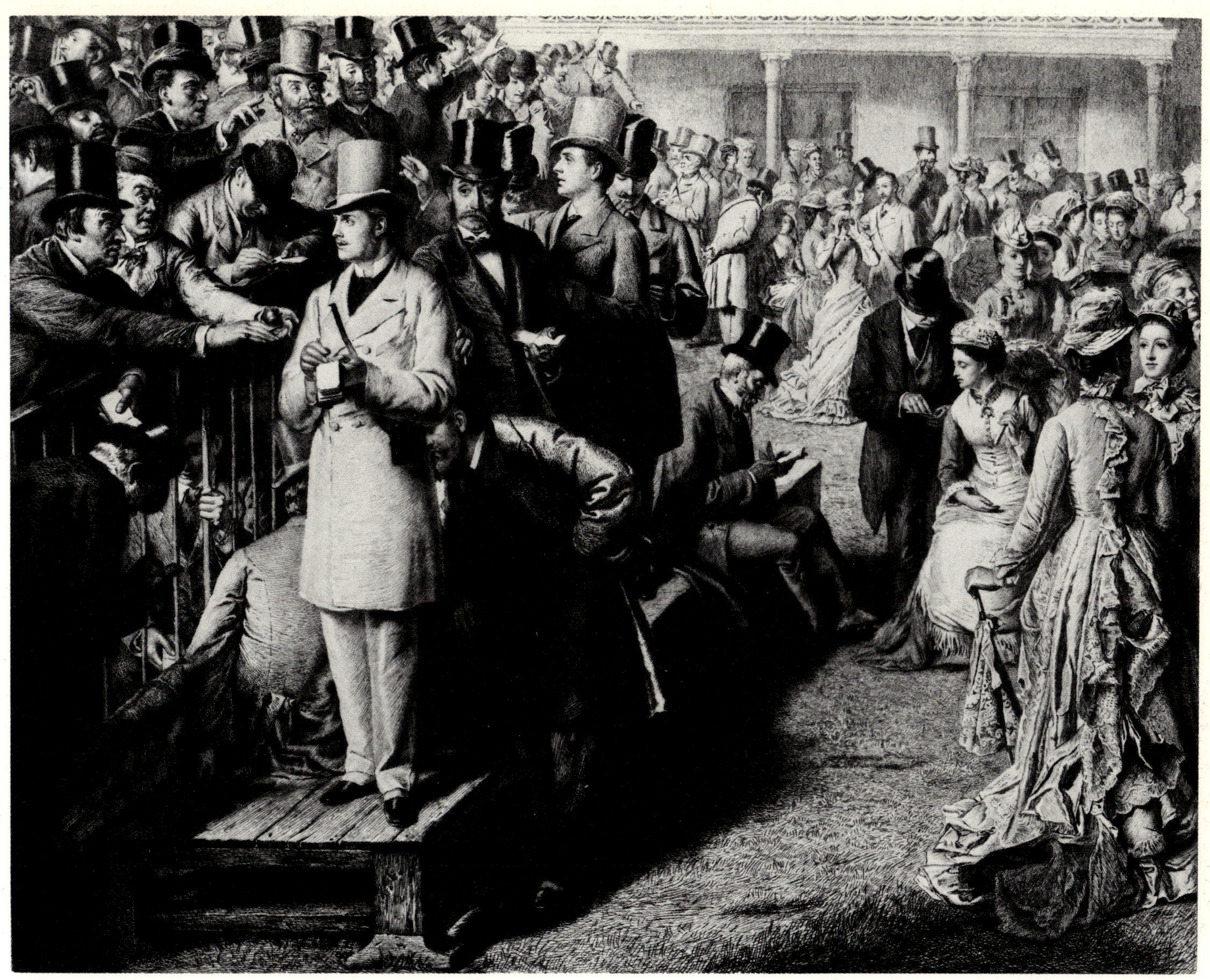

The Road to Ruin: The Royal Enclosure at Ascot

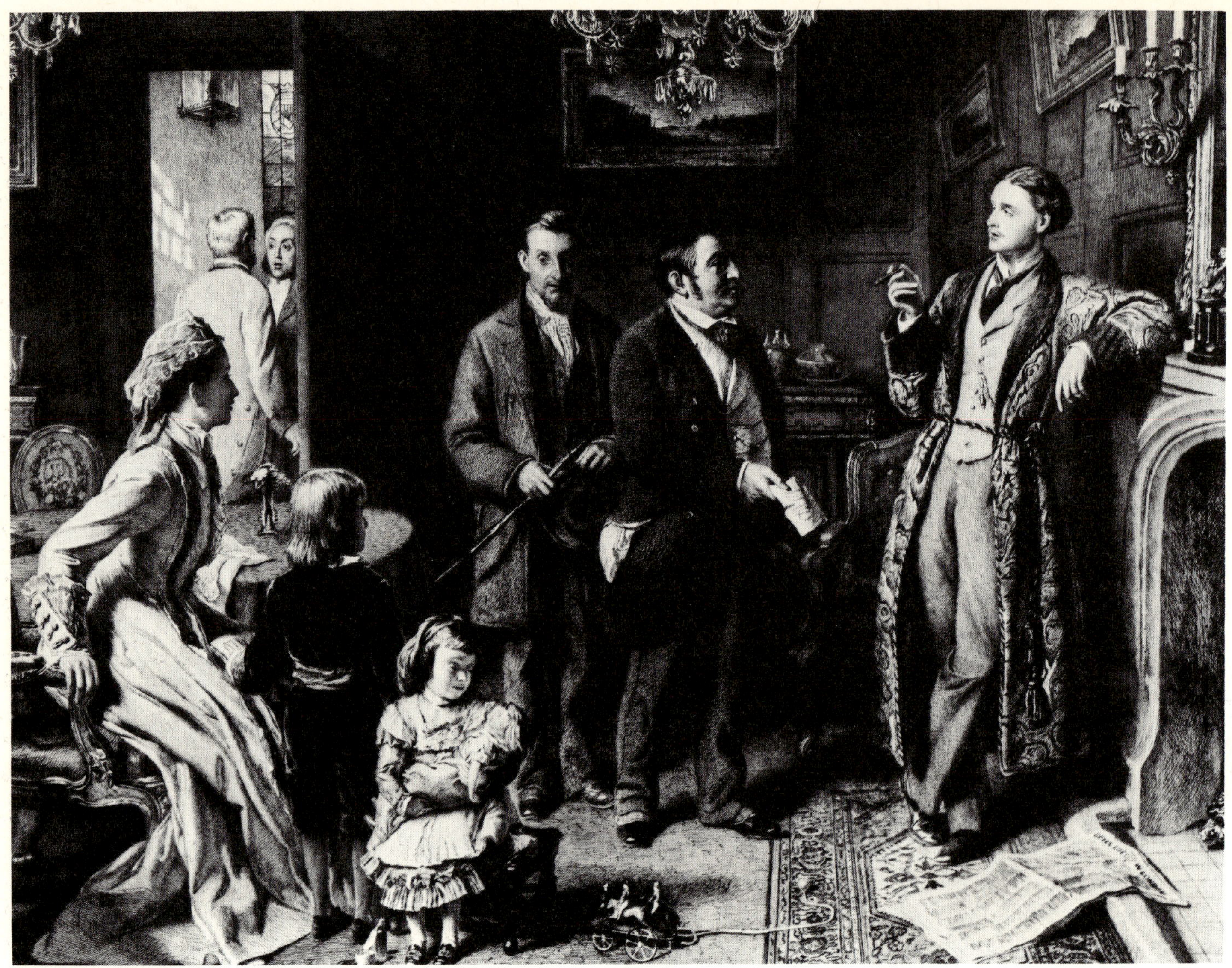

The Road to Ruin: Arrest

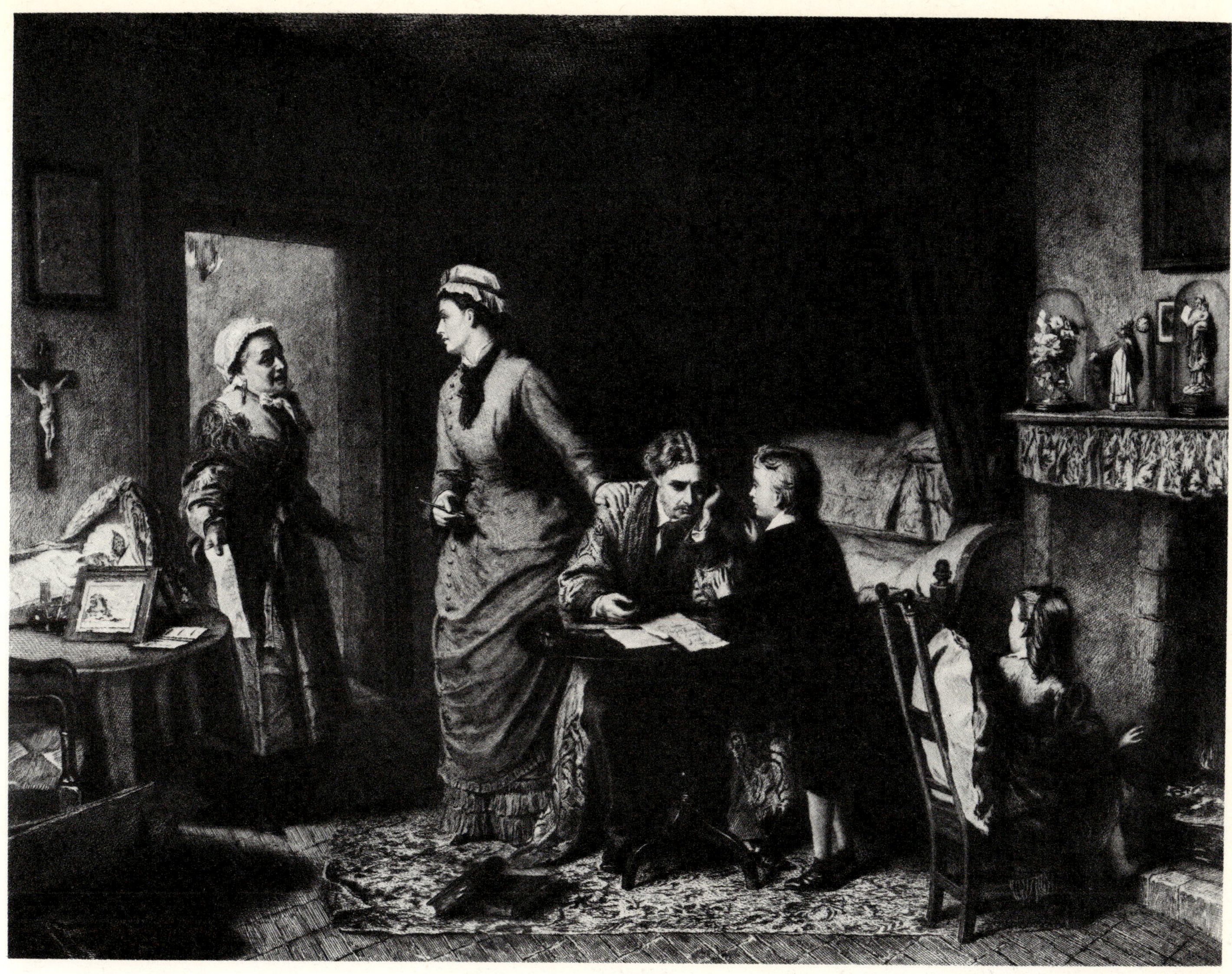

The Road to Ruin: Struggles

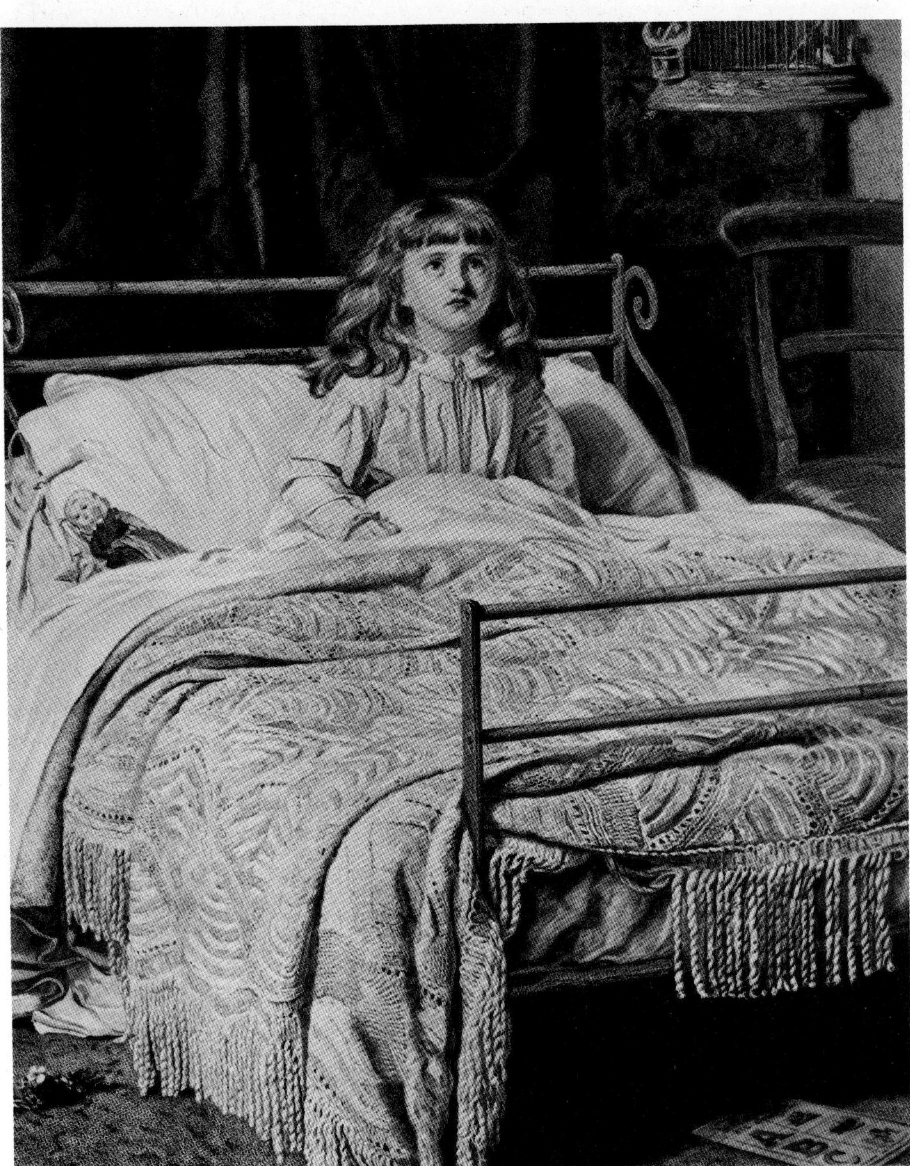

Thomas Oldham Barlow R.A. (1824–1889) *Awake!* mezzotint
After the painting (R.A. 1867) by Sir John Everett Millais (1829–1896). Published with its companion piece *Asleep* by Thos. Agnew and Sons, who bought the plate and copyright for the latter from H. Graves for £1,050. The agreement included six artist's proofs to be given to the owner of the picture, 'the usual number to the painter and engraver' and one each to members of the Agnew family. Barlow was a much sought after mezzotint engraver with over fifty-two plates registered by 1894 at the Printsellers' Association, including works after Frith, Landseer, R. Ansdell and J. Phillip.

William Holl, the younger (1807–1871) *An English Merry-making in the Olden Time* (with detail) line and stipple engraving
After the painting by William Powell Frith R.A. (1819–1909), published for the Art Union of London in 1852. Holl was the son of a prominent engraver. He exhibited twenty-two prints at the Royal Academy from 1860 to 1871 and engraved after F. Goodall, G. Richmond and J. Absolon in the stipple technique, perfecting the use of a meshwork of tiny dots to gain rich depth of surface.

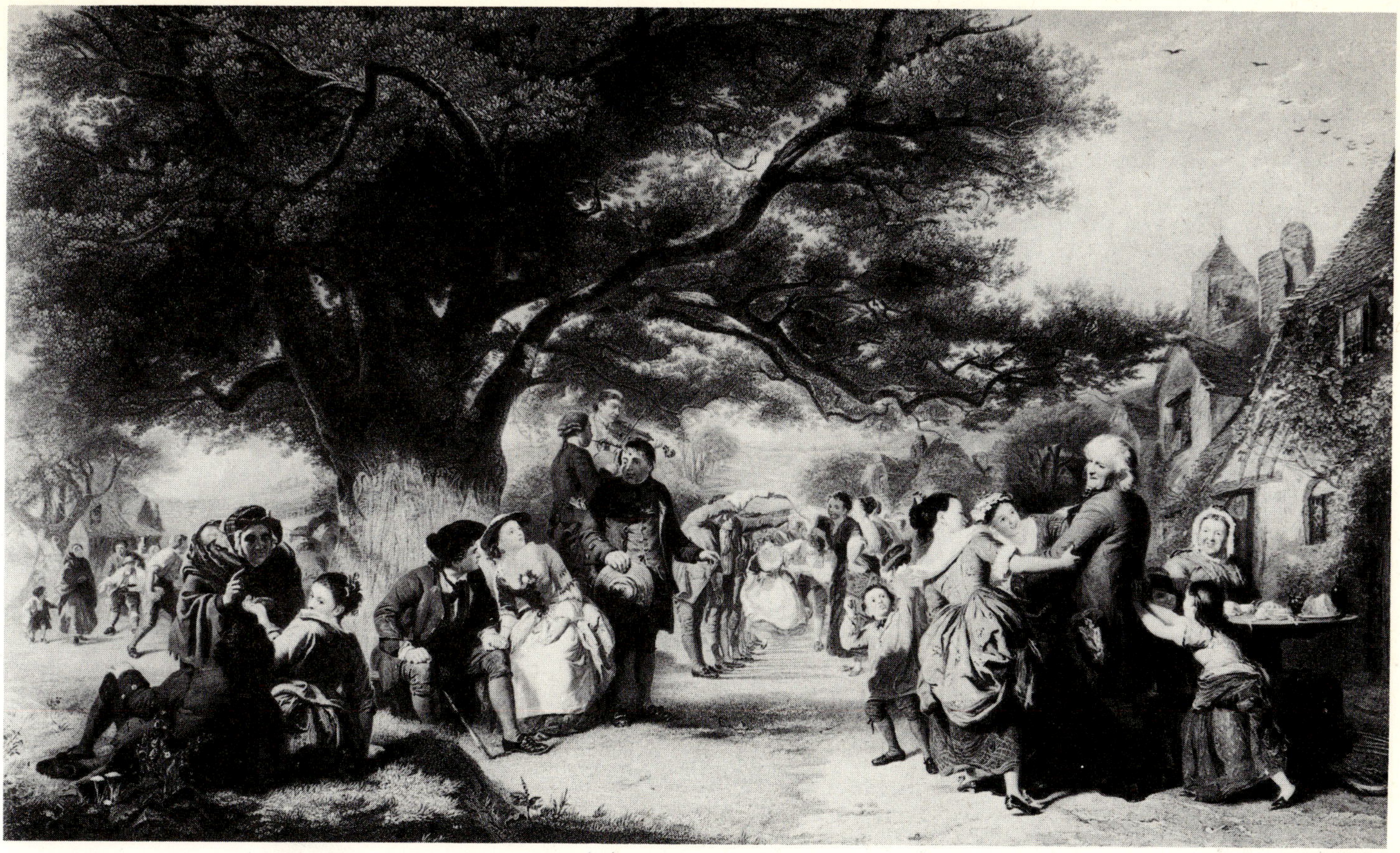

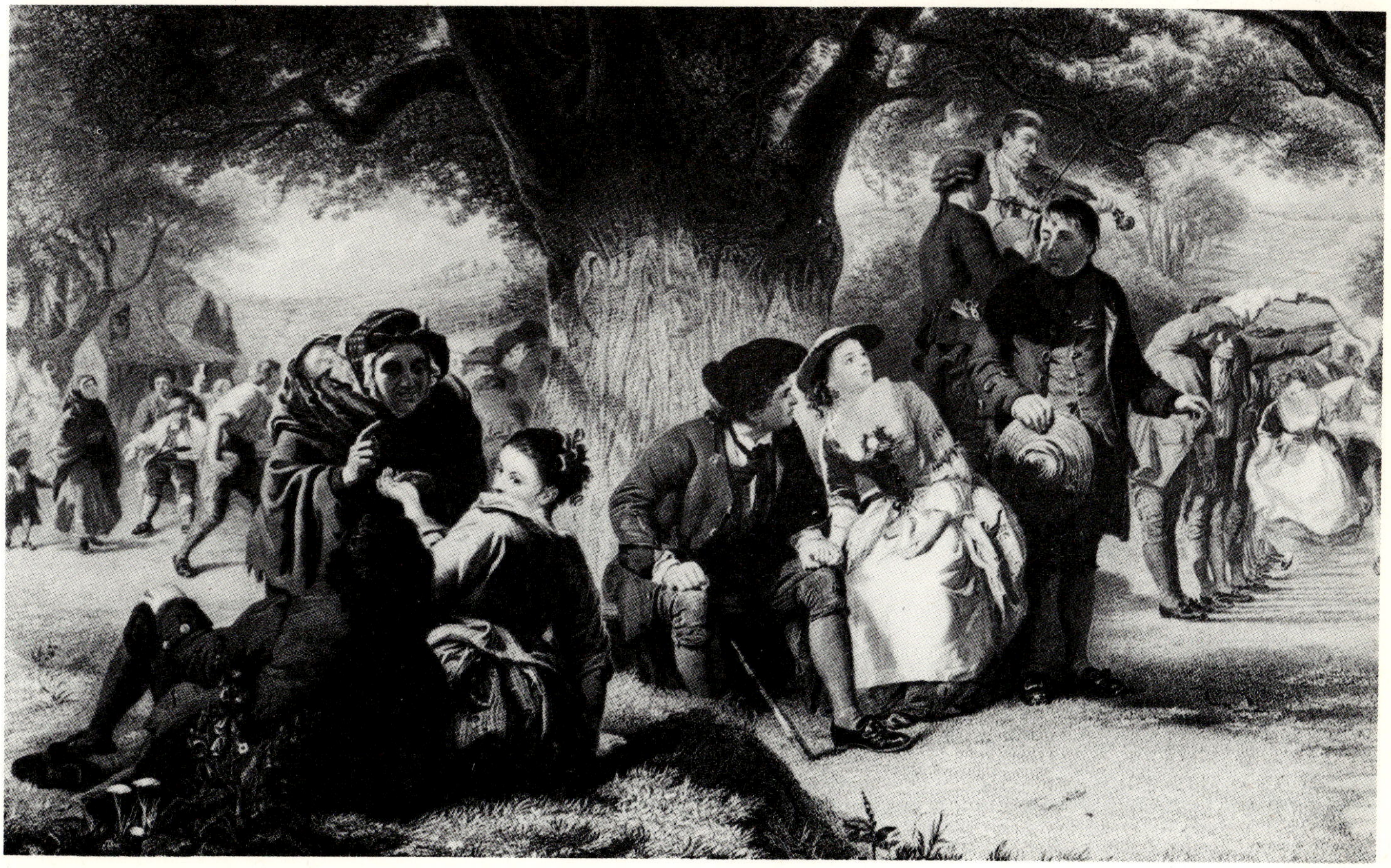

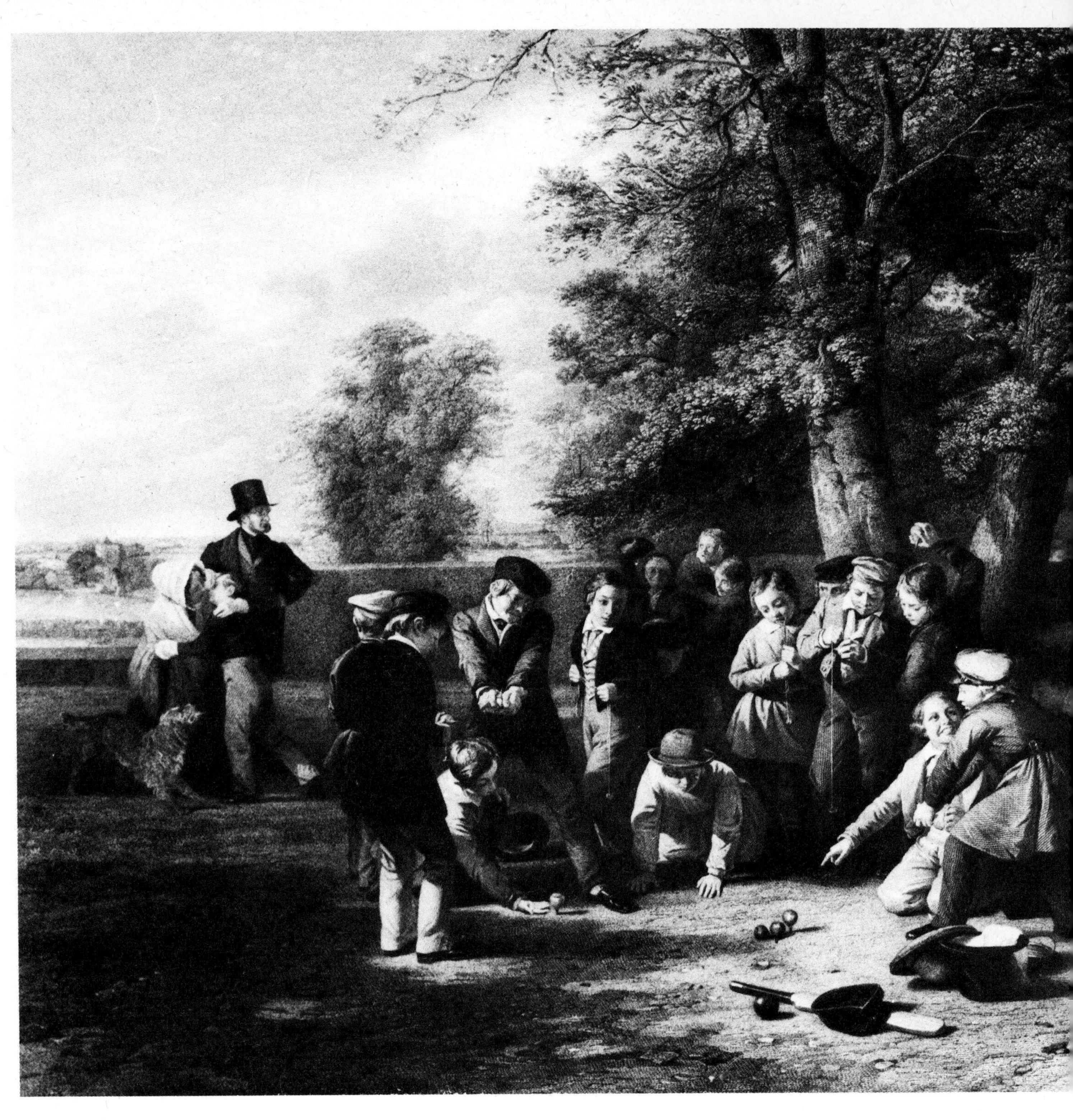

Ferdinand Jean Joubert F.S.A. (1810–1884) *The Playground* line engraving
After the painting by Thomas Webster R.A. (1800–1886), published for the Art Union of Glasgow in 1859. The subject indicates the strong link between Dutch seventeenth-century genre scenes and the popularity of recorded aspects of daily Victorian life. Joubert was one of the many French engravers who studied in London, and exhibited at the Royal Academy from 1855 to 1881, including works after Poynter, R. Thornburn and E. U. Eddis.

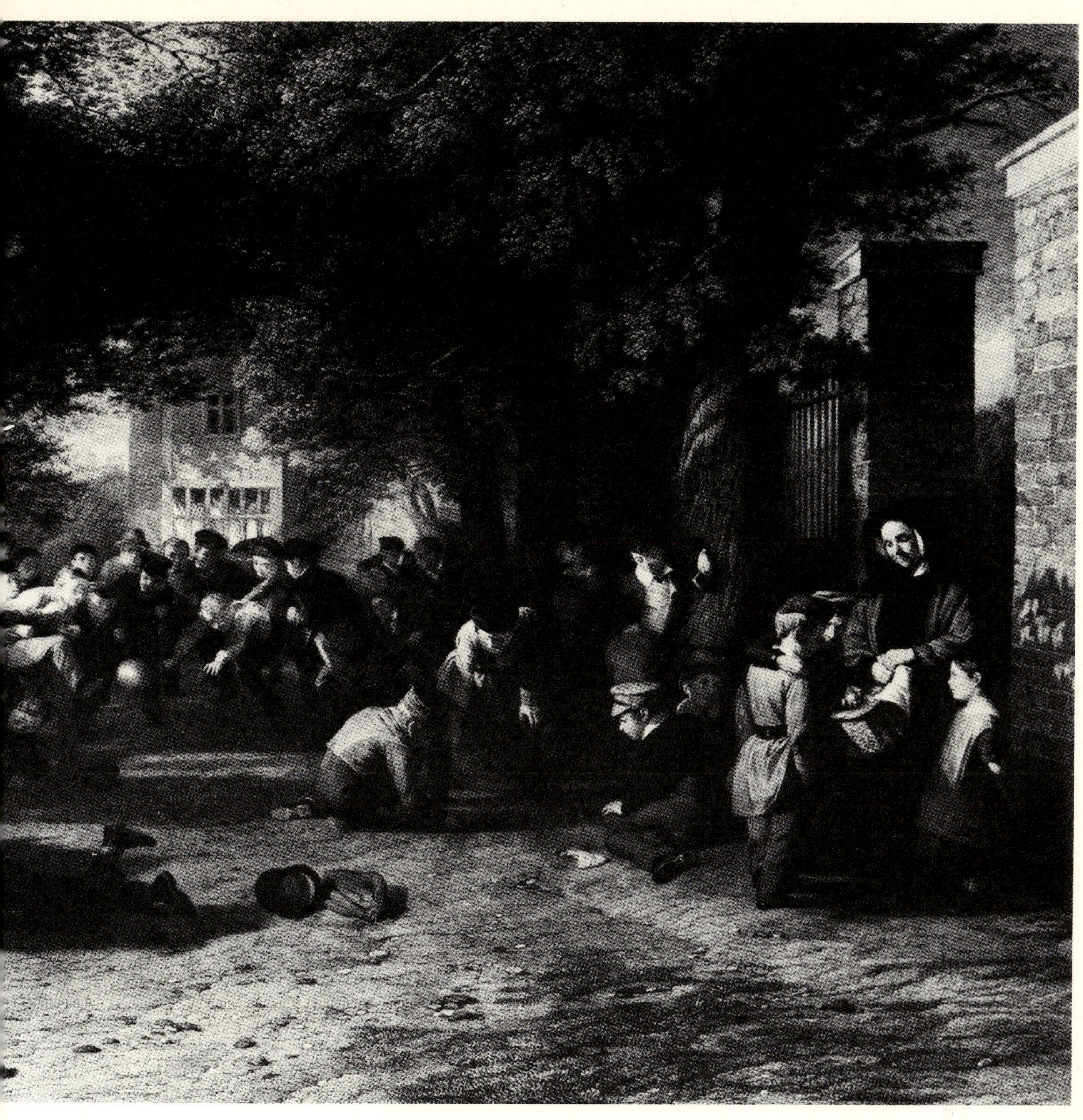

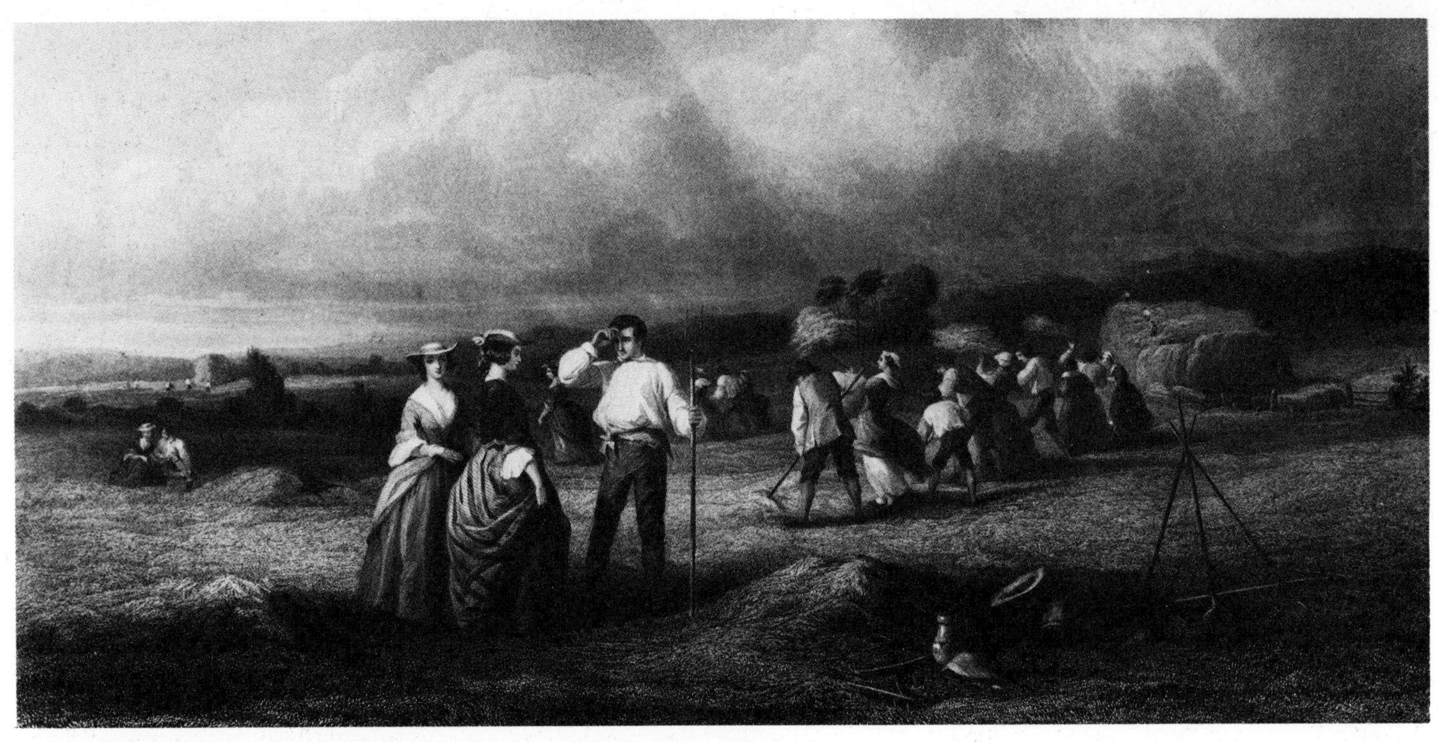

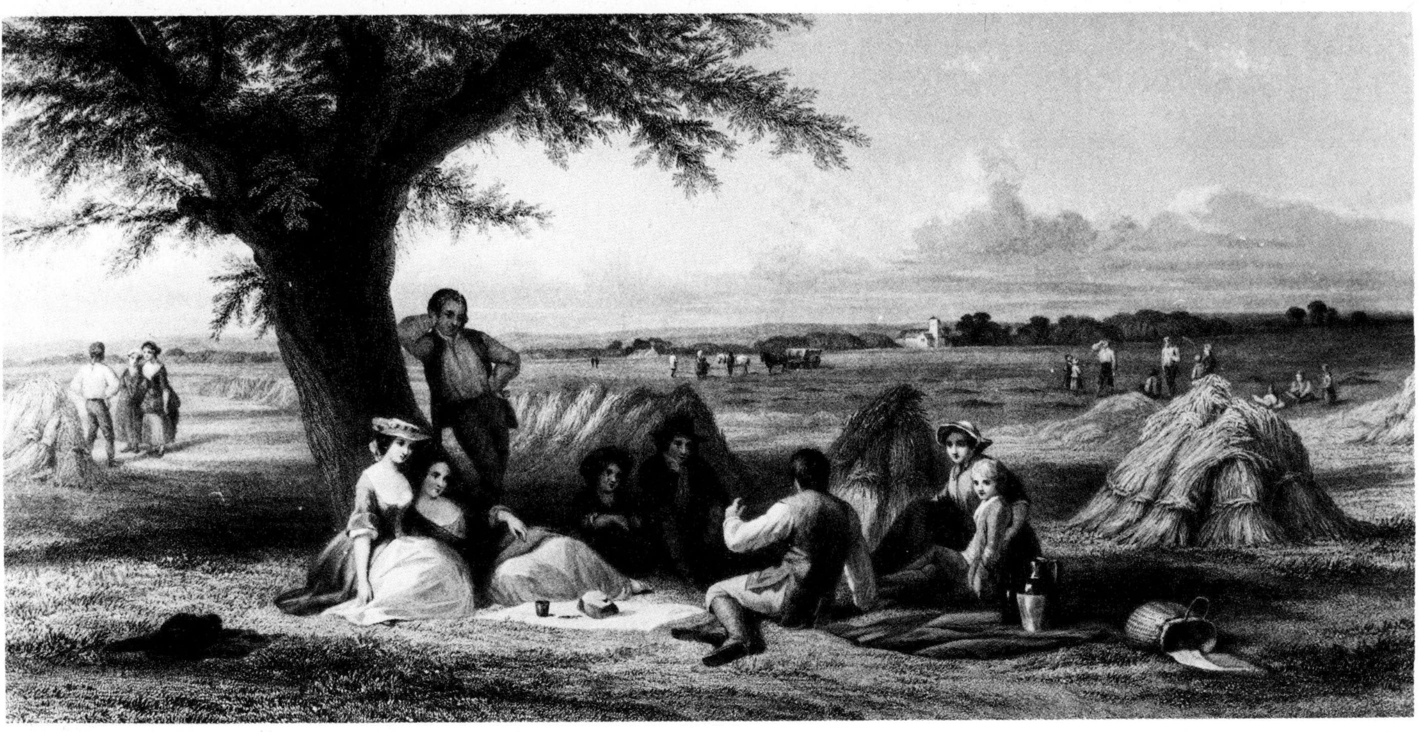

Edward Radclyffe (1809–1863) *Labour* and *Rest* mezzotints
After the paintings by John Absolon (1815–1895), published in 1870. Radclyffe engraved for the *Art Journal* and the Art Union of London, and exhibited works after David Cox at the Royal Academy from 1859 to 1863.

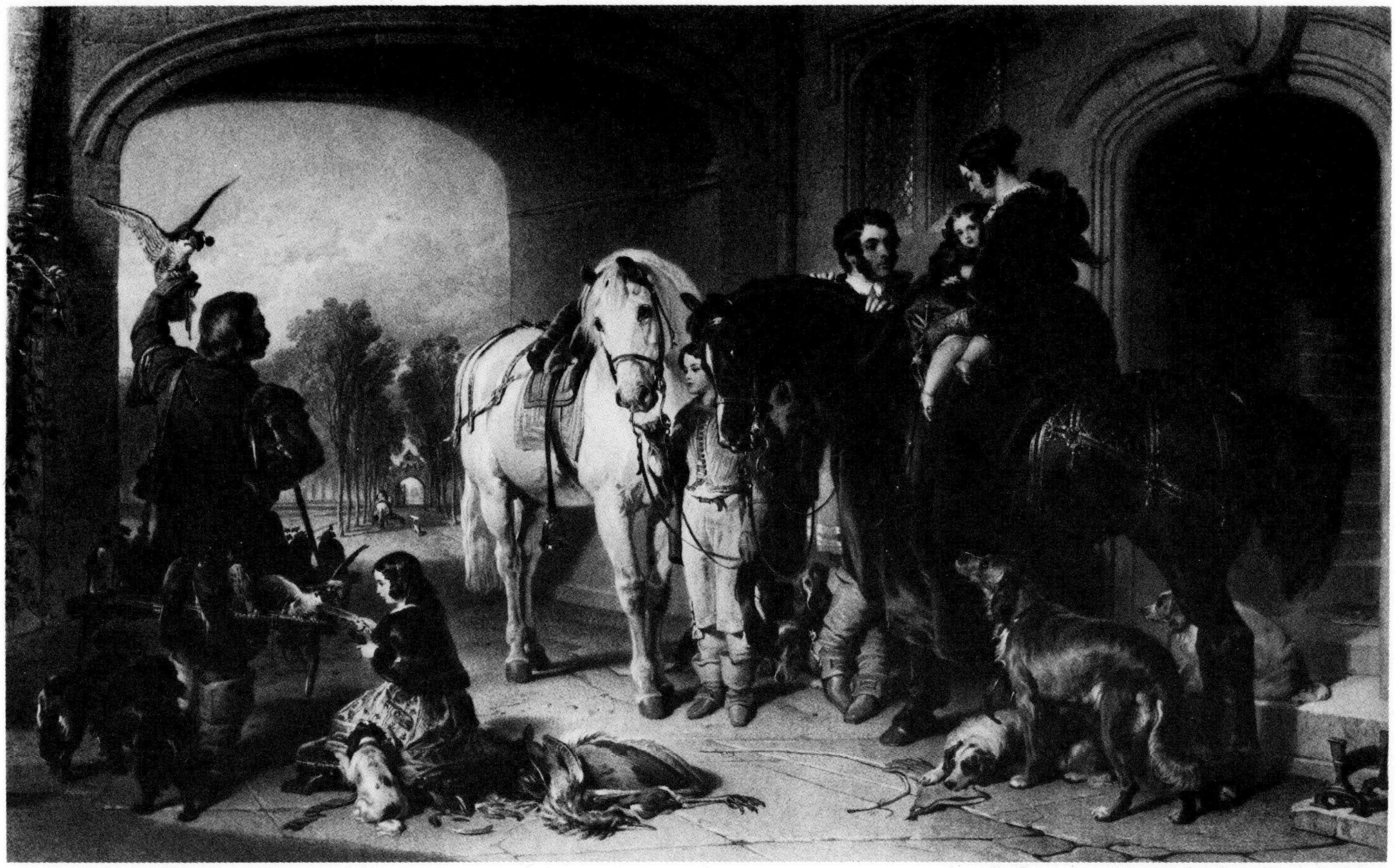

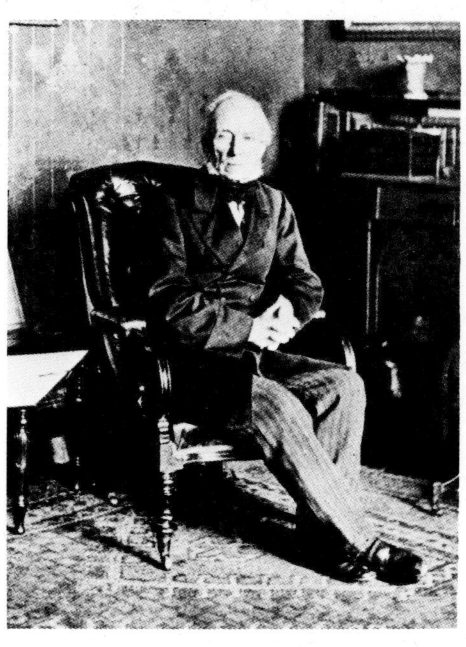

Samuel Cousins R.A. (1801–1887) *Return from Hawking* mezzotint
After the painting (R.A. 1837) by Sir Edwin Landseer R.A. (1802–1873), published by F. G. Moon in 1839. Cousins was the first engraver to receive full Royal Academician status in 1855. His mezzotints – the Printsellers' Association (1894) records sixty-eight – were after Lawrence, Reynolds and Wilkie, and the popular contemporary painters Millais, Leighton, Dicksee and Briton Riviere.

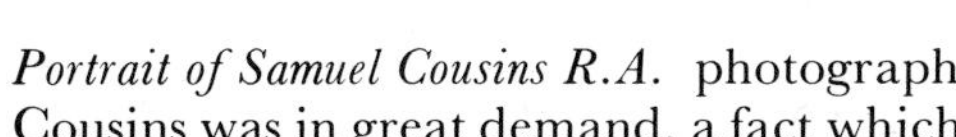

Portrait of Samuel Cousins R.A. photograph
Cousins was in great demand, a fact which allowed him to determine his own terms with publishers. In 1873 Thos. Agnew and Sons commissioned him to engrave Millais's *Yes or No*, for which he required half his fee (600 guineas) when the plate was half completed, and the balance on its completion. He commented on the beauty of certain sized proportions when engraved: 'I find that the head will be four and a quarter inches long, a handsome proportion.' (*Artists at Home*, 1886)

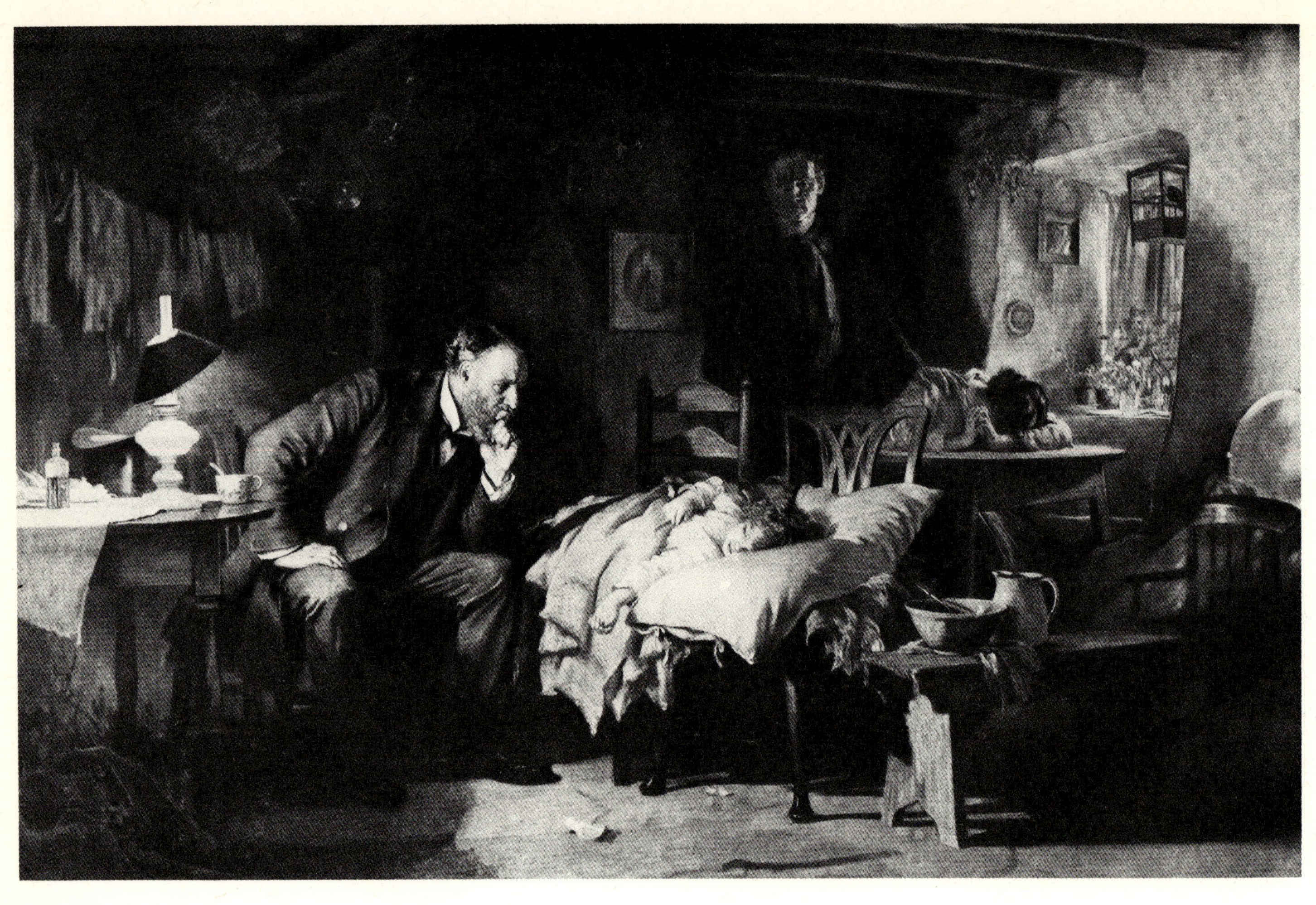

The Doctor photogravure
After the painting of 1891 by Sir Luke Fildes R.A. (1843–1927), published by Thos. Agnew and Sons in a declared edition of 625. The work was subsequently published in America, where it was claimed to have sold over a million copies and was then reproduced as a postage stamp. Fildes however received no royalties, for there were no copyright laws at the time in America.

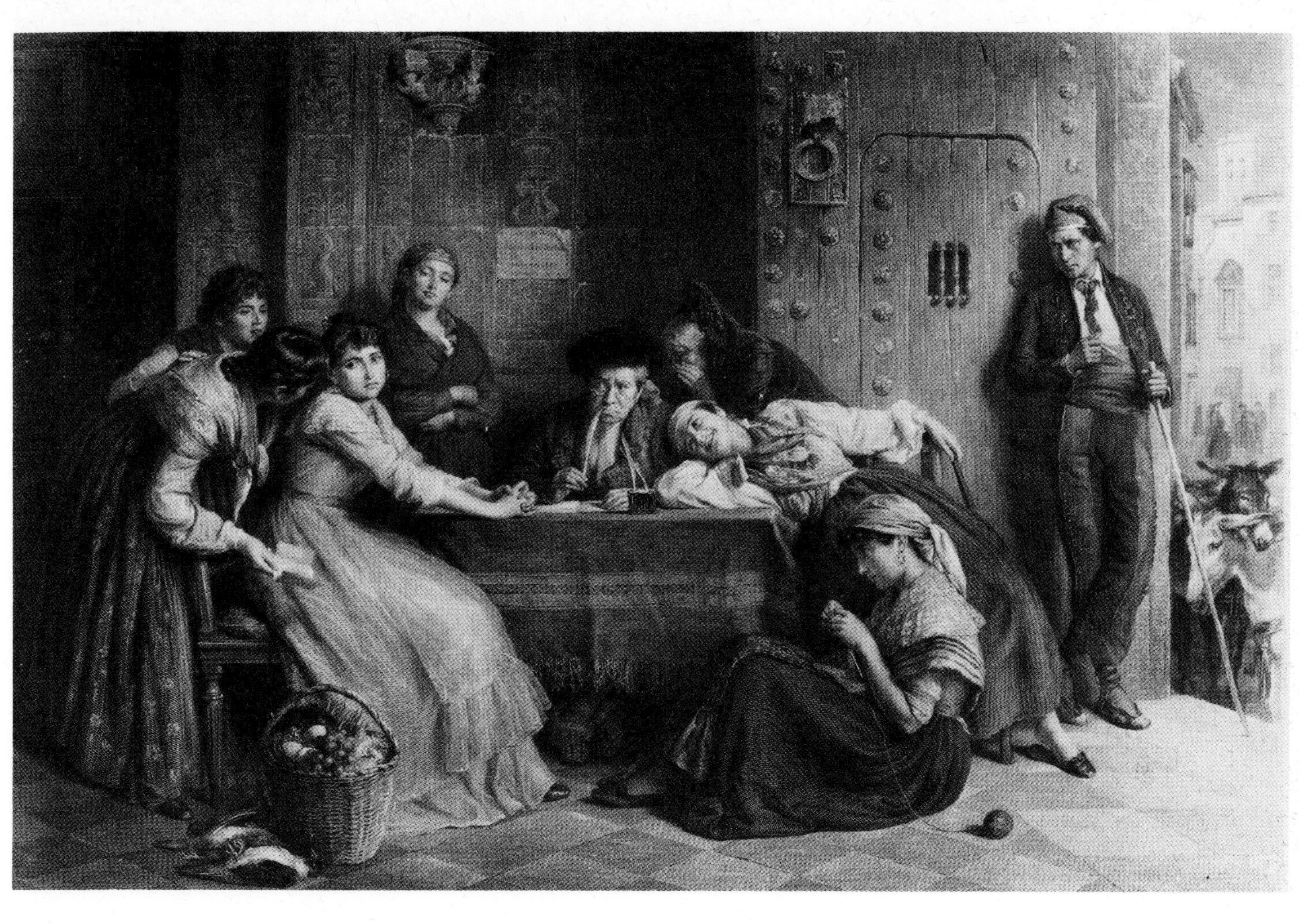

Lumb Stocks R.A. (1812–1892) *A Spanish Letter-Writer* line engraving
After the painting by John Bagnold Burgess R.A. (1830–1897), published for the Art Union of London in 1888. Stocks had a model career as engraver. He began with a six year apprenticeship, graduated to book and periodical illustration, and from 1852 obtained commissions to engrave after the popular paintings of the day. Finally elected a Royal Academician in 1872.

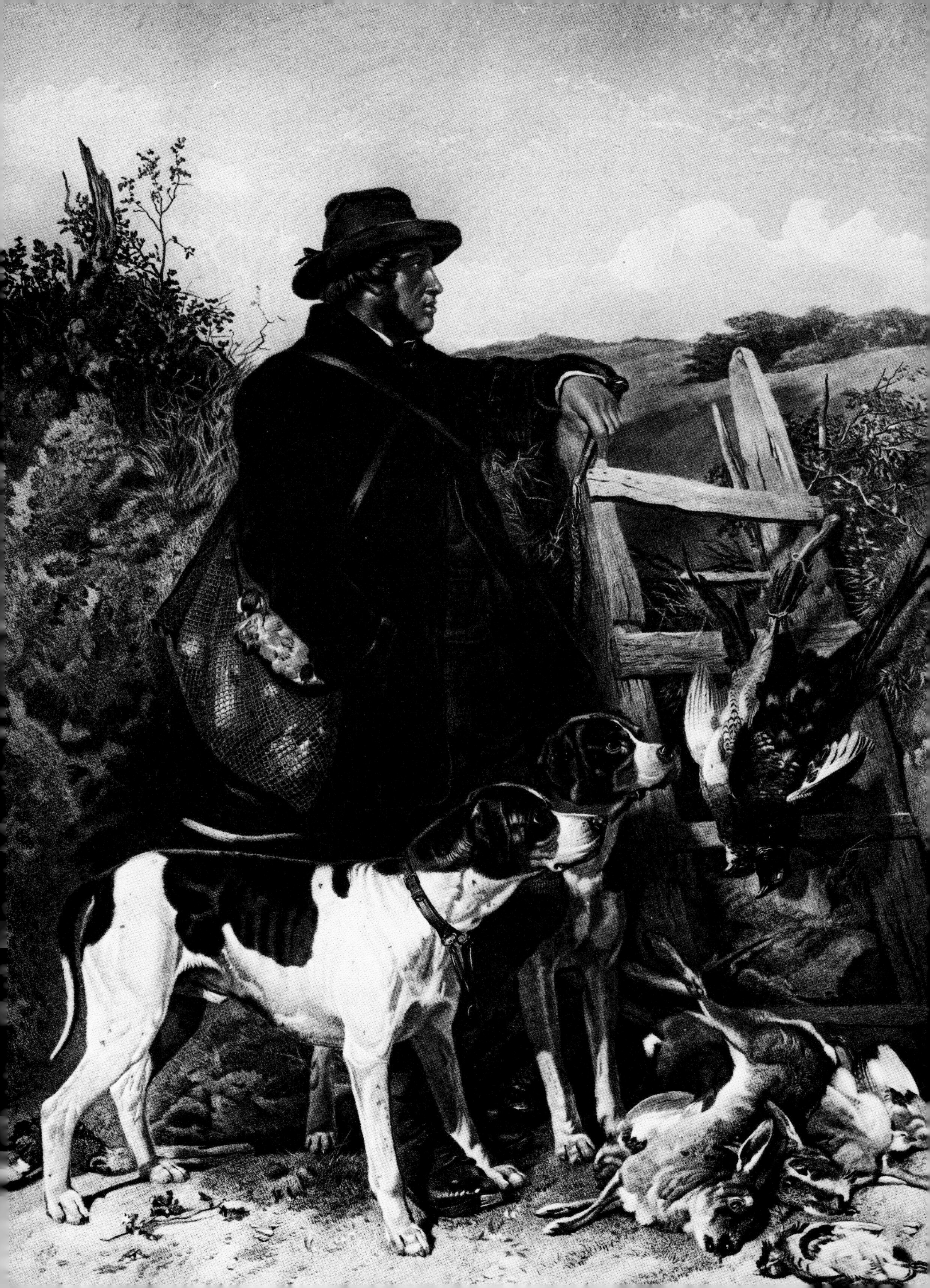

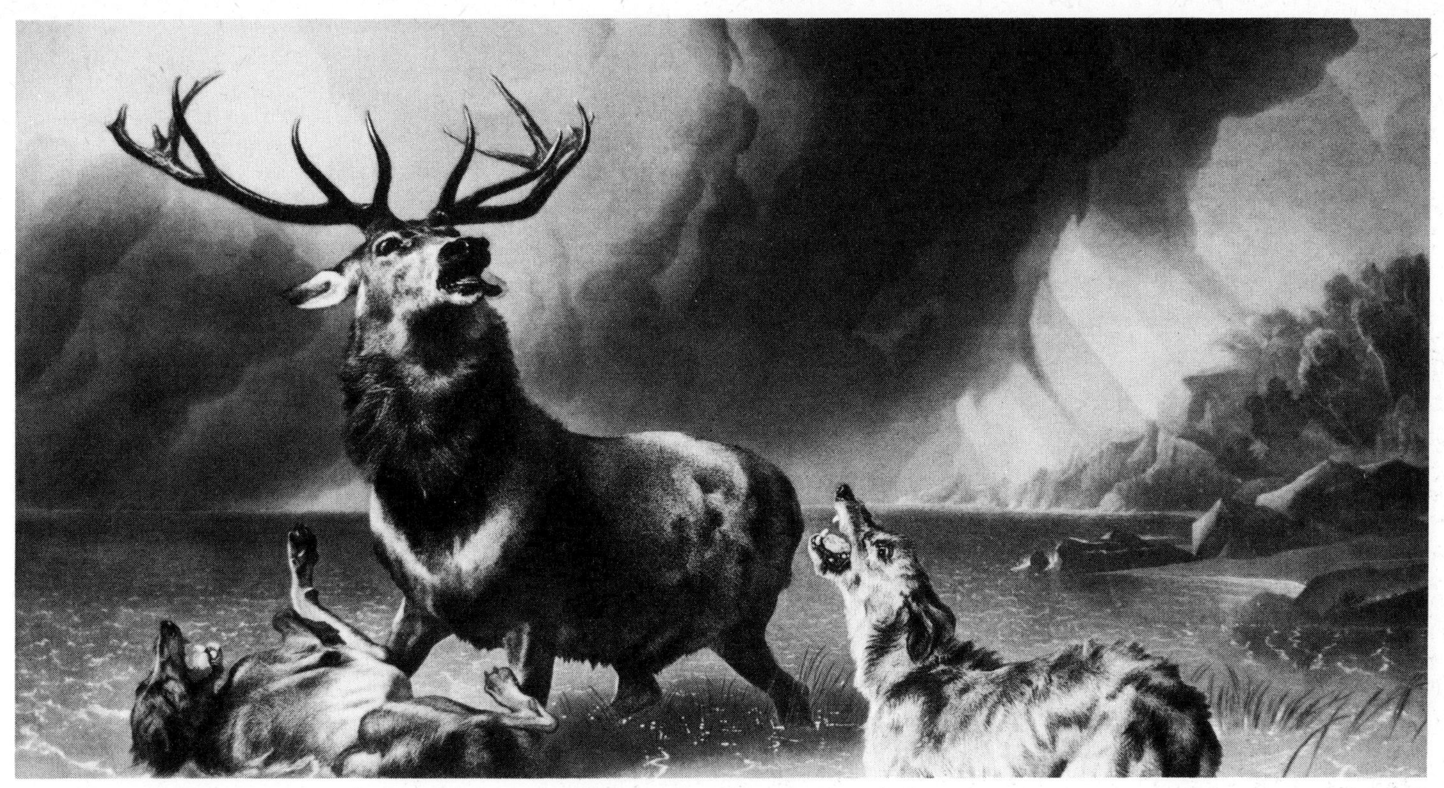

Thomas Landseer A.R.A. (1795–1880) *The Stag at Bay* line engraving
After the painting (R.A. 1846) by Sir Edwin Landseer R.A. (1802–1873). Originally published in 1847, republished in 1865.
The work was engraved three times, first by Landseer, and then by Charles Mottram in 1852 and George Zober in 1866,
with three different publishers paying for copyrights. Thomas was the son of a noted line engraver and the brother of
Edwin, whose works he reproduced in line and etching throughout his life. A recognised master of all engraving techniques
on metal, he was famous for his truthful rendering of the textures of fur and hides. His commissions were numerous – the
Printsellers' Association (1894) registers fifty-five prints – including the following invitation by Thos. Agnew and Sons in
1871:

Dear Mr. Landseer,
    We rejoice greatly to have it in our power to give you the commission to engrave your brother's noble pictures of a
deer family and the Ptarmigan Hill, and we have the fullest confidence that your splendid talent of rendering your great
brother's works will be executed to its full extent in the engraving of these two pictures. We gladly accept your terms –
namely three hundred pounds for the Deer, four hundred for the Ptarmigan Hill, and remain
Ever yours truly
Thos. Agnew and Sons

Frederick Stacpoole A.R.A. (1813–1907) *English Gamekeeper* mezzotint (LEFT)
After the painting by Richard Ansdell R.A. (1815–1885), and a companion to *Scotch Gamekeeper* published by Graves and Co.
in 1858. Stacpoole was a major interpretative engraver who exhibited at the Academy from 1842 until 1899 works after
Landseer, B. Riviere, F. Goodall, J. Sant and T. Faed. The Printsellers' Association (1894) registered sixty prints in stipple,
line and mezzotint techniques.

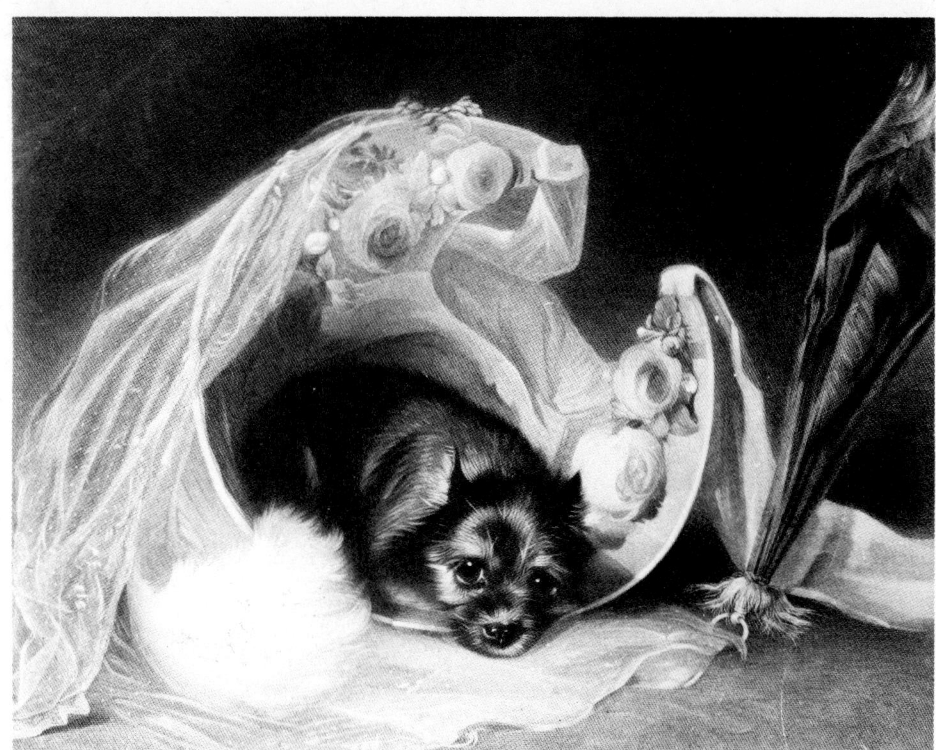

George Salisbury Shury (1815–1880)
The Bed of Roses mezzotint
After the painting by Thomas Earl (fl. 1836–1885) a noted animal painter. Published in 1854. Fur, drapery and feathers were especially suitable for the mezzotint technique. The lined plate was burnished with rocker tools for highlights, while the carefully ruled plate produced rich, full black backgrounds.

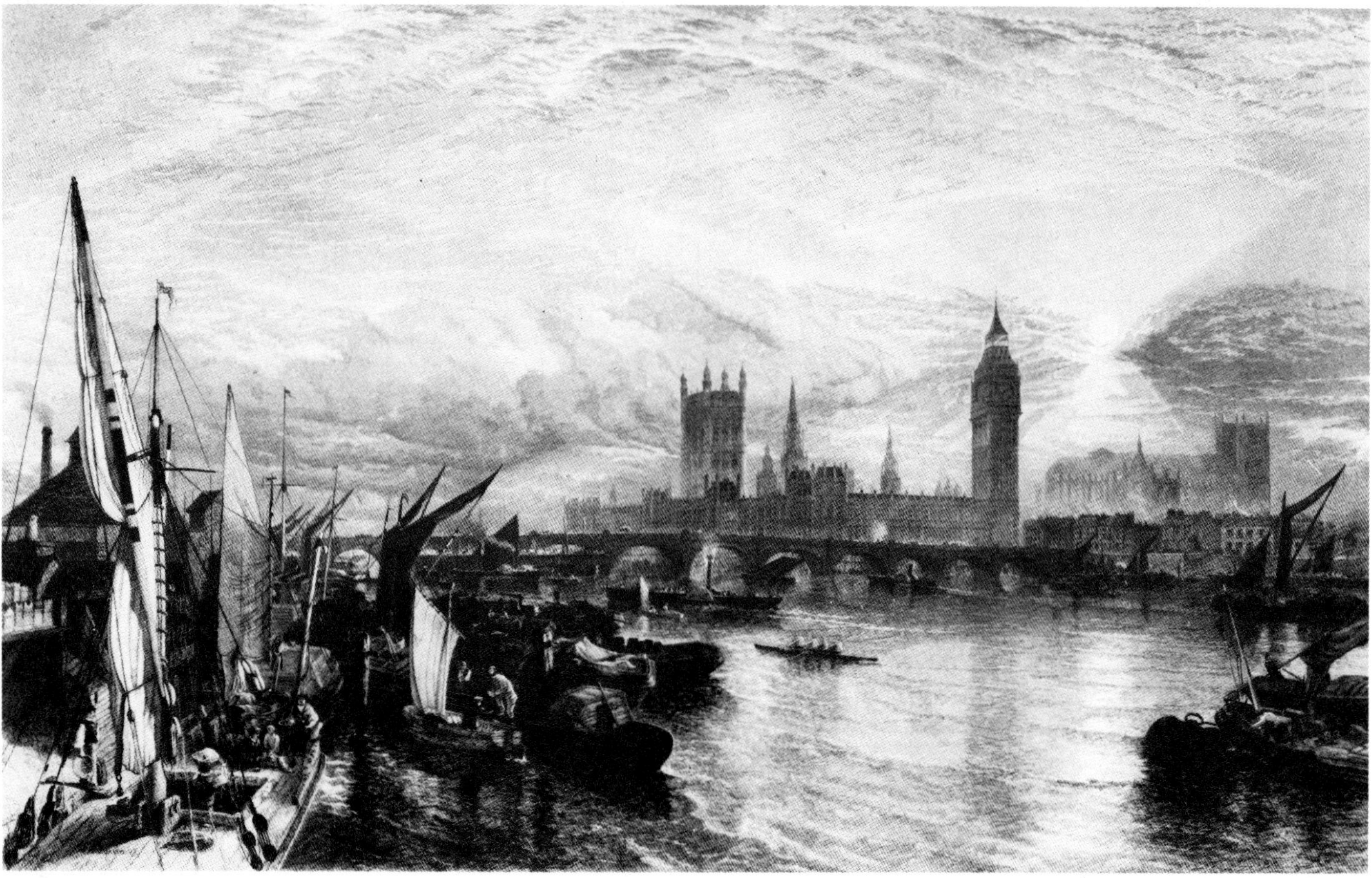

William Chapman York *Waiting for the Tide* line engraving
After the painting of 1857 by Henry Dawson (1811–1878), published in 1865. Such harbour scenes anticipated the popularity of Whistler's series of sixteen etchings, *The Thames Set*, which was issued in 1871 and sold by the Fine Art Society.

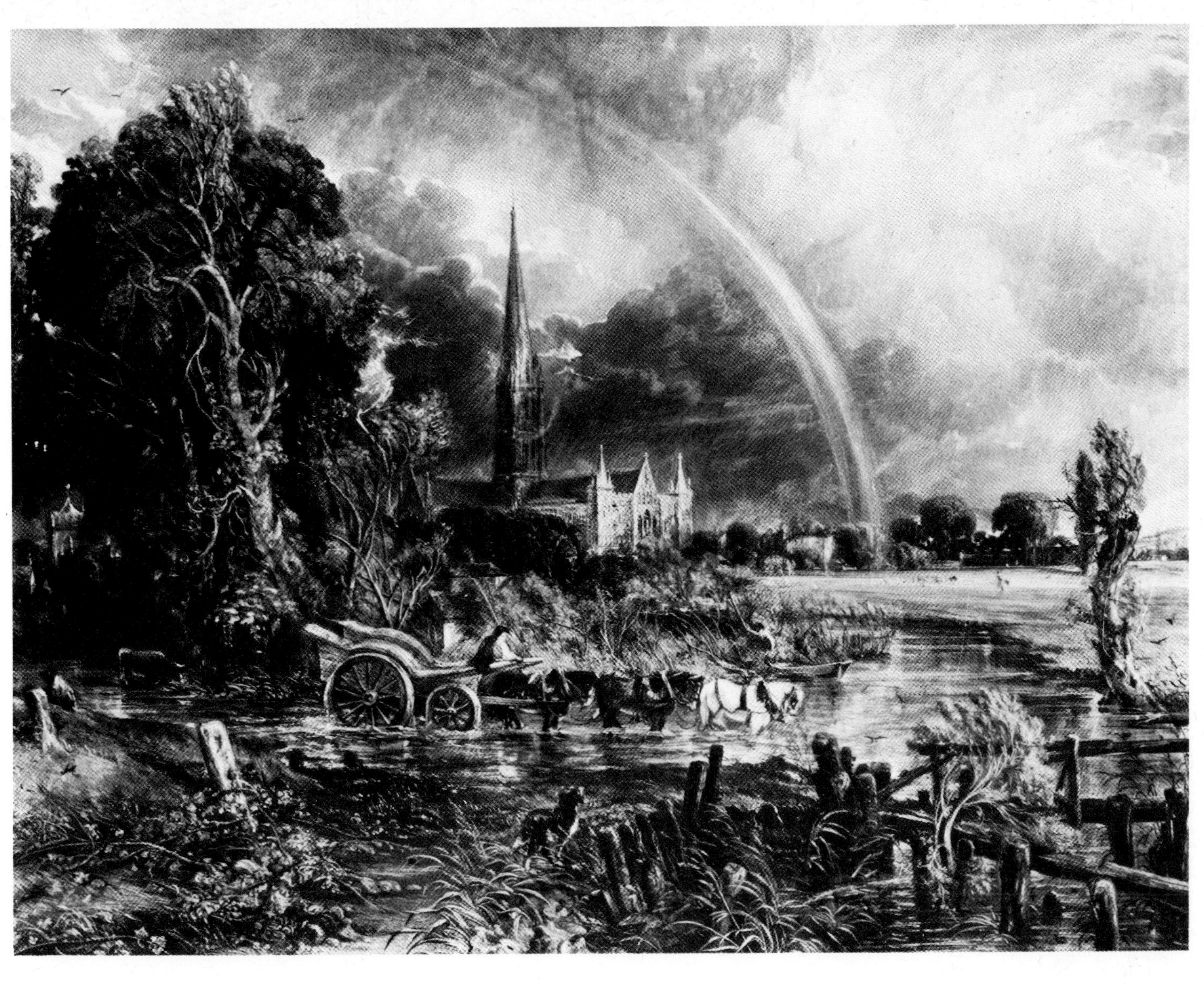

David Lucas (1802–1881) *The Rainbow – Salisbury Cathedral* mezzotint
After the painting by John Constable (1776–1837). Lucas, who was known as Constable's engraver, worked with the painter on a series of mezzotints issued as *English Landscape* between 1830 and 1832, and developed an interpretative style of chiaroscuro mezzotint which used strong dark patches with flecks of white in a combination of etching and mezzotint techniques. This technique was criticized as giving new order to the often overworked painting surfaces.

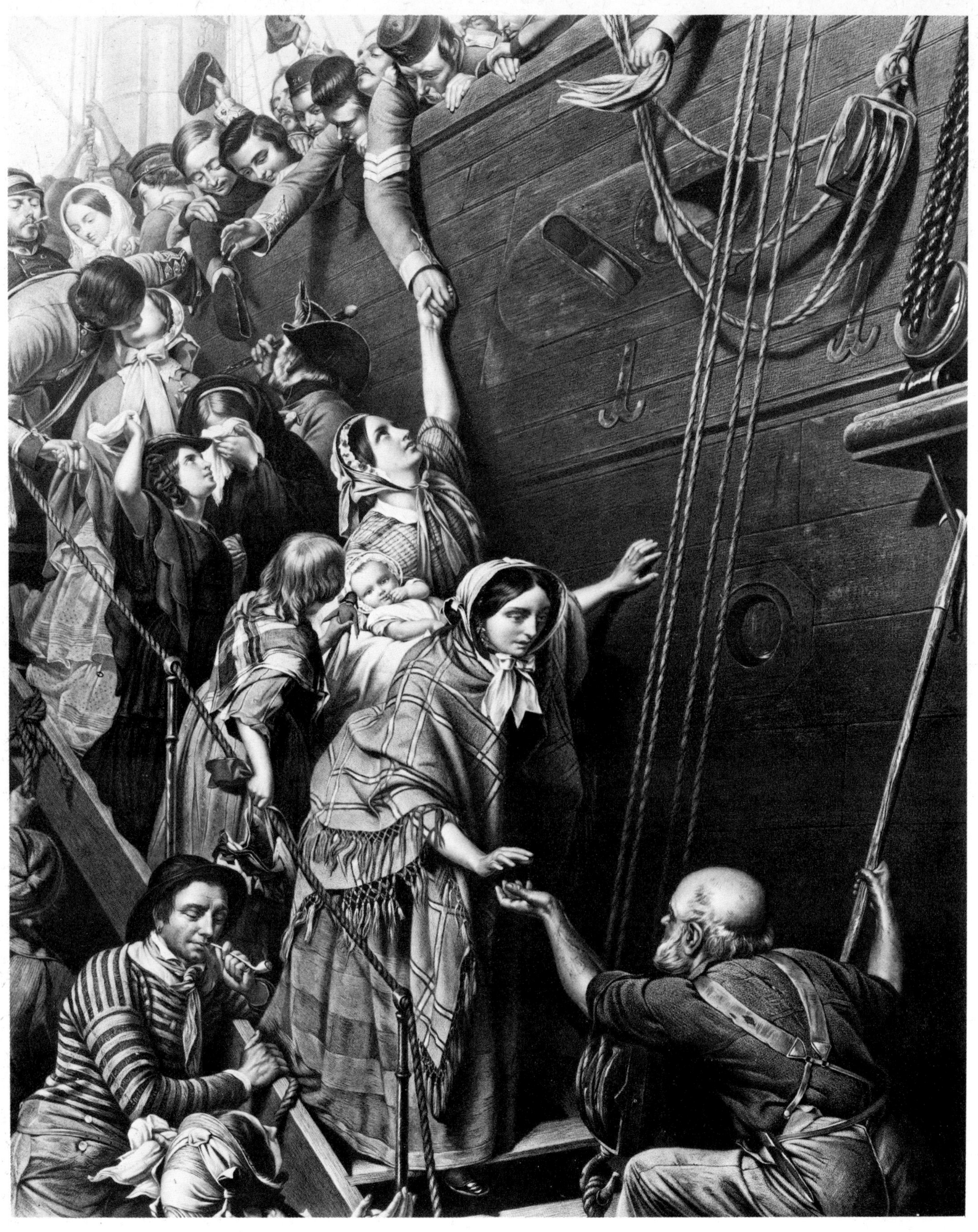

William Turner Davey (1818–1890) *Eastward Ho! August 1857* (with detail opposite) mezzotint and etching
After the painting of 1858 by Henry Nelson O'Neil A.R.A. (1817–1880), published in 1860 with a companion print *Home Again, 1858* (R.A. 1858). The Printsellers' Association registered an edition of 1,475. Historical themes gained in popularity as reporter-engravers were commissioned to record events for such periodicals as *The Illustrated London News*. Engravings of

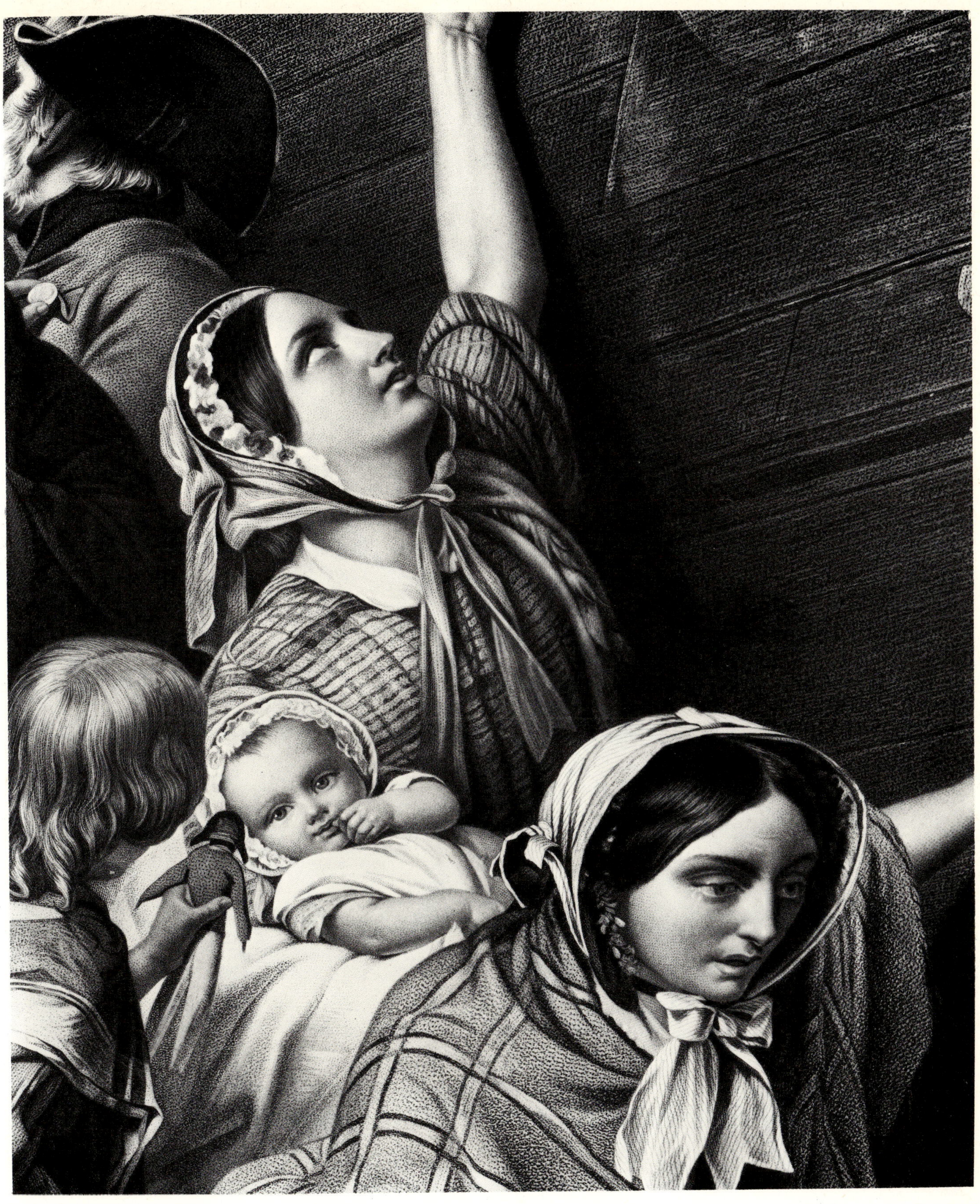

battle scenes from the Crimean war, the Indian Uprising of 1857, and Napoleonic campaigns were particularly popular. The combined technique seen in the detail shows the crisp delineation of etched lines against the soft mottled mezzotinted background.

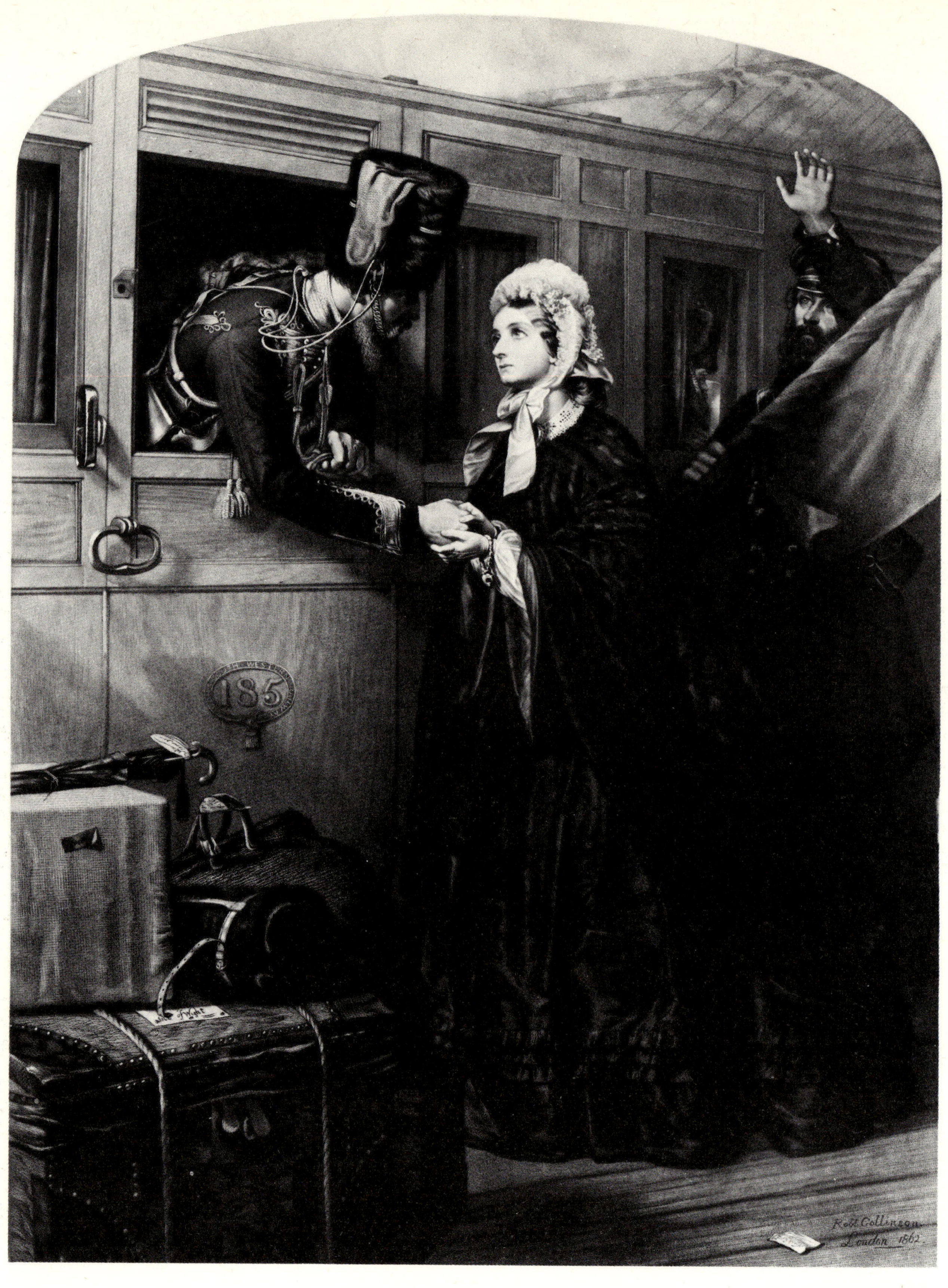

Charles Algernon Tomkins (1812–c.1897) *Ordered on Foreign Service* mezzotint
After the painting by Robert Collinson (1832–c.1890), published in 1865. Tomkins engraved some ninety-one
works registered with the Printsellers'' Association (1894), including works after F. Goodall, T. Faed and R.
Ansdell, which he exhibited at the Academy from 1872 to 1893.

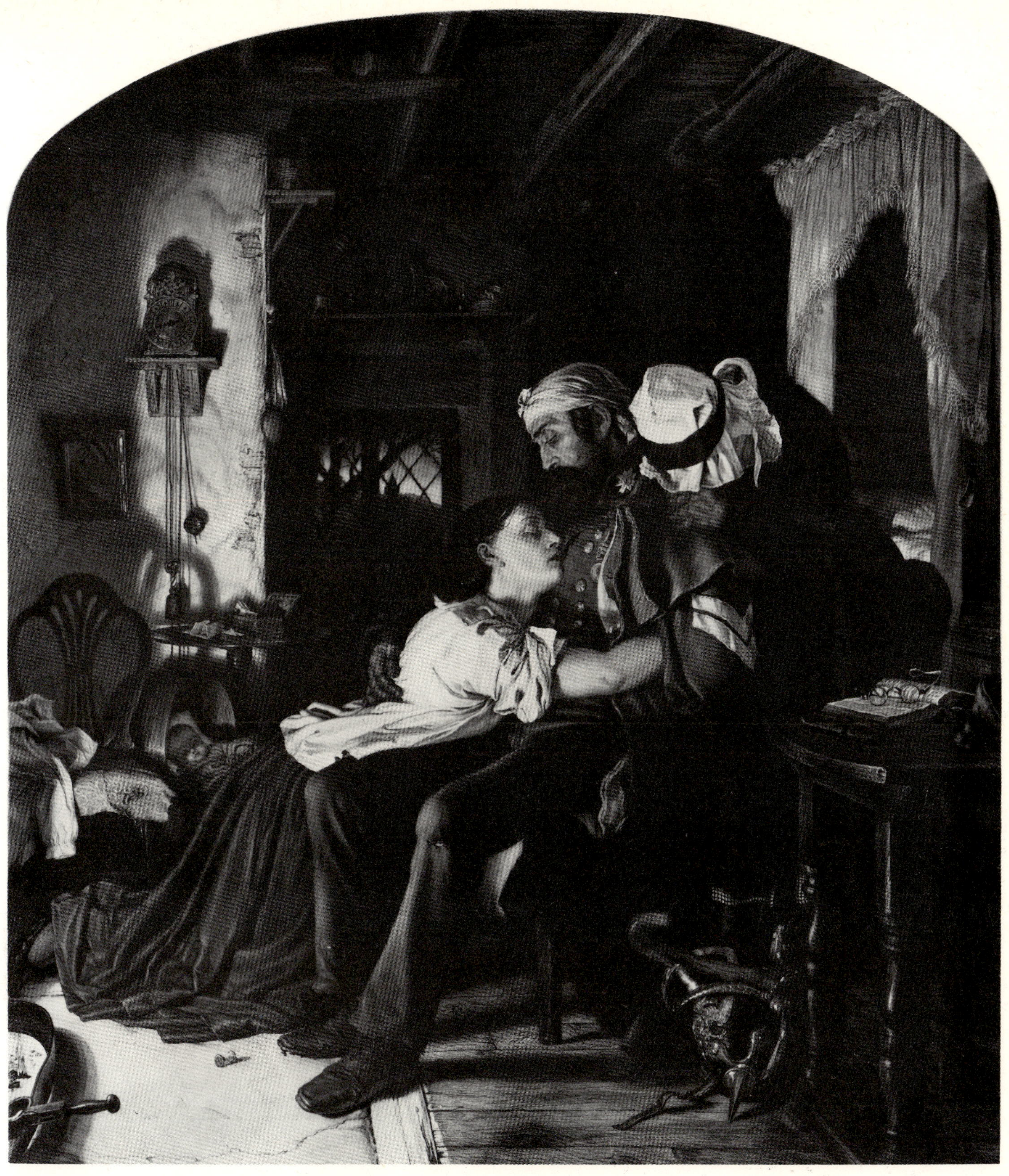

Henry Thomas Ryall (1811–1867) *'Home!' Return from the Crimea* mezzotint
After the painting (R.A. 1856) by Sir Noël Paton R.S.A. (1821–1901), published in 1856. Ryall was popular for his mezzotint. He was appointed historical engraver to the Queen and worked after Landseer, R. Ansdell and Frith. The Crimean war was a popular subject among painters as well as engravers. *The Roll Call*, 1874, a painting of soldiers in the Crimean War by Lady Butler (1846–1933) was the most important picture of the year. The artist's research into the correct military uniforms and manoeuvres, and her interviews with surviving soldiers, produced such an accurate and moving picture that it was purchased by the Queen. Florence Nightingale asked for the painting to be brought to her bedside before she died so that she could relive the memory of the conflict, and extra guards were needed when the picture was exhibited at the Academy to prevent the crowds from damaging it. The copyright of the picture was sold for £1,200.

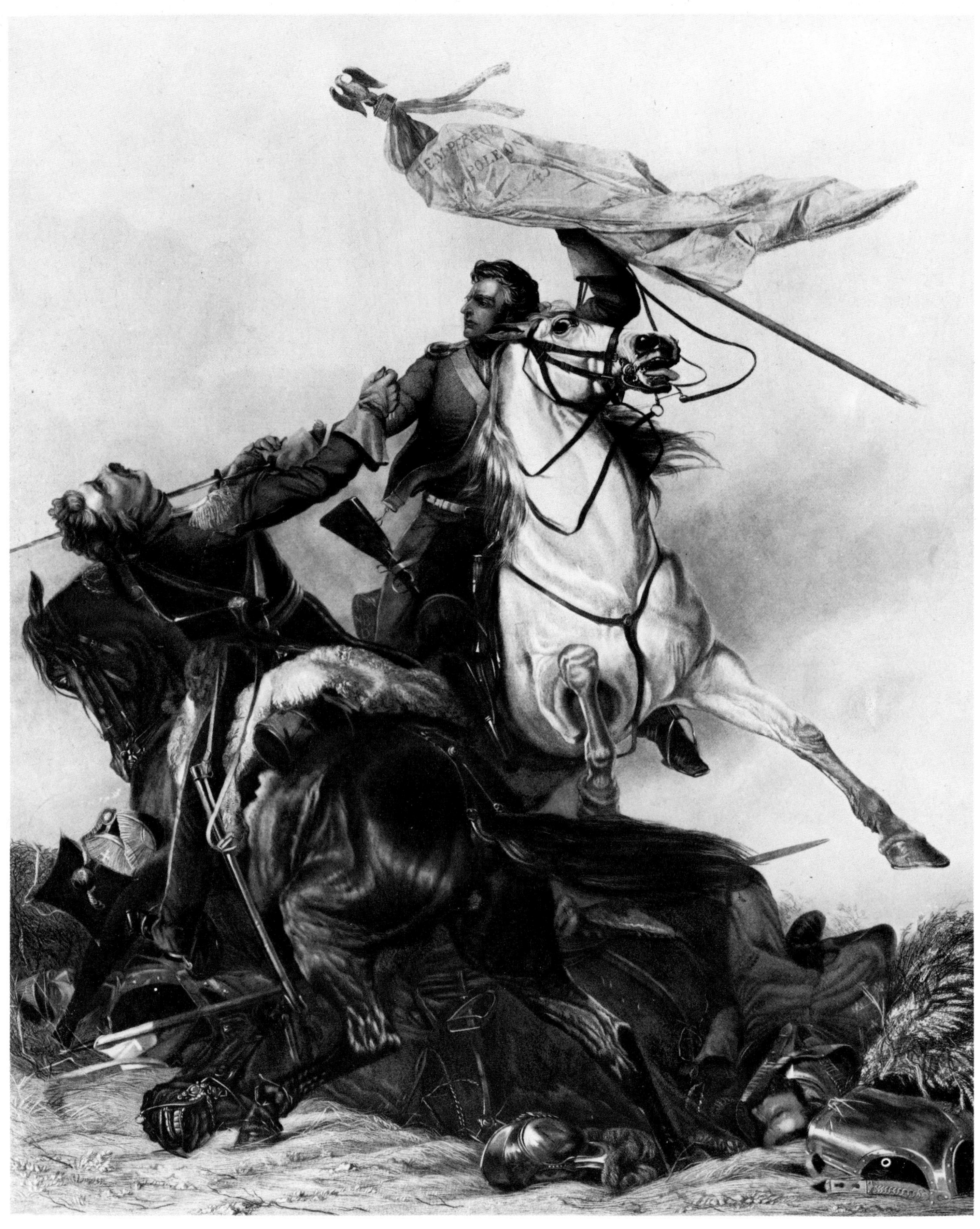

Henry Thomas Ryall (1811–1867) *Fight for the Standard* mezzotint, stipple and line
After the painting by Richard Ansdell A.R.A. (1815–1885), published in 1854. Sergeant Ewart of the Scots Greys is shown capturing the Eagle from the 45th Regiment, 'The Invincibles', at Waterloo, 18 June 1815. Themes of military triumph encouraged a sense of national pride and patriotism as the British Empire expanded.

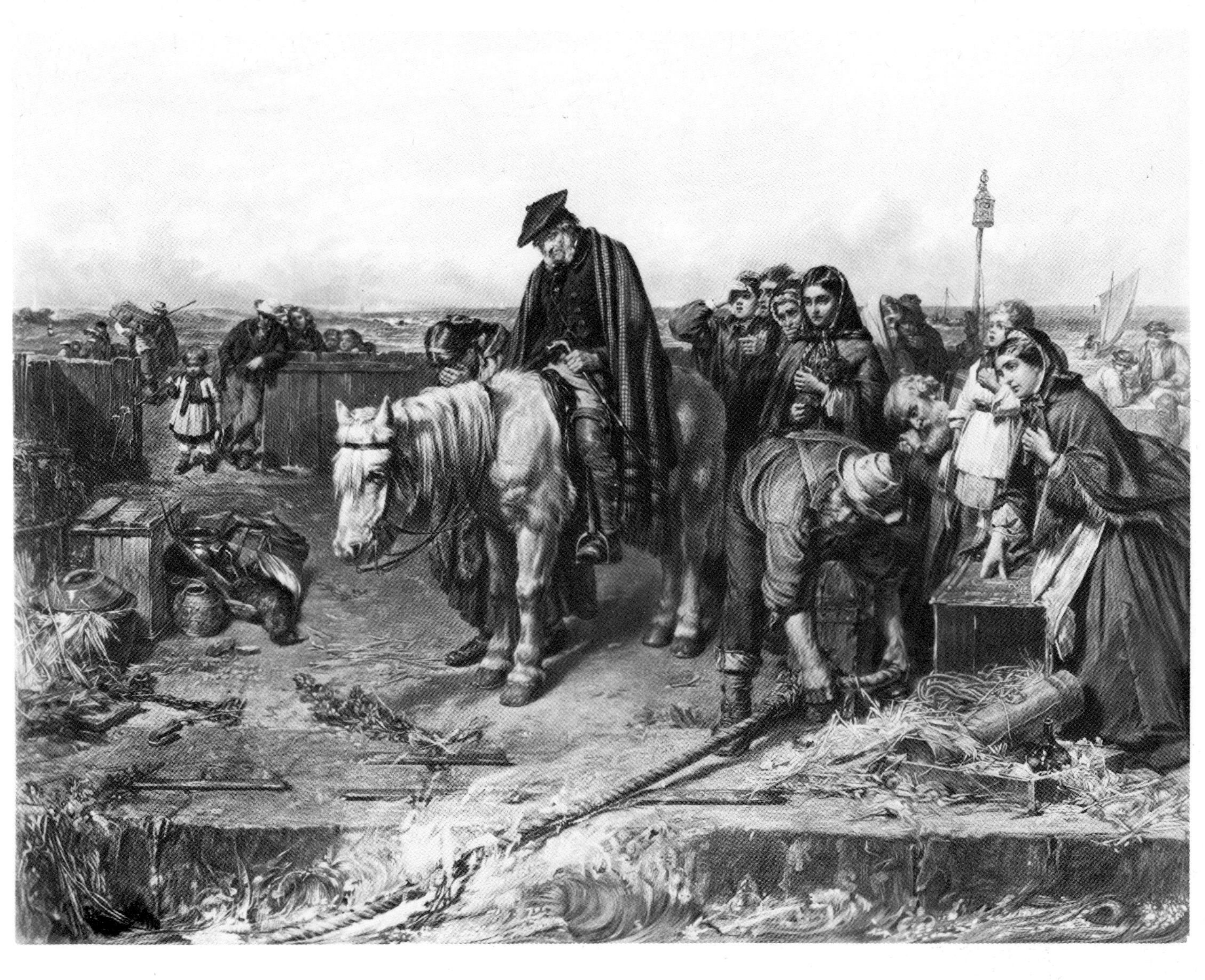

William Henry Simmons (1811–1882) *The Last of the Clan* mixed mezzotint
After the painting (R.A. 1865) by Thomas Faed R.A. (1826–1900), published in 1868 in a registered edition of 300. Faed was a Scotsman who painted domestic scenes in the highlands. Especially popular was his work *The Mitherless Bairn*, published in numerous engraved editions.

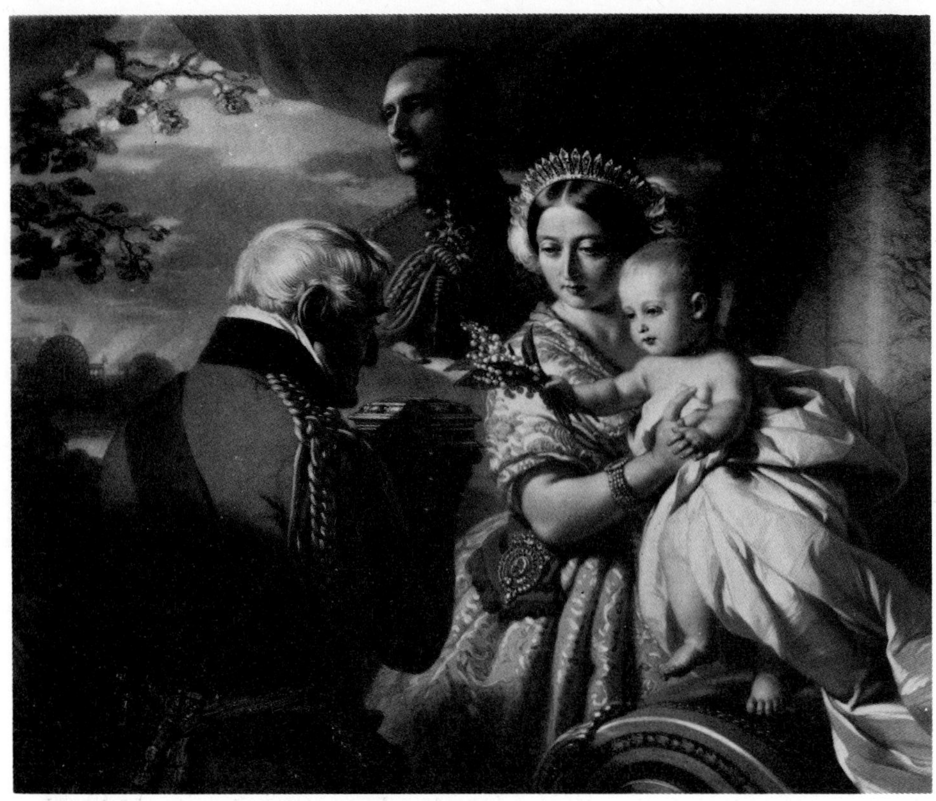

Prince Albert (1819–1861) *Eos and Cairnach* and *Old Woman in a Cloak* etchings
After drawings by Sir Edwin Landseer R.A. Printed privately in 1843 and 1844. Landseer taught Queen Victoria and Albert to etch, giving them the drawings he made of their pets to practise copying on the metal plates. Albert completed forty plates after these drawings and after drawings by Victoria. The subjects were mostly souvenirs of married life and observations from their travels, but when exhibited they were considered not far from being as good as the etchings of Thackeray. The print *Isaly* sold for £22 in 1849. (*The Printseller*, December 1903)

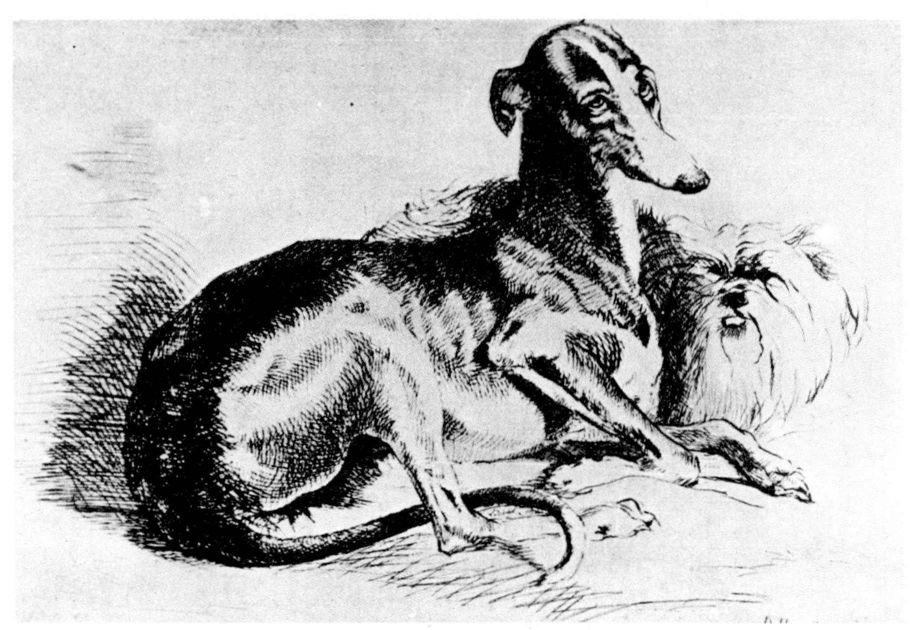

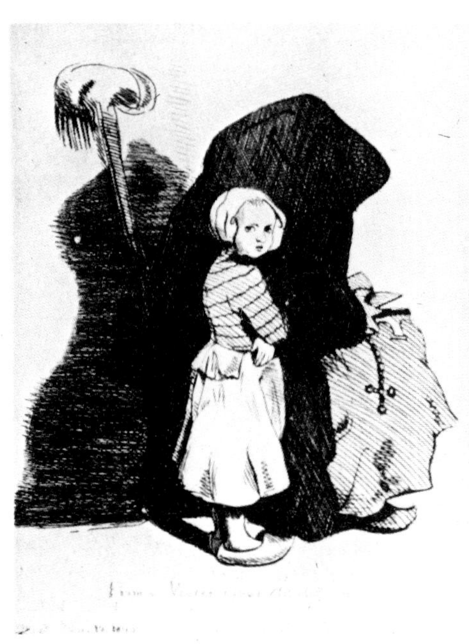

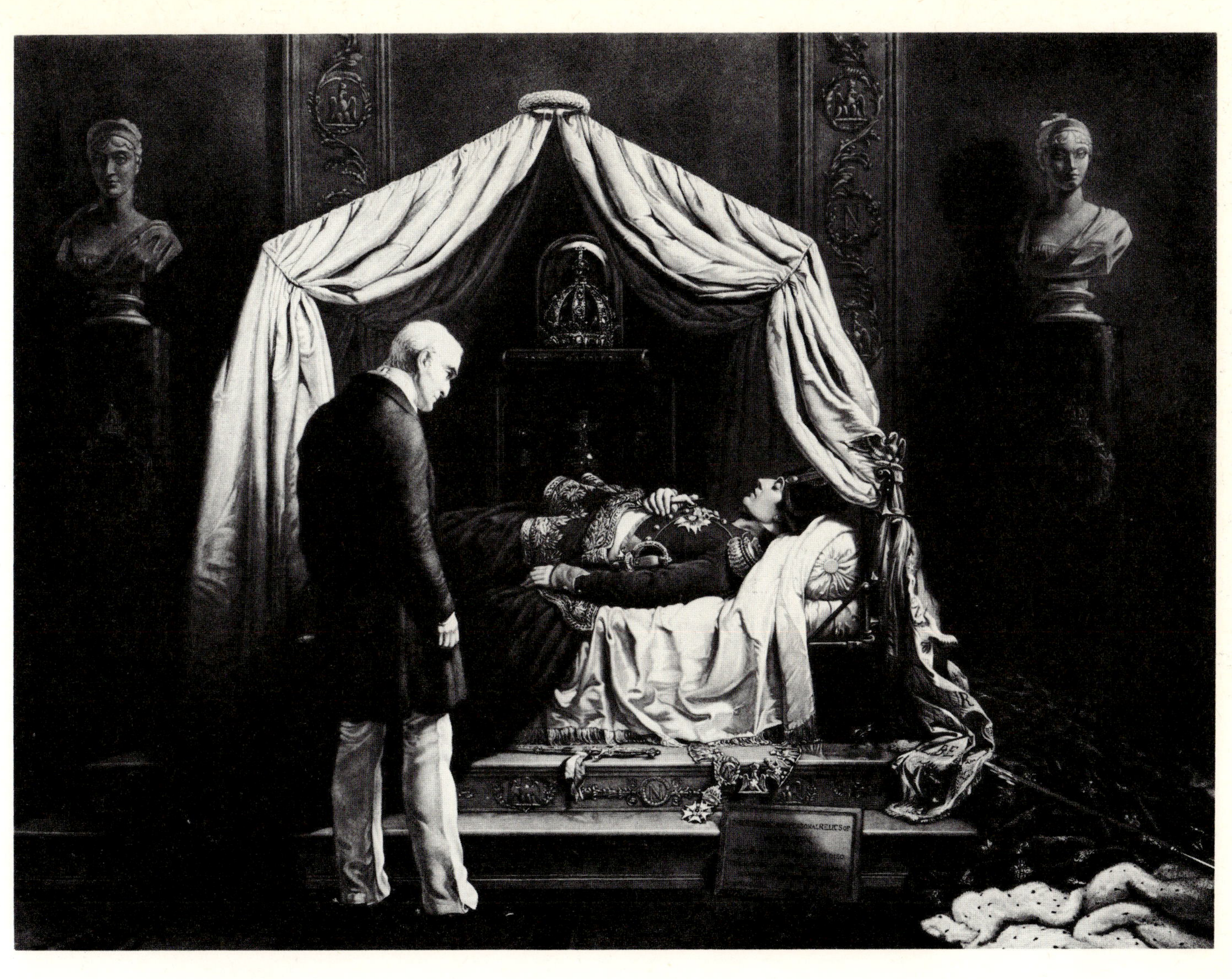

James Scott (1809–1889) *Duke of Wellington visiting the Effigy and Personal Relics of Napoleon* mezzotint
After the painting by Sir George Hayter (1792–1871), published in a declared edition of 450 in 1854. The scene represents
Wellington visiting Madame Tussaud's wax works. Wellington was a particularly popular figure for engravings. Three
colour lithographed prints of his funeral in 1852 were engraved by William Simpson and Thomas Picken.

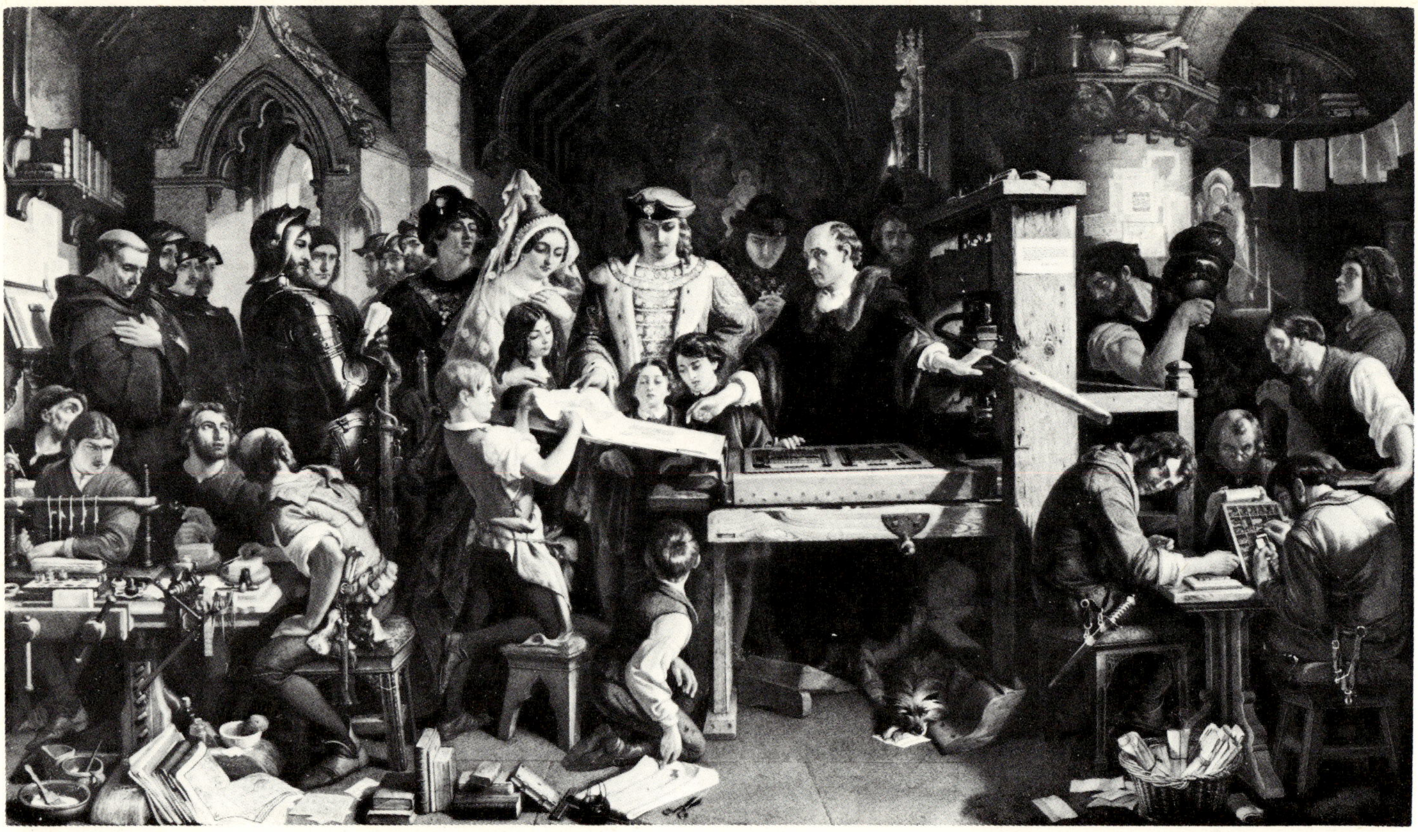

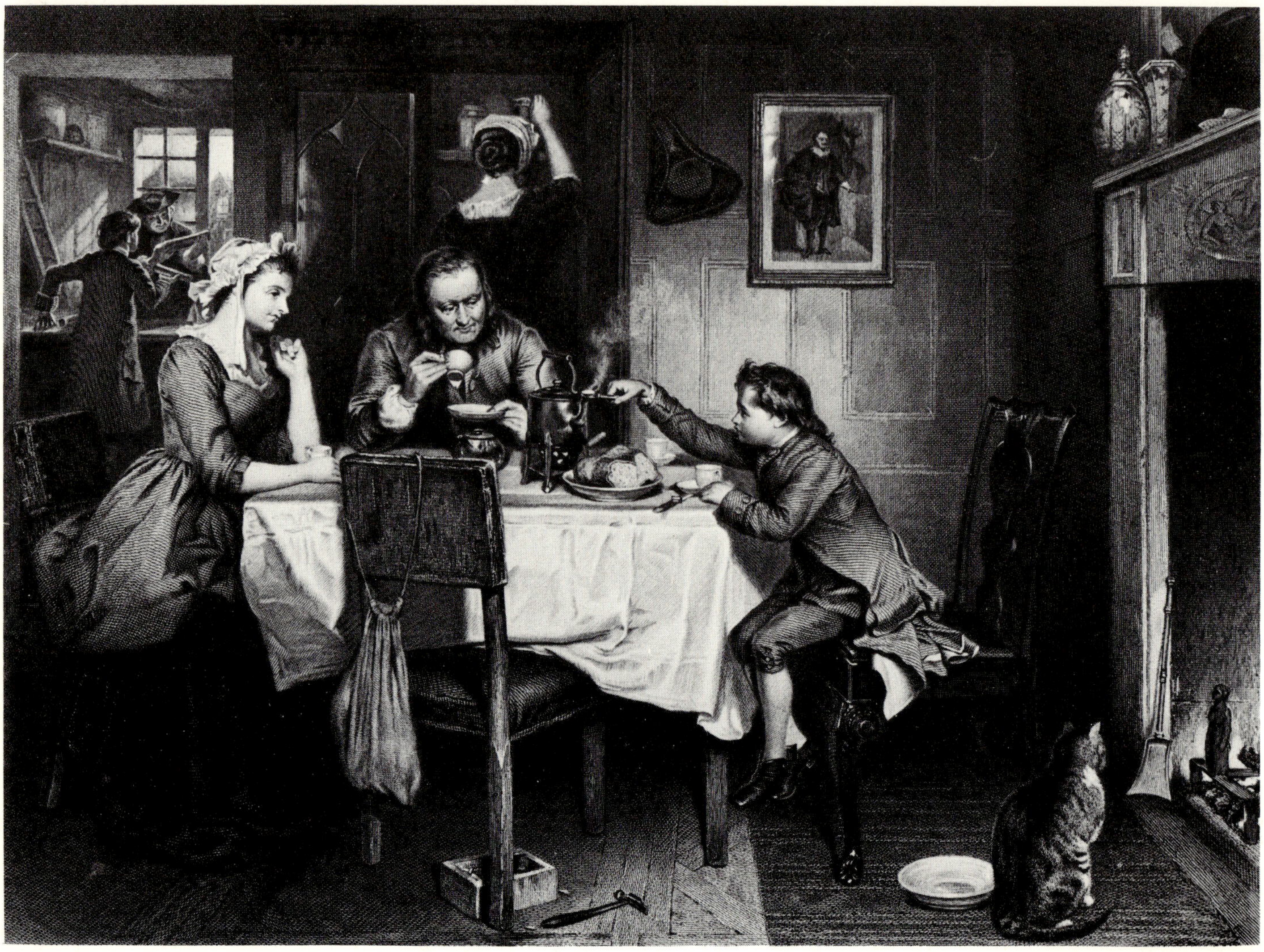

Frederick Bromley (fl. 1856–1860) *Caxton showing the First Specimen of his Printing to King Edward the Fourth at the Almonry at Westminster* mixed mezzotint (LEFT)
After the painting by Daniel Maclise R.A. (1806–1870). The engraving was exhibited at the Royal Academy in 1858. Bromley was the son of John Charles Bromley (1795–1839), noted mezzotinter and etcher. He engraved works after J. P. Knight, J. R. Herbert, C. Landseer and W. C. T. Dobson.

Herbert Bourne (1820–c.1885) *Watt's First Experiment (on steam)* mezzotint (BELOW LEFT)
After the painting by Marcus Stone R.A. (1840–1921). Bourne engraved after Millais, Frederick Leighton, Frith and Doré.

John Charles Bromley (1795–1839) *The Reform Banquet 1832* mezzotint
After the painting by Benjamin Robert Haydon (1786–1846), engraved in 1837. Bromley was from a noted family of four engravers. His father was William Bromley (1769–1842). The Reform Bill was a major impetus in changing the lives of those destined to become members of the rising middle class.

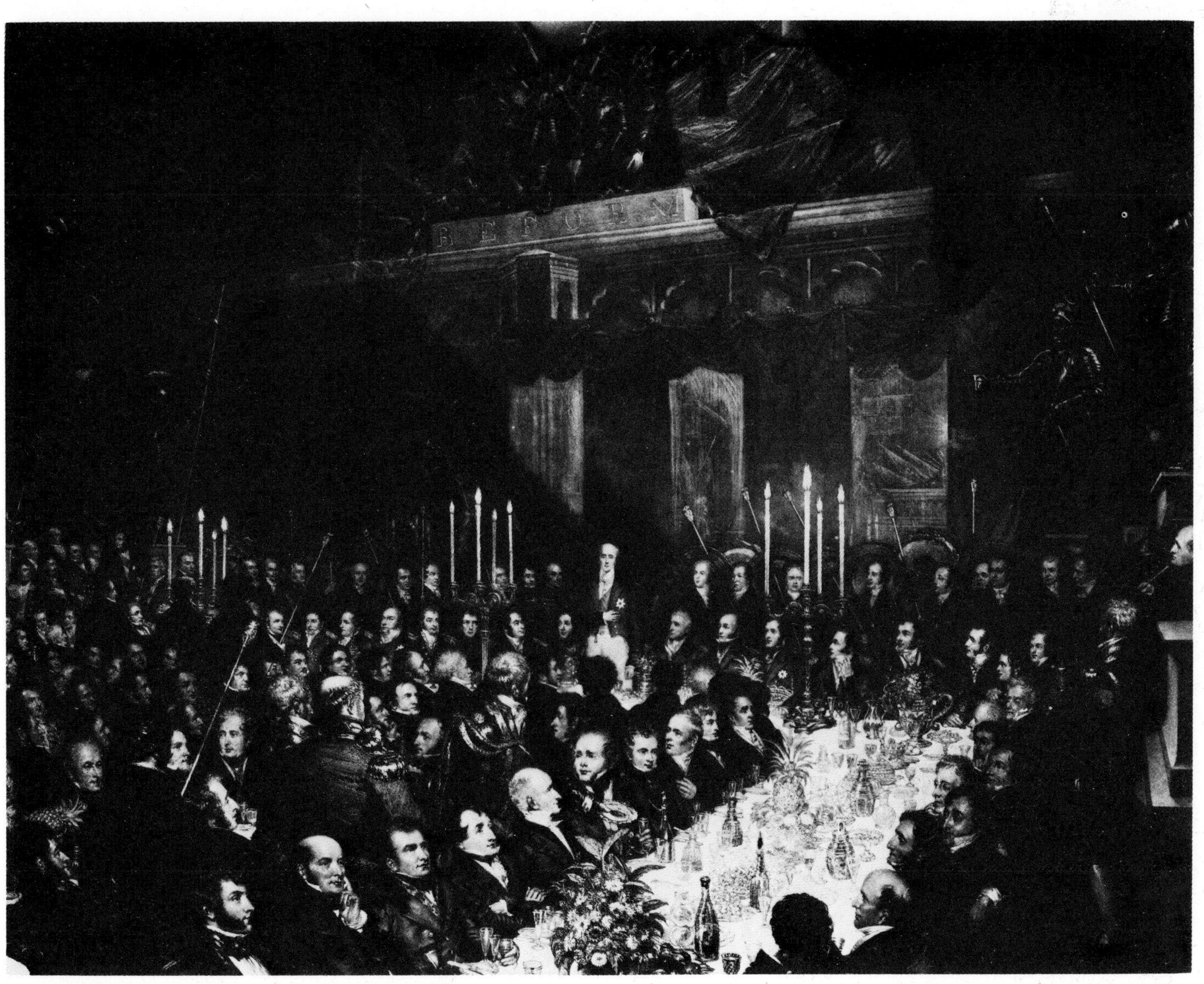

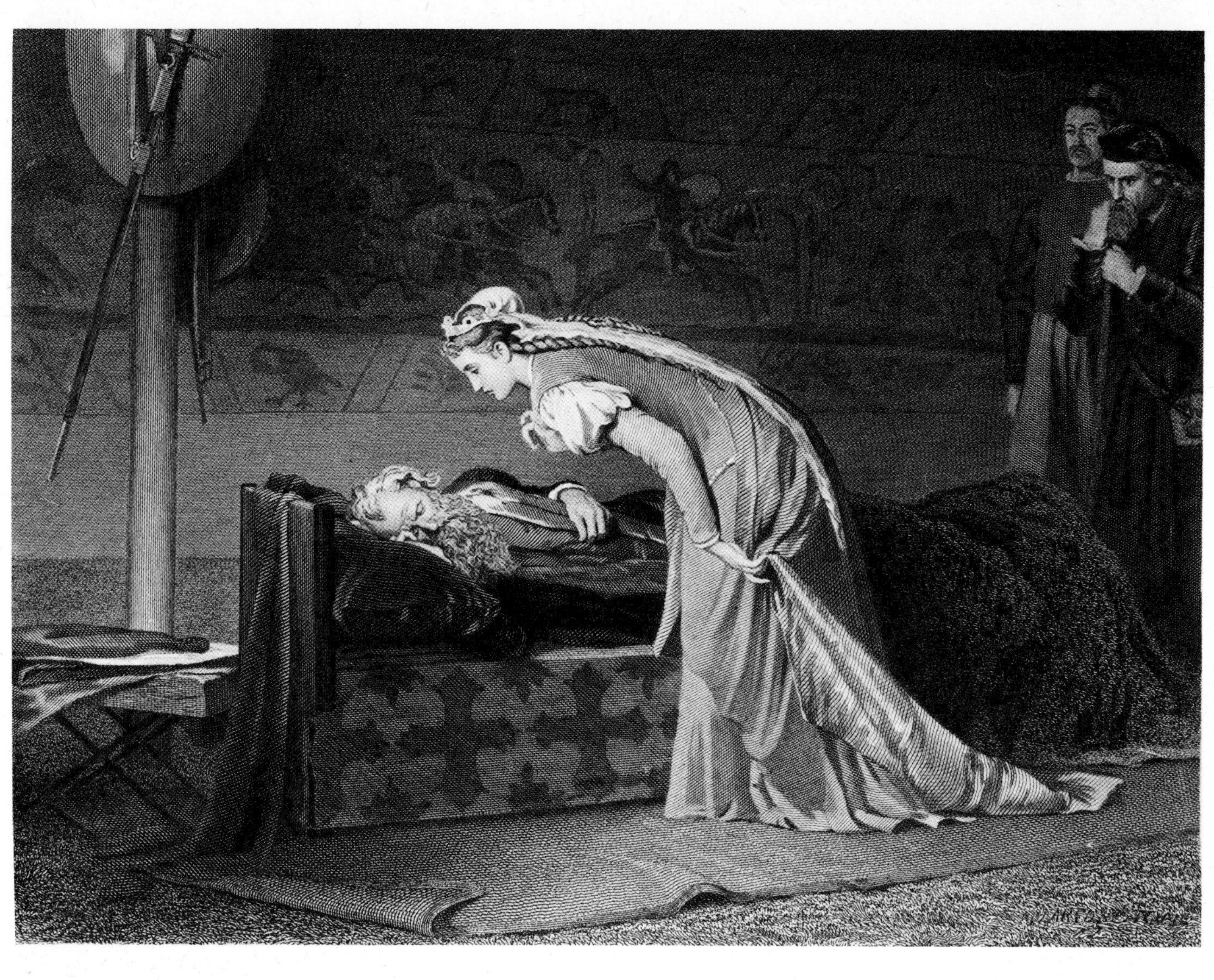

Herbert Bourne (1820–c.1885) *Lear and Cordelia* line engraving
After the painting (R.A. 1794) by Benjamin West (1738–1820) entitled *Cordelia making herself known to her father King Lear*.
The growing popularity of the theatre, and the strong moral overtones of the often elaborate productions, meant that
Shakespearean themes were often engraved.

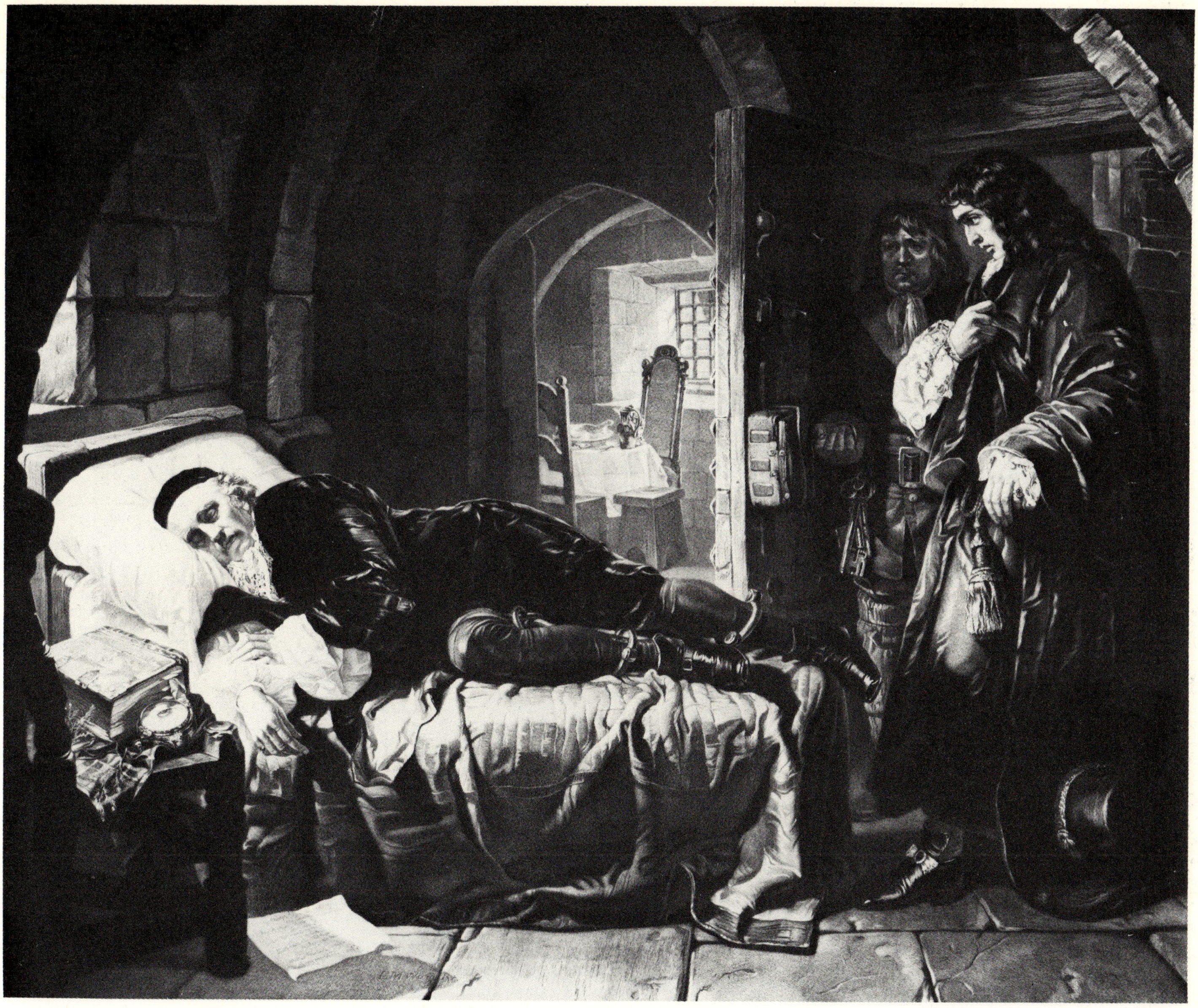

William Turner Davey (1818–1890) *Last Sleep of Argyle* (with detail) mezzotint After the painting by Edward Matthew Ward R.A. (1816–1879), painter of French and English historical subjects. The print was published in 1861 in an edition of 725. Davey usually worked on large plates after Charles Baxter, Land-seer, Ansdell, R. Bonheur and Lady Butler.

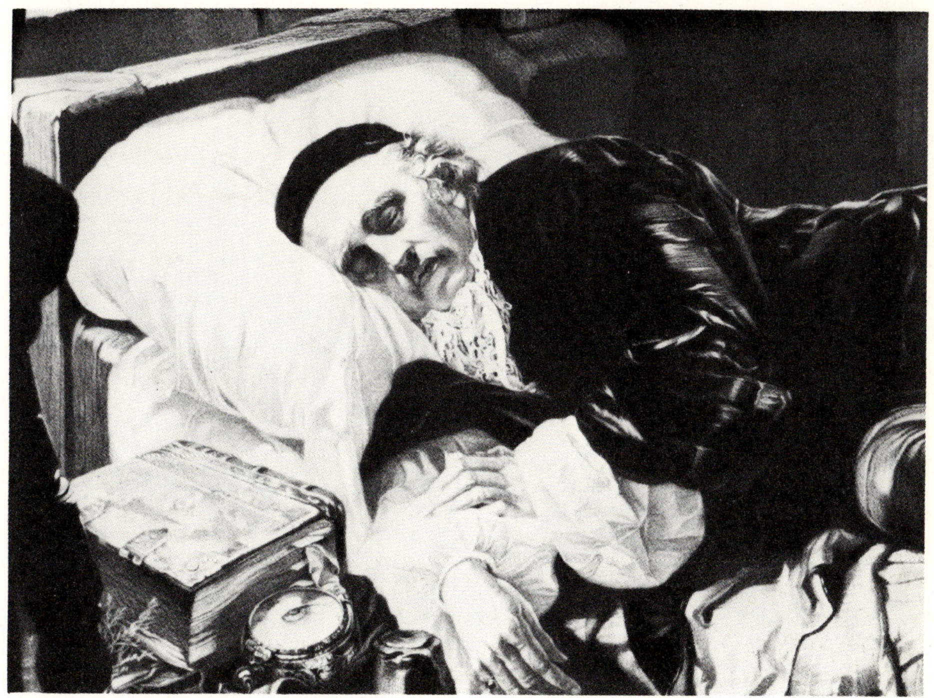

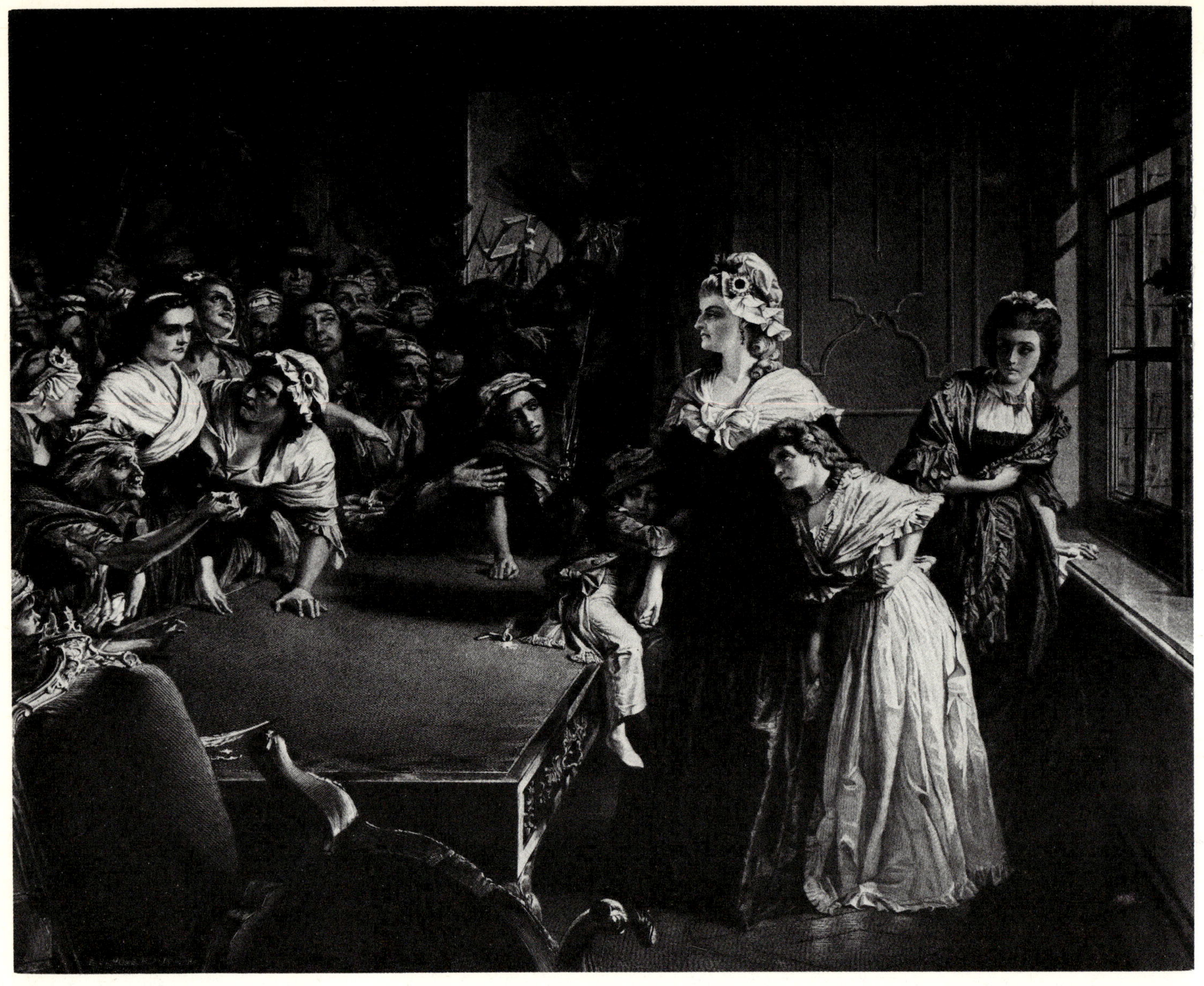

Charles William Sharpe (1818–1899) *Tuileries, 20 June 1792* line engraving
After the painting (R.A. 1860) by Alfred Elmore R.A. (1815–1881), and published for the Art Union of London in 1883.
Sharpe exhibited engravings at the Academy from 1858–83, working after Frith, Maclise, T. Faed, Wilkie, Etty and
Eastlake. The following text accompanied the painting:

> They brought the Queen's children to her, in order that their presence, by softening the mob, might serve as a buckler
> to their mother. They placed them in the depth of the window. They wheeled in front of this the Council table.
> Preserving a noble and becoming demeanour in this dreadful situation, she held the Dauphin before her, seated upon the
> table. Madame was at her side.
>
> A young girl of pleasing appearance, and respectably attired came forth and bitterly reviled in the coarsest terms
> *L'Autrichienne*. The Queen, struck by the contrast between the rage of this young girl and the gentleness of her face,
> said to her in a kind tone, 'Why do you hate me? Have I ever done you any injury?' 'No, not to me,' replied the
> pretty patriot, 'but it is you who cause the misery of the nation.' 'Poor child!' replied the Queen, 'someone has told you so,
> and deceived you. What interest can I have in making the people miserable? The wife of the King, mother of the Dauphin,
> I am a Frenchwoman in all the feelings of my heart as a wife and mother. I shall never again see my own country. I can
> only be happy or unhappy in France. I was happy when you loved me.' This gentle reproach affected the heart of the
> young girl, and her anger was effaced. She asked the Queen's pardon saying, 'I did not know you, but I see that you are
> good.'

Frederick Bromley (fl. 1856–1860) *The Alarm Bell* mezzotint and etching (RIGHT)
After the painting (R.A. 1846) by John Rogers Herbert R.A. (1810–1890), published in 1849. Herbert's paintings were
predominantly based upon biblical themes, some being engraved for *The Keepsake* books.

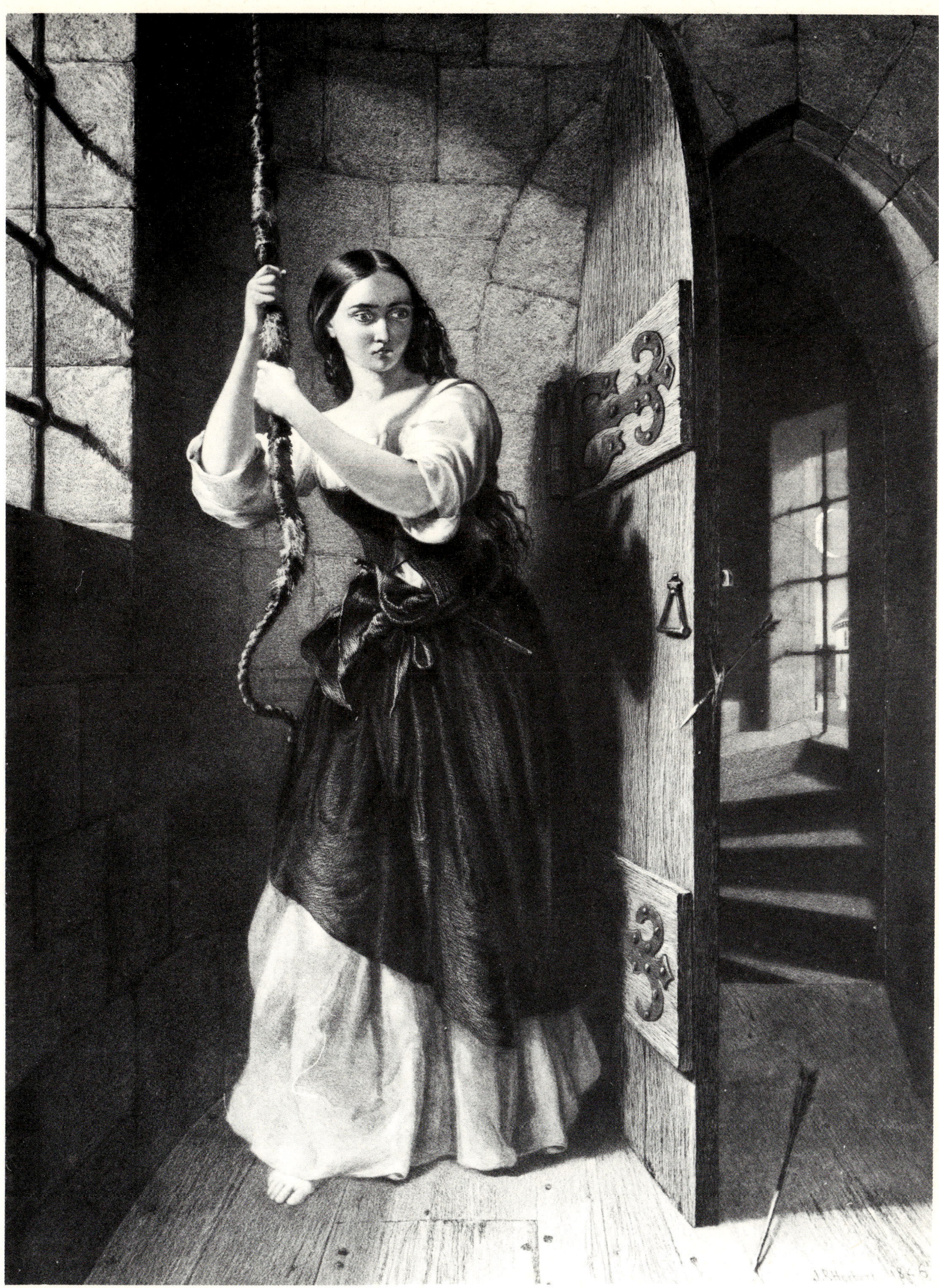

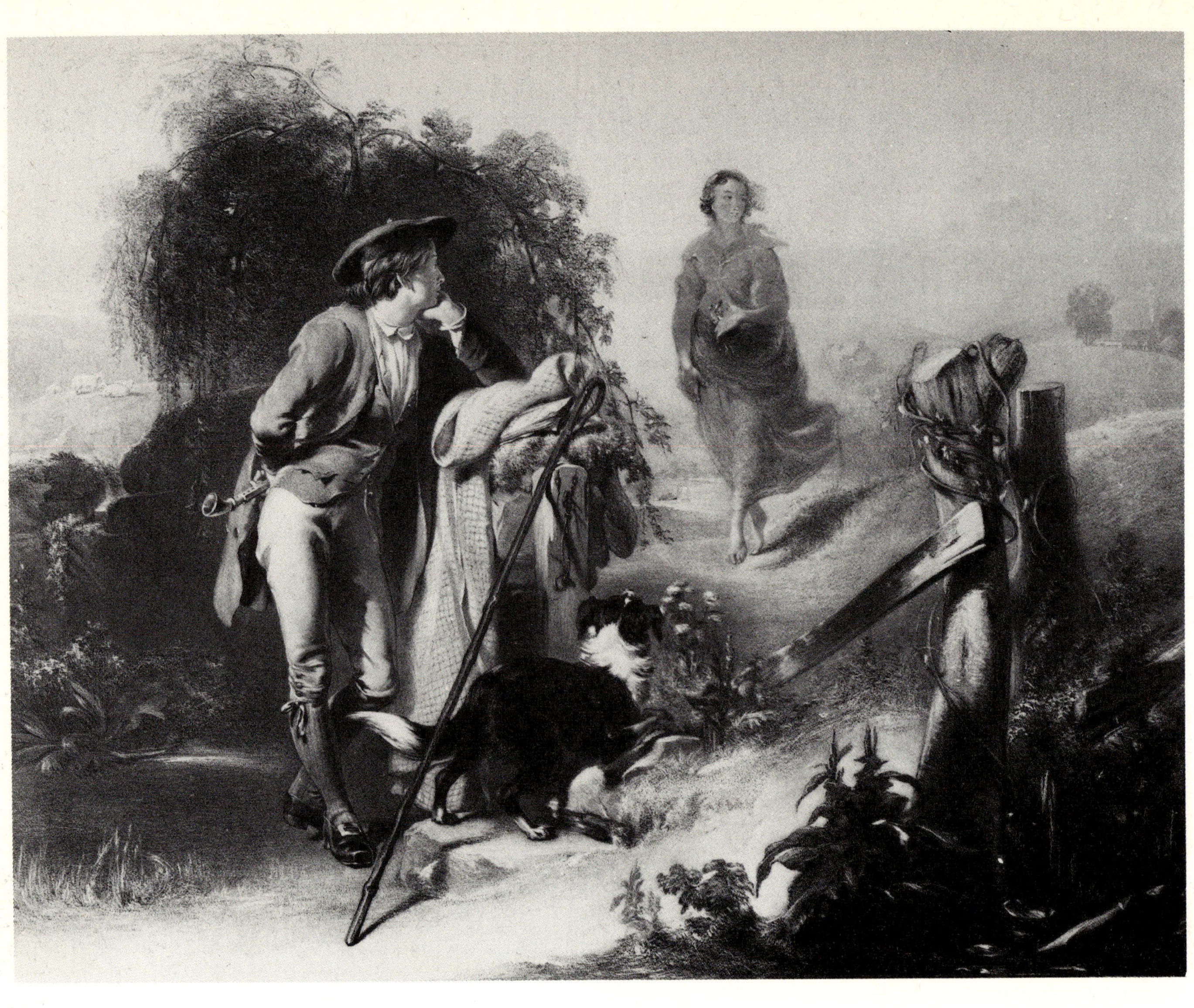

Frederick Bromley (fl.1856–1860) *The Gentle Shepherd* mezzotint
After the painting by Alexander Johnston (1815–1891), a Scottish painter of historical and genre scenes. The verse accompanying the print read:

Last morning I was gay and early out,
Upon a Dyke I leaned, glow'ring about;
I saw my Meg come linkan o'er the lee;
I saw my Meg, but Meggy saw na me.

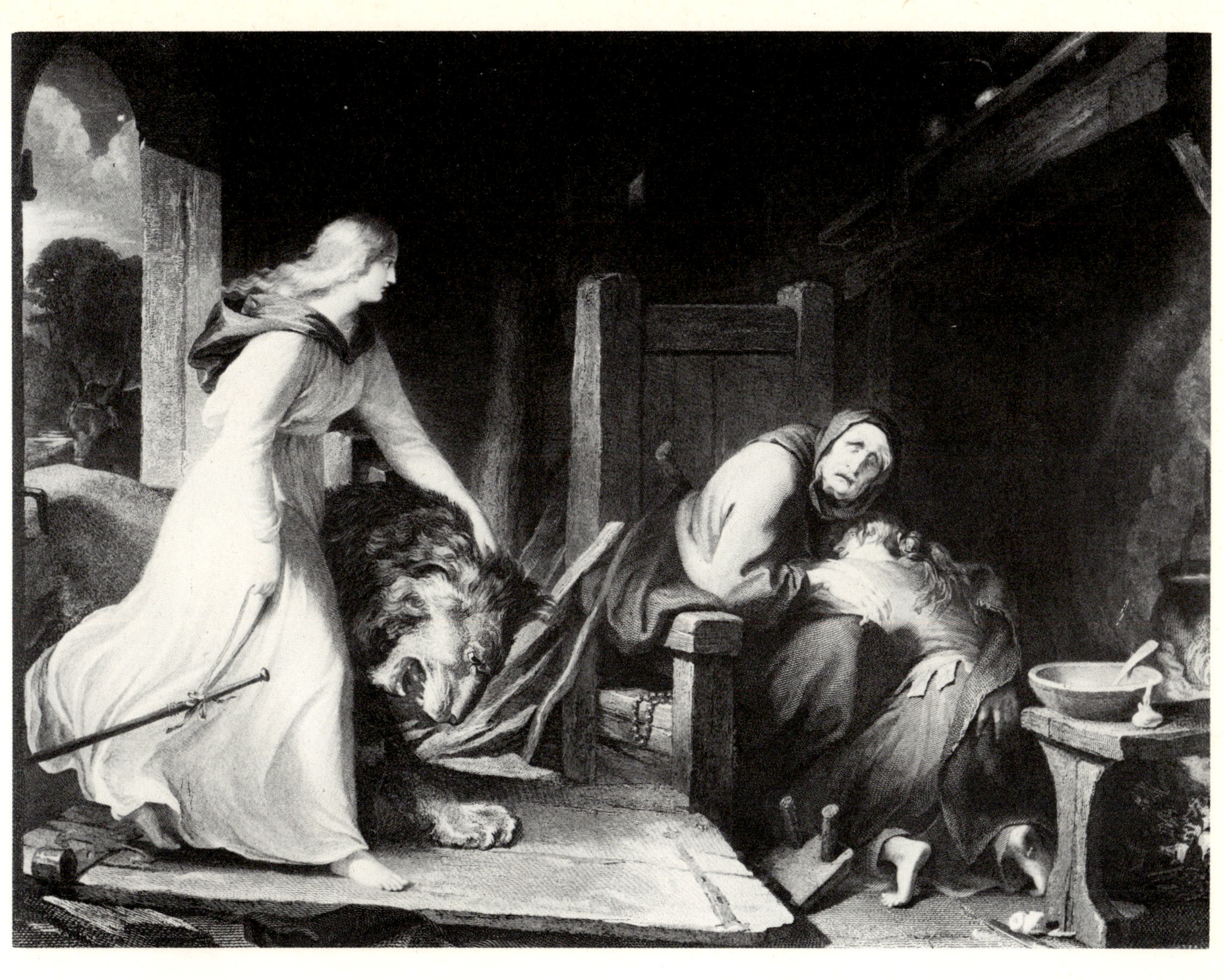

William Henry Watt (1804–1845) *Una and the Lion* line engraving
After the painting (R.A. 1832) by William Hilton (1786–1839), published for the Art Union of London in 1842. The subject was taken from an episode in Spenser's *Faerie Queen* in which Una seeks shelter in the cave of Corceca.

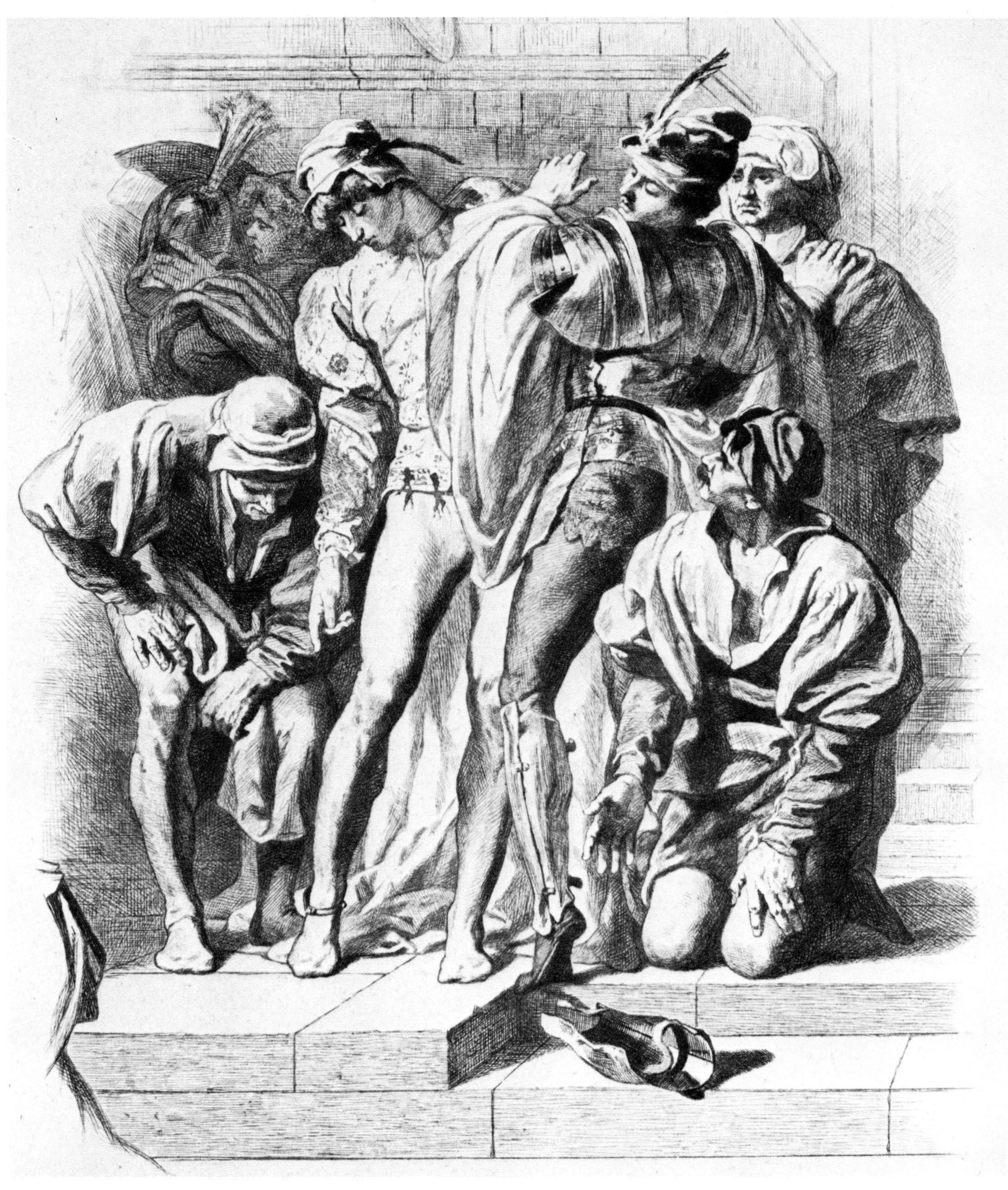

Achille-Isidore Gilbert (1828–1899) *The Arts of War* etching
After the fresco for the Victoria and Albert Museum designed by Lord Leighton P.R.A. (1830–1896) in 1873–79. Published for the British and Foreign Artists Association in 1881, in a registered edition of 1,500. Leighton did not allow many of his works to be engraved, believing that their popularization would vulgarize the importance of their classical and Italianate themes. He designed a companion fresco *The Arts of Peace*, 1883–85. Both depicted figures which were criticized as vulgar and affected. 'Their exaggerated amplitude about the dresses is anything but Greek,' wrote Pepys Cockerall. Gilbert was a Parisian who exhibited works at the Academy from 1877 to 1884, including an etching of Leighton's famed sculpture *Athlete struggling with a Python* which was published in a declared edition of 1,490 in 1881.

46

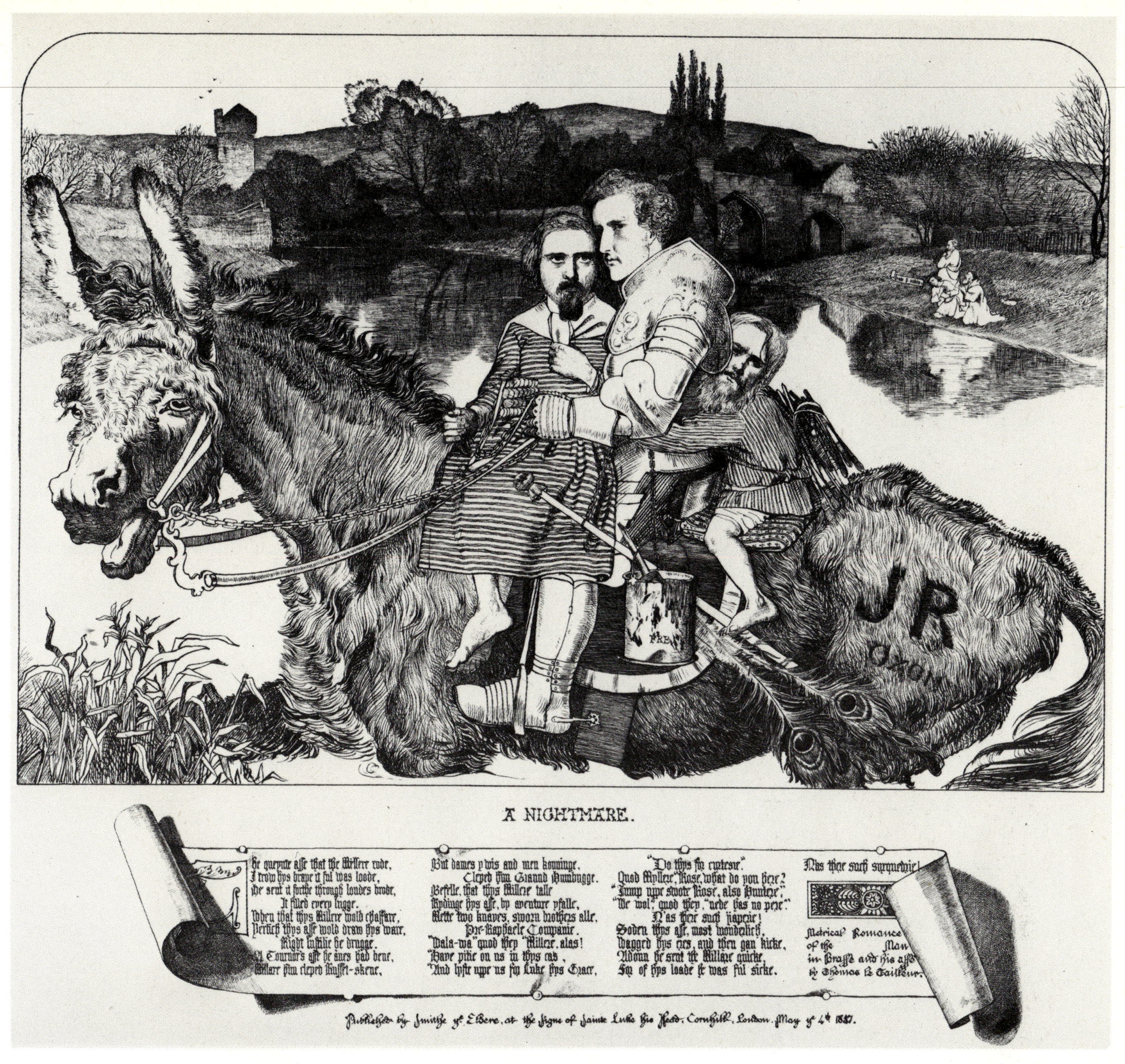

Frederick Sandys (1829–1904) *A Nightmare* line engraving
Intended as a parody of Millais's painting *A Dream of the Past: Sir Isumbras at the Ford*, 1857, the painting which Ruskin attacked as 'not merely Fall – it is Catastrophe', for Millais's loosened style and obvious sentimentality. Sandys, a noted painter and wood engraver, produced this zinc engraving which was issued as a broadsheet depicting three figures – Rossetti, Millais in armour, and Holman Hunt astride a braying jackass. From the saddle hangs a bucket of paint, stamped 'P.R.B.' (Pre-Raphaelite Brotherhood). On the opposite bank of the stream sit Titian, Raphael and Michelangelo begging to be carried across with the Pre-Raphaelites. As a result of this print Sandys became friends with Rossetti, and his succeeding work adopted characteristics of the Pre-Raphaelite style.

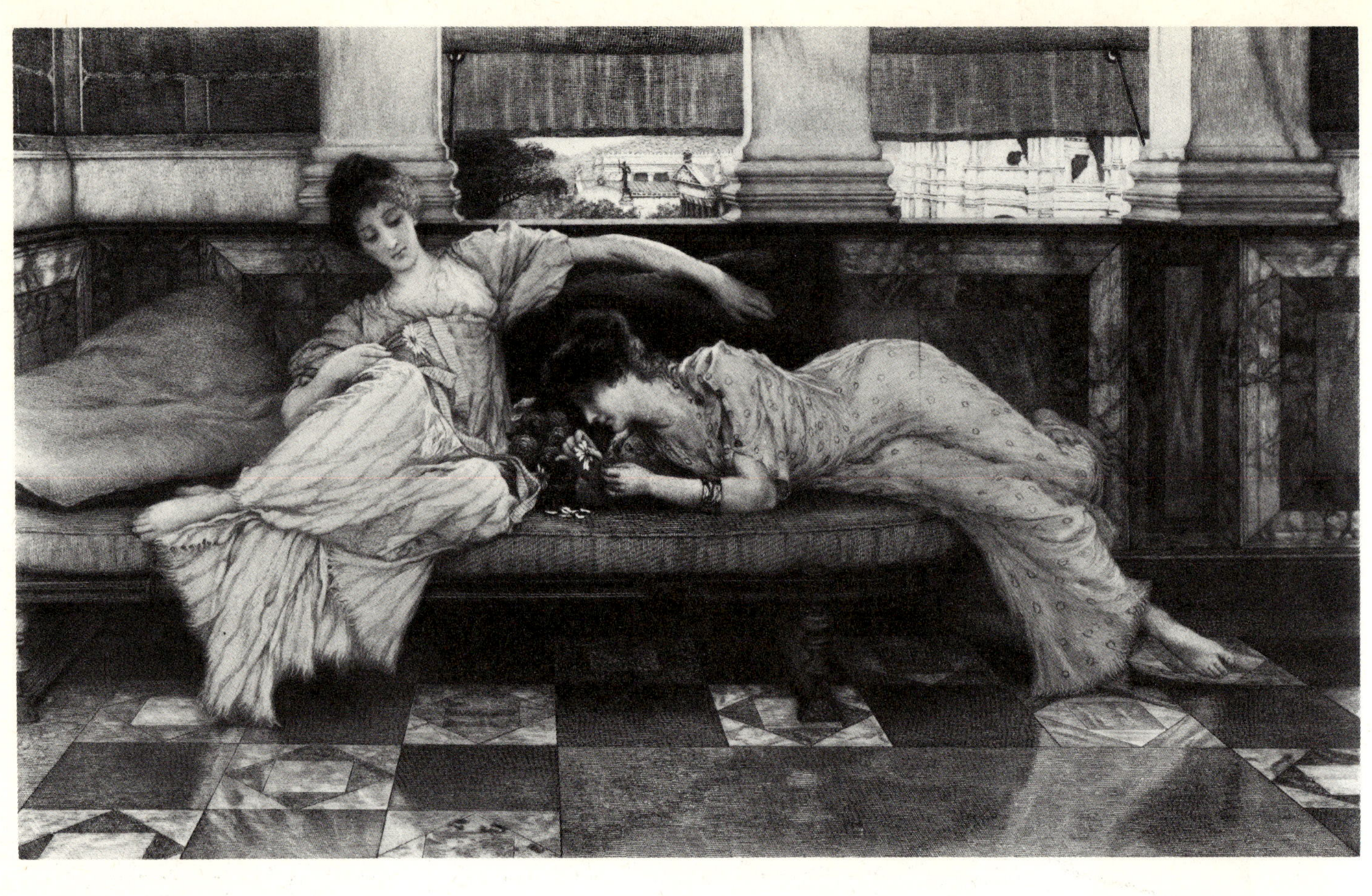

Leopold Lowenstam (1842–1898) *He loves me – He loves me not!* etching
After the painting by Sir Lawrence Alma-Tadema R.A. (1836–1912). Published in 1893. Lowenstam was a popular etcher who taught in Sweden until 1873. In London he exhibited works after Alma-Tadema, Sadler, Bonheur and Poynter. Alma-Tadema was a noted painter of genre paintings in the classical style, and occasionally etched illustrations for books (e.g. Firdusi's *Epic of Kings*, reprinted in 1889). His skill in painting marble was adequately reproduced in the etching.

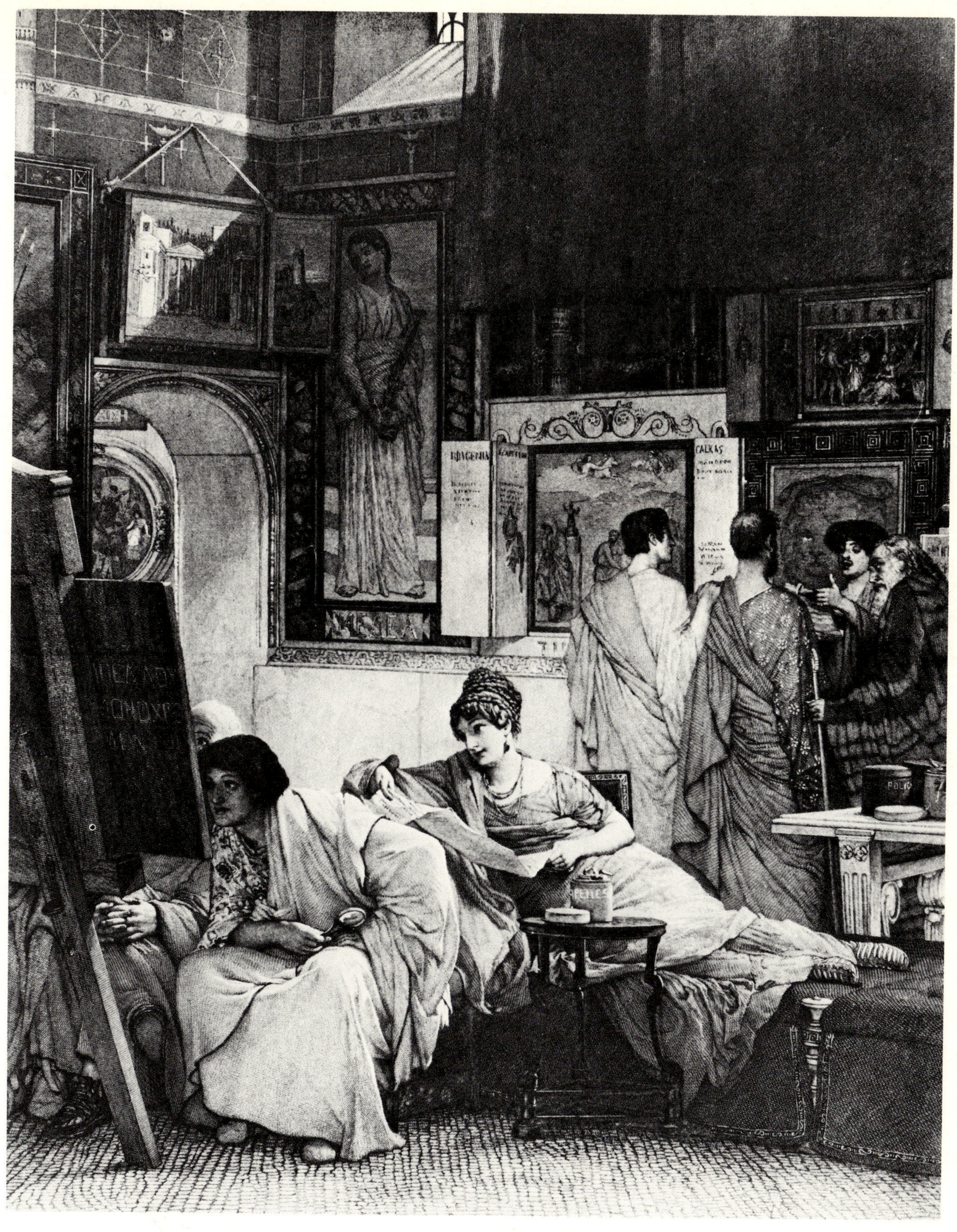

Auguste Blanchard (1819–1898) *The Antique Studio of Painting* line engraving
After the painting by Sir Lawrence Alma-Tadema R.A. (1836–1912). Published in 1875 as a companion to *The Sculpture Gallery* in a declared edition of 450. Blanchard was a Parisian who engraved over ninety-three plates registered by the Printsellers' Association (1894) including works after Holman Hunt, Maclise, Alma-Tadema and Frith. The most noted of his works was *The Derby Day* after Frith, declared in 1858 in an edition of 8,025.

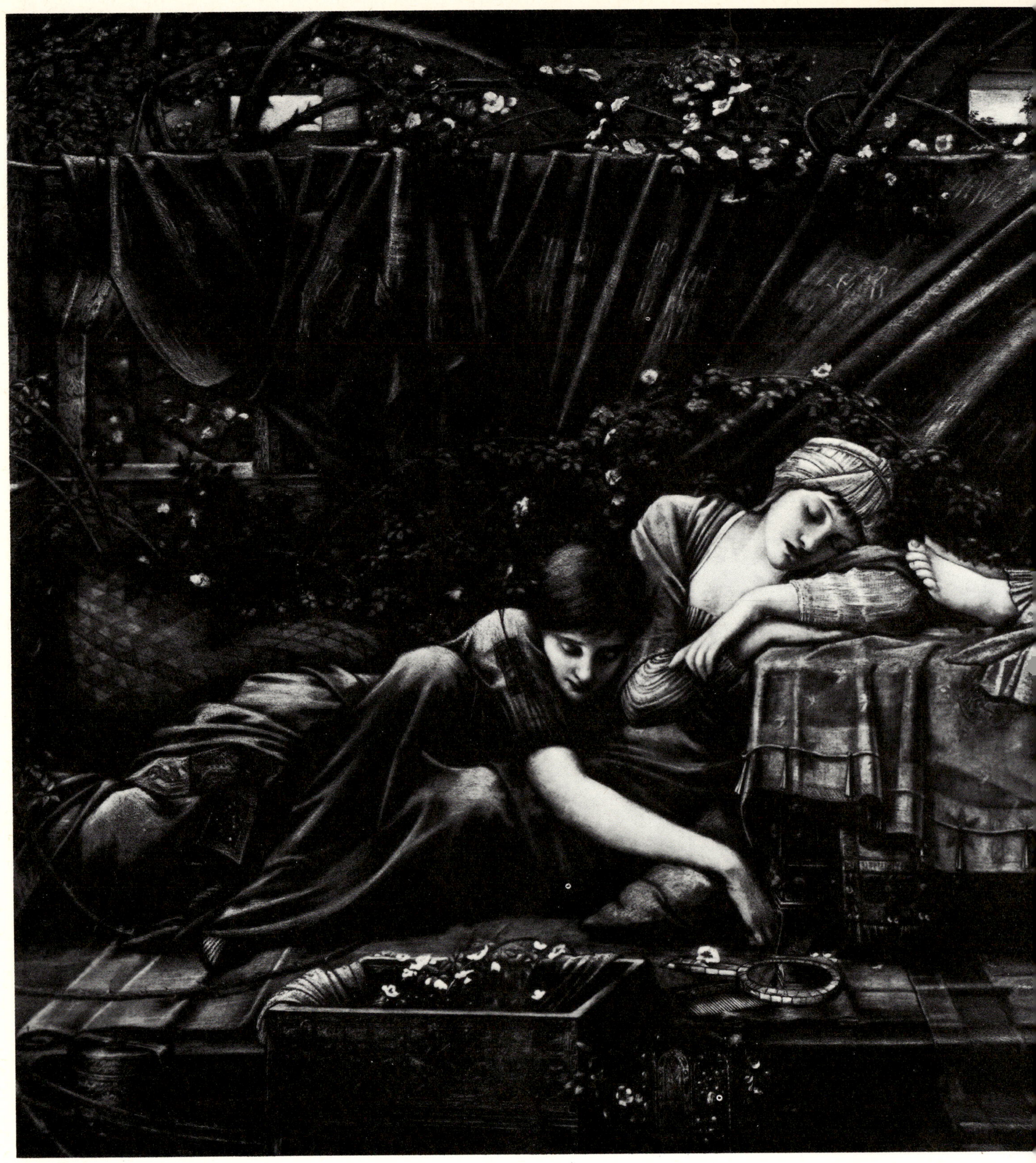

The Rose Bower photogravure
After Sir Edward Coley Burne-Jones, Bart, R.W.S. (1833–1898), from *The Legend of the Briar Rose*, a series of four paintings of 1890, published in 1892 in a declared edition of 525 sets. The series included *The Briar Wood*, *The Council Room*, and *The Garden Court*, with verses by William Morris:

Here lies the hoarded love, the key
To all the treasure that shall be.
Come, fated hand, the gift to take
And smite the sleeping world awake.

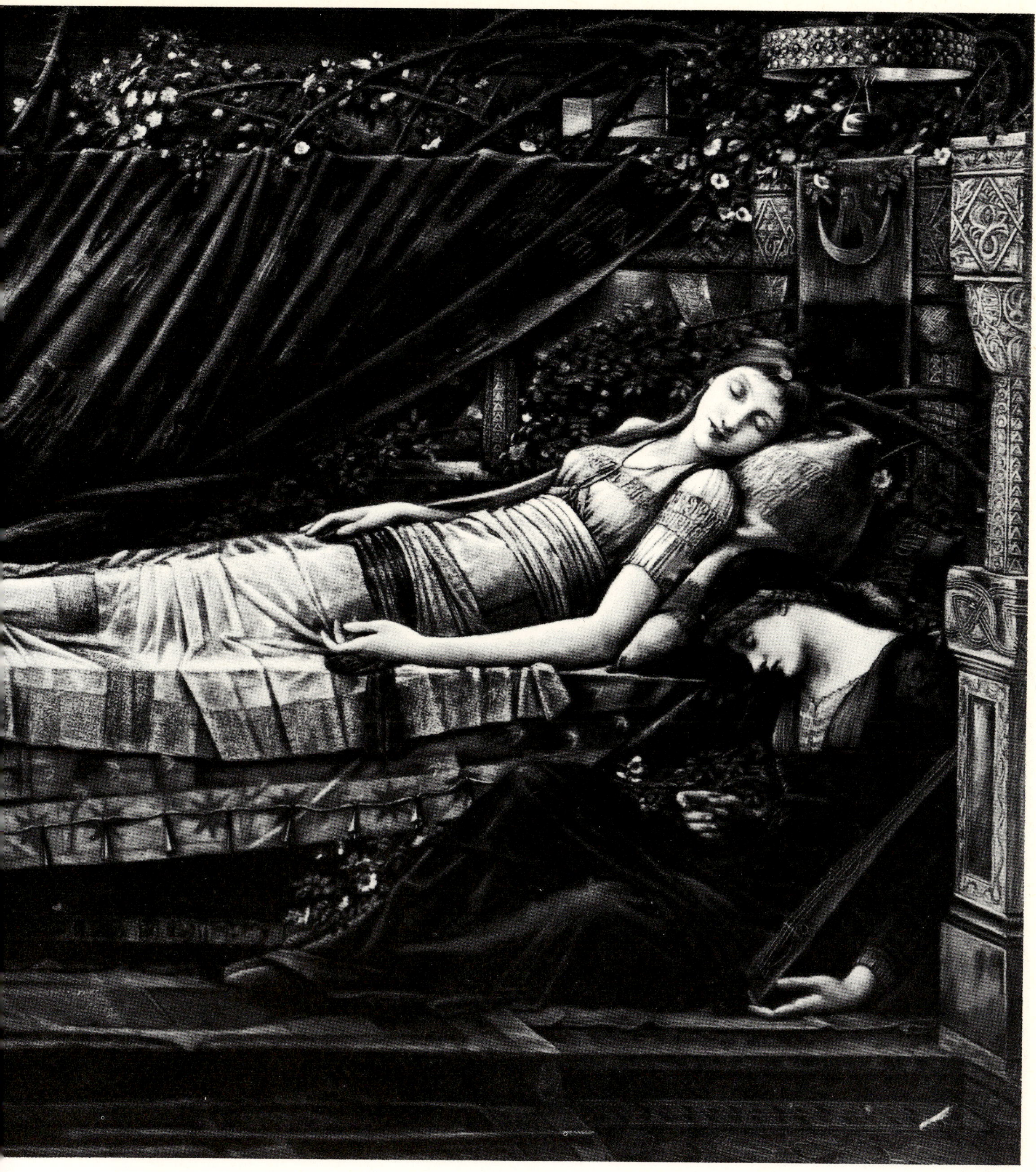

Burne-Jones's paintings were etched in small editions or published as photogravures in very large editions, which were printed in Paris in sepia or green-toned inks.

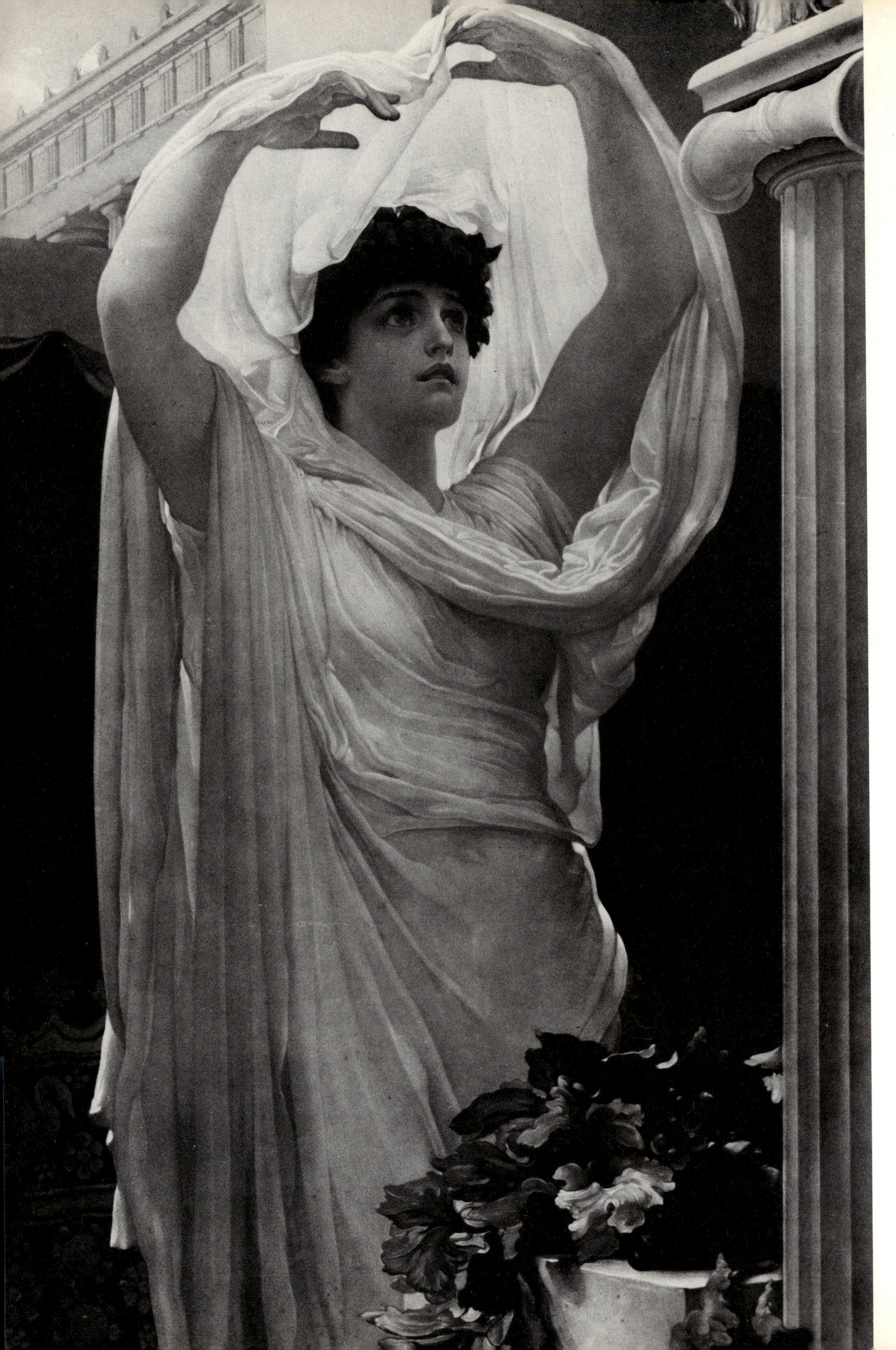

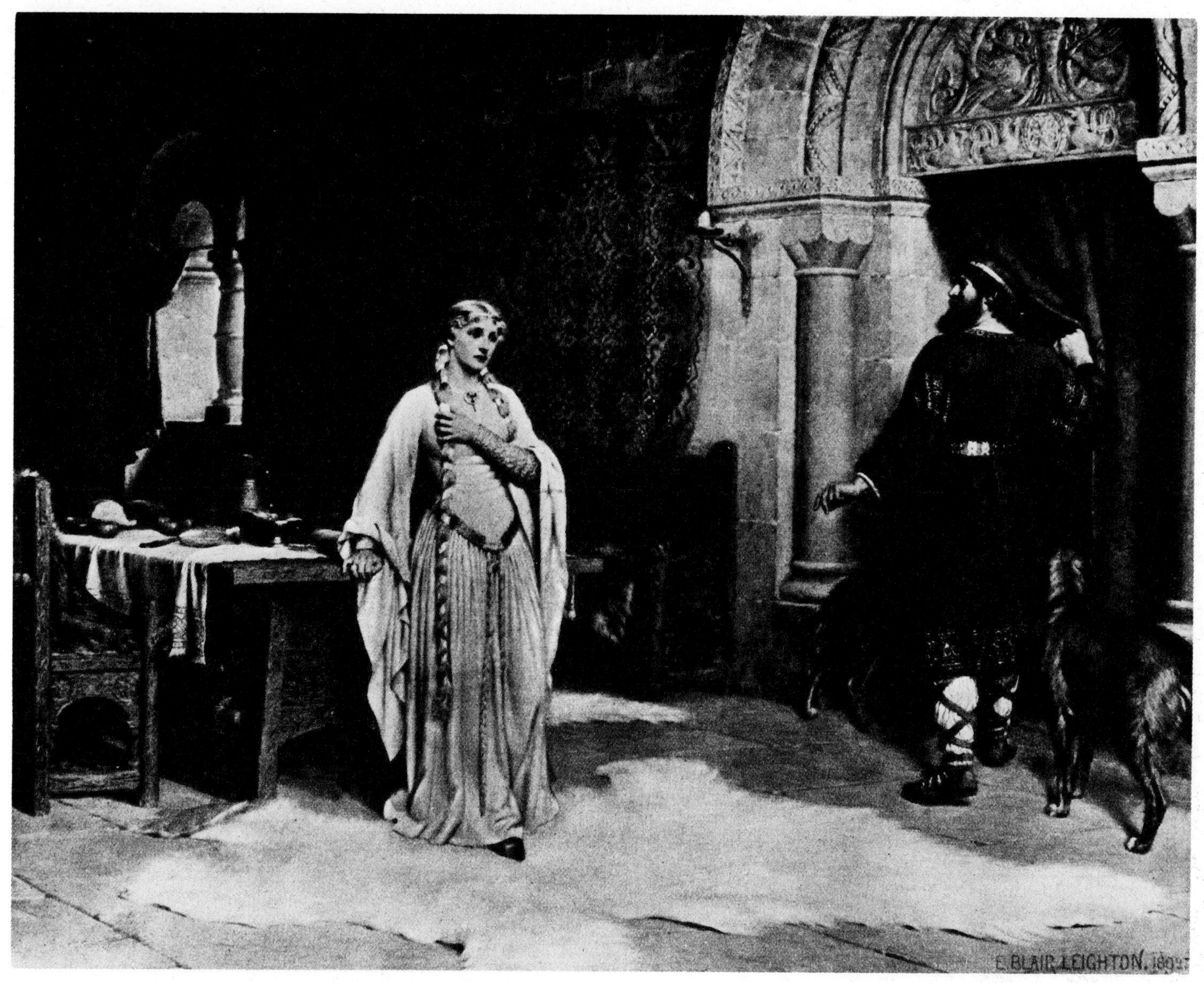

Lady Godiva photogravure
From the *Magazine of Art* after the painting (R.A. 1892) by Edmund Blair Leighton (1853–1922), based upon the lines:

He answered, 'Ride You naked thro' the town and I repeal it', and, nodding as in scorn, he parted, with great strides, among his dogs. (Tennyson)

John Douglas Miller (c.1872–c.1903) *Invocation* mezzotint (LEFT)
After the painting (R.A. 1889) by Lord Leighton P.R.A. (1830–1896). Published in an edition of 925 in 1893, after which the plate was destroyed. The print was exhibited at the Academy in 1893. Miller also engraved after the works of Fildes, F. Dicksee, and W. B. Richmond. This print is a particularly fine example of Leighton's style of figure drawing which was so admired by his aristocratic contemporaries.

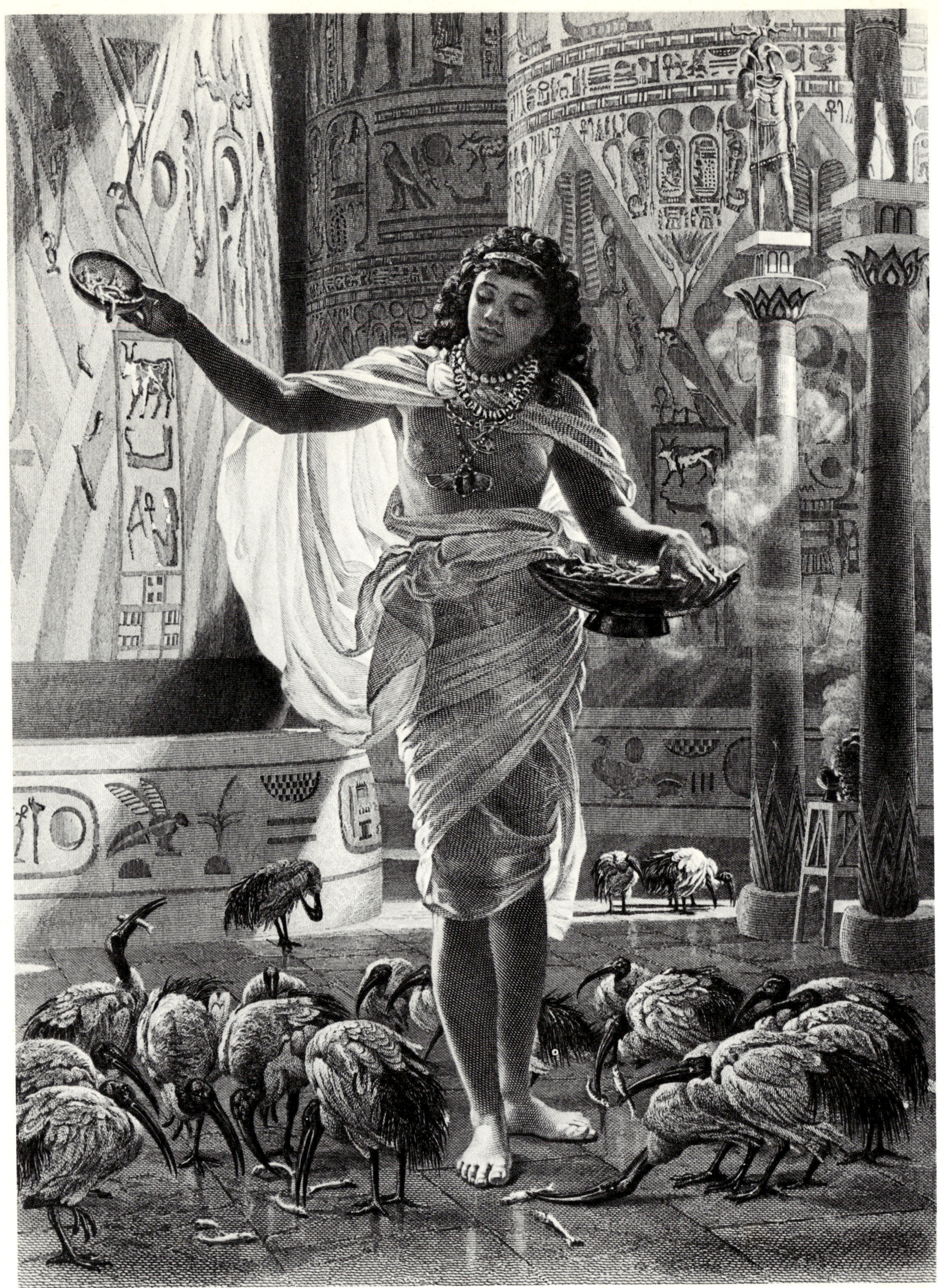

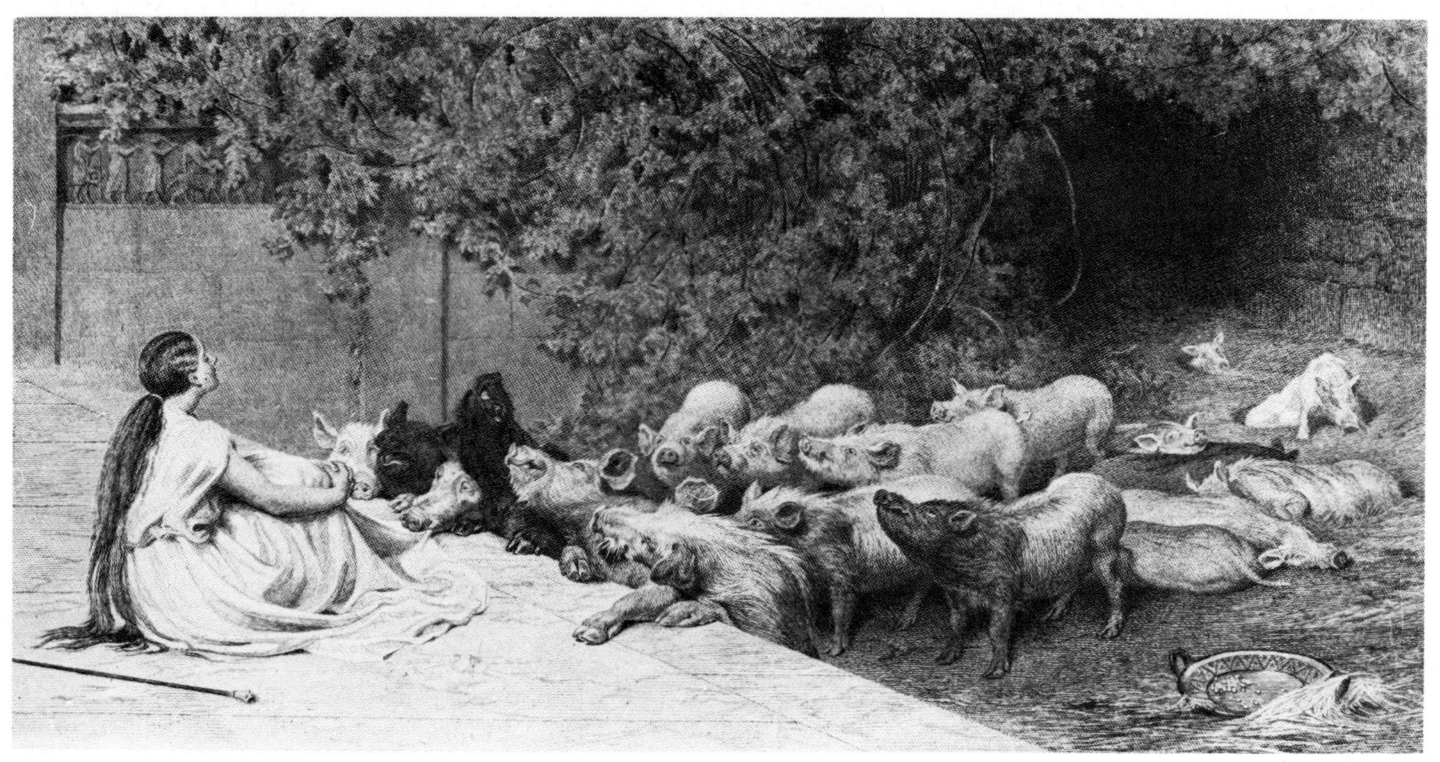

James Dobie (1849–c.1893) *Circe and the Companions of Ulysses* etching
After the painting (R.A. 1871) by Briton Riviere R.A. (1840–1920). Published here from *Art Journal*. Other popular periodicals including *The Studio, The Graphic,* and *The Illustrated London News* commissioned prominent contemporary engravers to reproduce in their pages the popular paintings of the year, often with whole issues devoted to an individual artist's work. This picture was also engraved in a mixture of styles for Thos. Agnew and Sons in 1872, who paid fifty guineas for the copyright and sold artist's proofs for eight pounds sixteen shillings each. The engraver Frederick Stacpoole, wrote: 'The shortest time I can name (to complete) will be 10 months! that surely can't frighten your friend. I should like to receive the picture the first week in June so as to put it in hand at once, and make the most of the long days.'

Feeding the Sacred Ibis in the Halls of Karnac line engraving (LEFT)
From the *Art Journal* after the painting (R.A. 1871) by Sir Edward John Poynter P.R.A. (1836–1919).

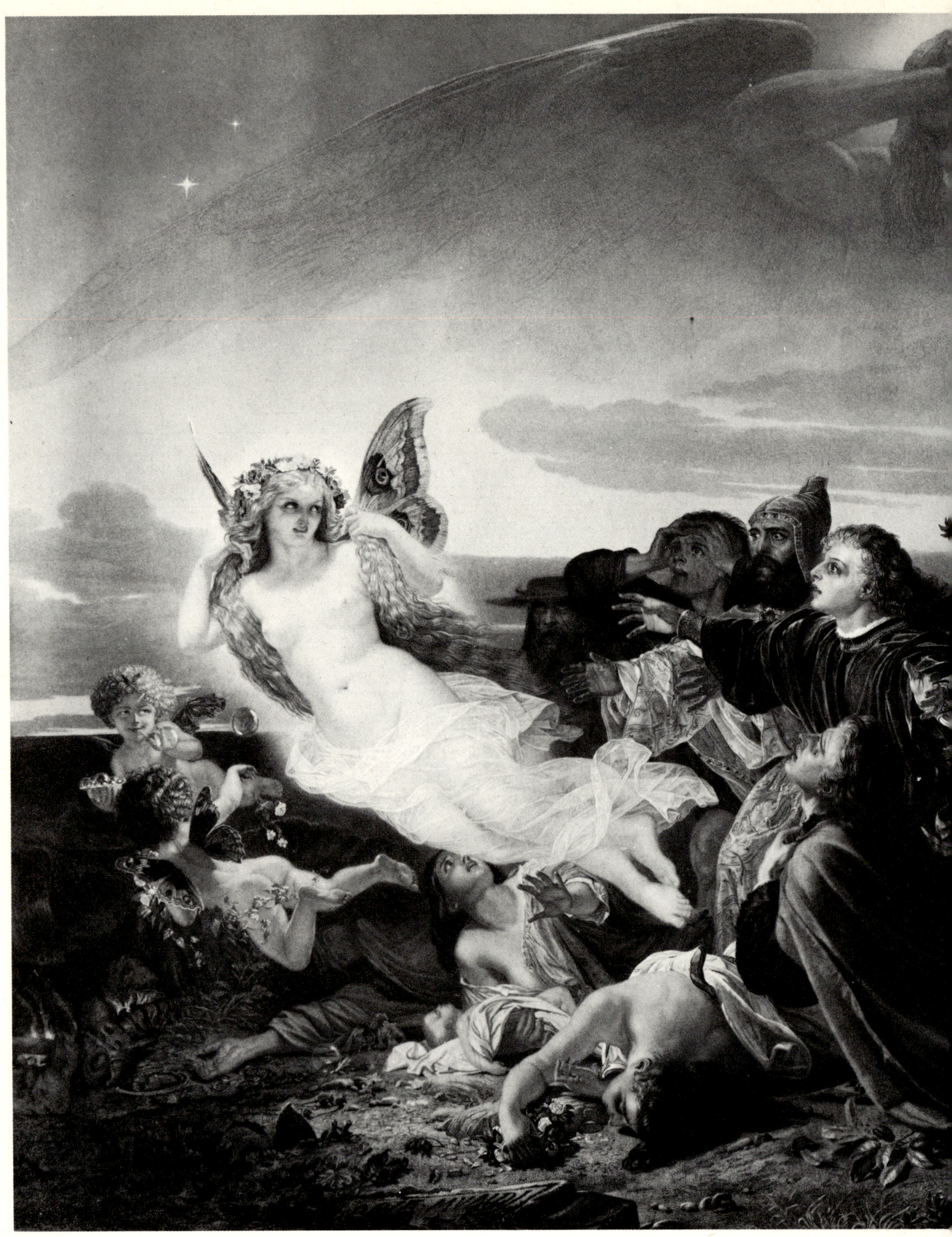

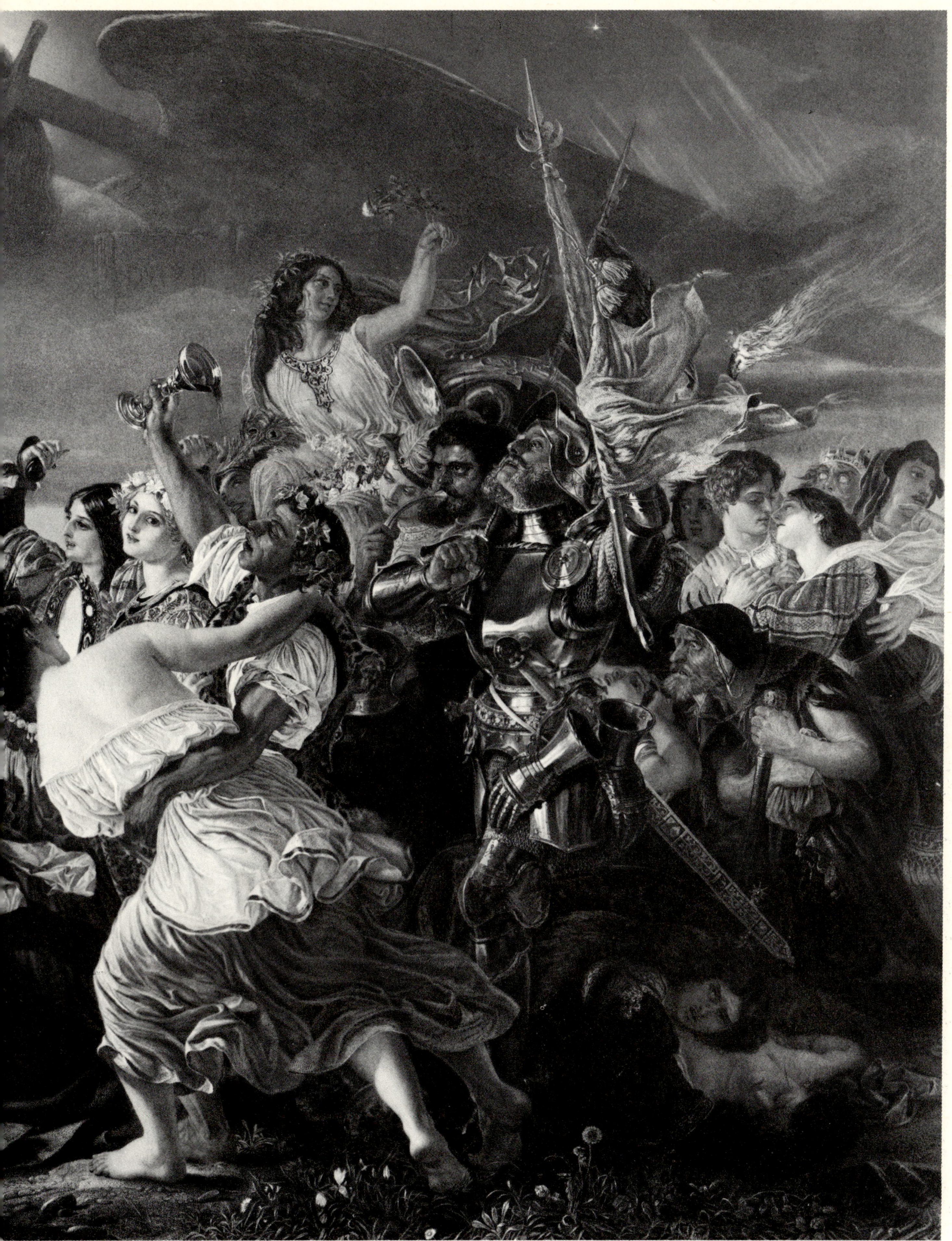

Henry Thomas Ryall (1811–1867) *The Pursuit of Pleasure (A Vision of Human Life)* line and stipple engraving
After the painting (R.S.A. 1855) by Sir Joseph Noël Paton R.S.A. (1821–1901), published by Alexander Hill in 1864.
Declared in 1859 for an edition of 1,325.

John Martin (1789–1854) *Satan arousing the Fallen Angels* mezzotint (RIGHT)
From Martin's own designs illustrating the Bible and Milton's *Paradise Lost* of 1827. Martin was a noted landscape and historical painter and mezzotint engraver. During the years 1823 to 1842 he engraved 100 plates. He was the first to make extensive use of soft steel plates for engraving, and attained a dramatic richness which was much admired and imitated by his contemporaries.

Edward Goodall (1795–1870) *The Angel's Whisper* mezzotint and etching (BELOW)
After a painting by Frederick Goodall R.A. (1822–1904). Engraved by his father in 1848, and published by H. Graves in 1849. The verse below the print reads:

The Dawn of the Morning
Saw Dermont Returning
And the wife wept with joy rake's Father to see
And closely caressing
Her child with a blessing said
'I knew that the Angels were whispering with thee.'

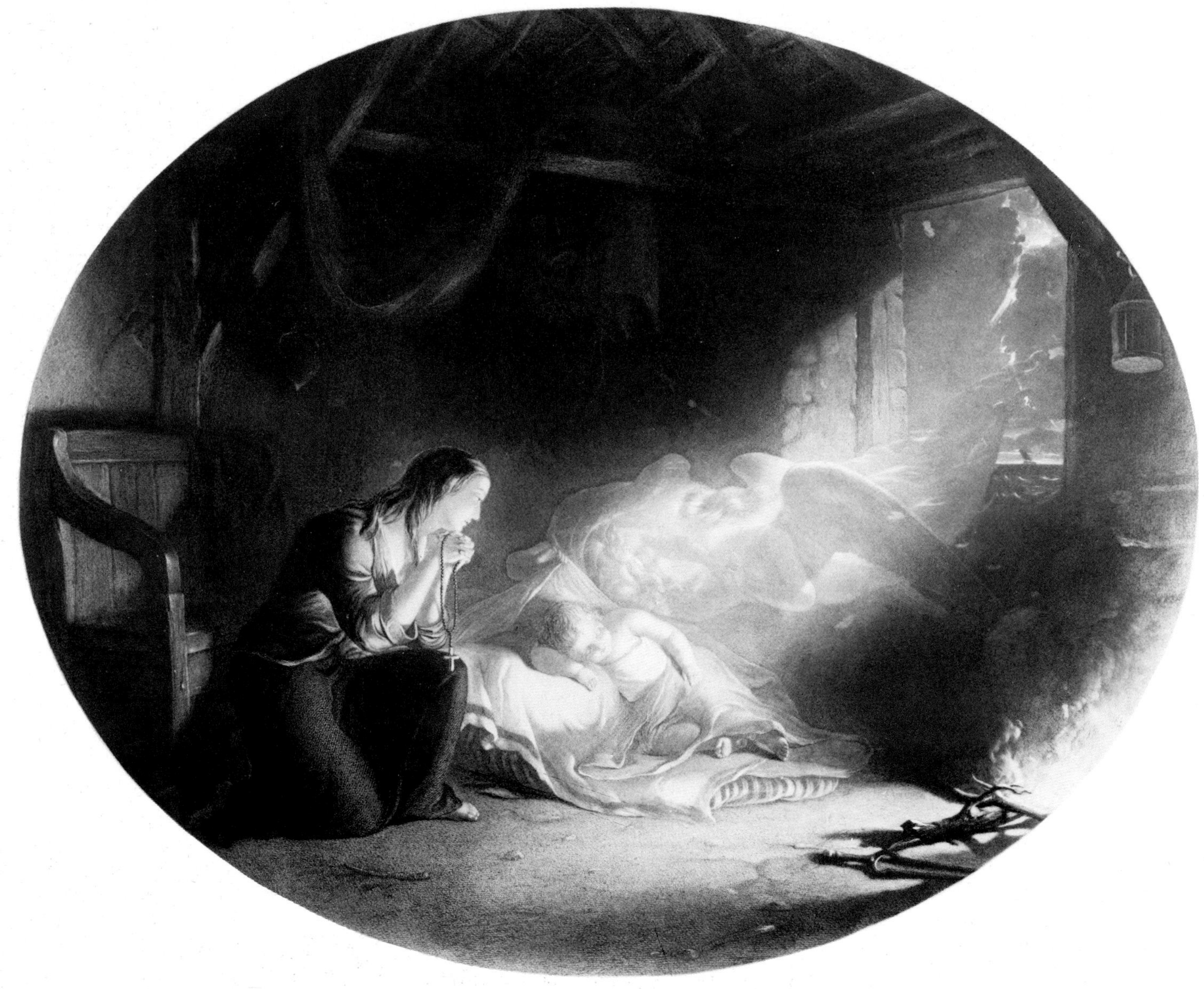

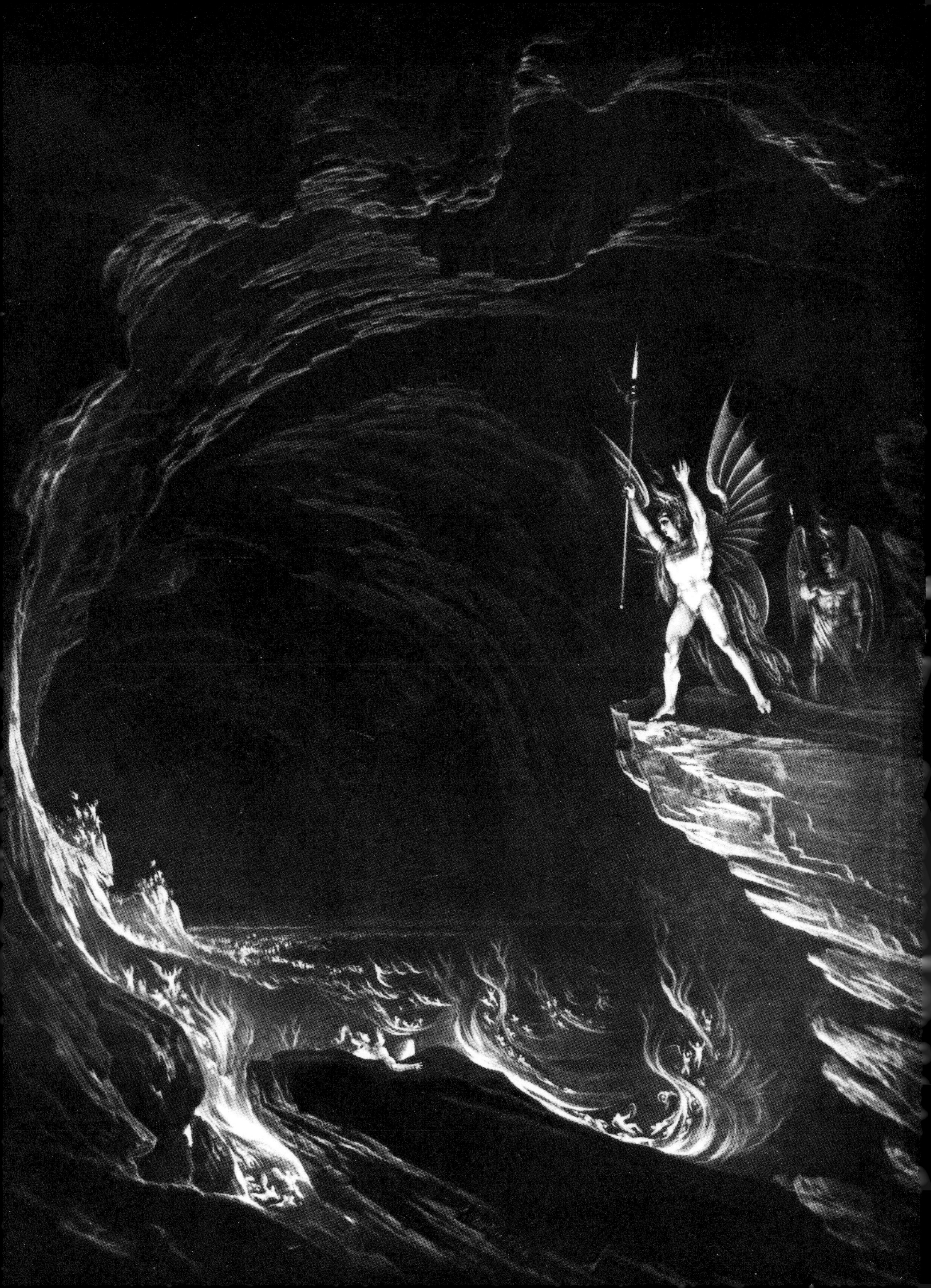

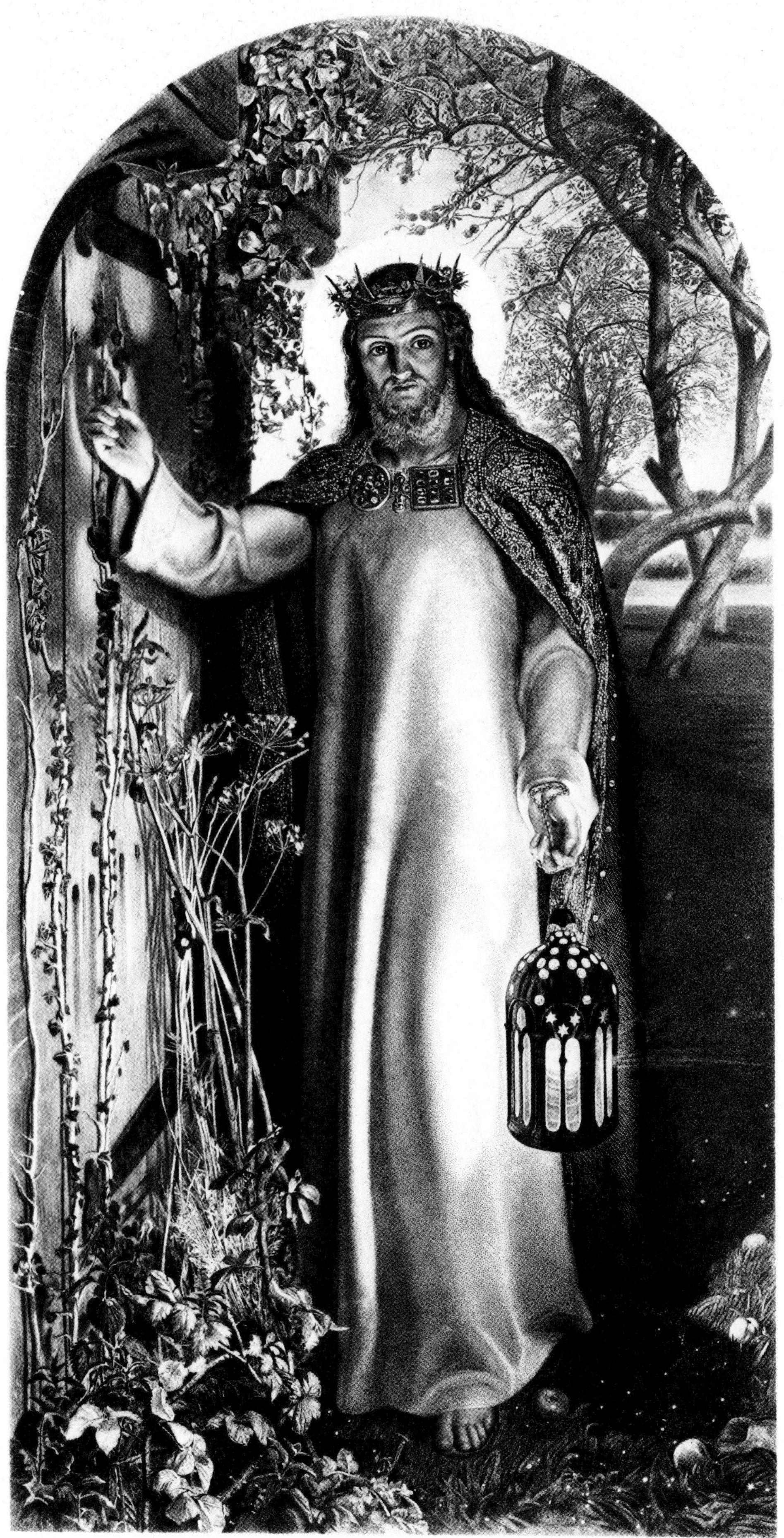

William Henry Simmons (1811–1882)
The Light of the World line and stipple
engraving
After the painting (R.A. 1854) by
William Holman Hunt O.M. (1827–
1910), published in 1860 by Gambart
and Co. in a declared edition of 1,025.
The painting was accompanied by the
text: 'Behold, I stand at the door and
knock: if any man hear my voice, and
open the door, I will sup with him and
he with me (Rev.III:20).' Ruskin considered the painting to be 'the most
wonderful picture I ever saw for intensity
of feeling and depth and fullness of mean-
ing'; and he wrote a treatise explain-
ing his full impressions which was published as a broadsheet promoting the
print. Holman Hunt wrote to Gambart
and Co. in 1860 in praise of the reproduction: '. . . how very much I approve
of the character of the work and (to)
thank [Simmons] for his kind and patient
attention to my criticisms throughout
its progress . . . how entire is my
satisfaction. All the parts of secondary
importance such as the vegetation, which
from the first I felt to be remarkably
successful, have retained their excellence
of drawing and truth of texture, with the
addition of force which has been given
to them in completion – while more
important points for instance: the head
and hands of the figure have been
steadily acquiring a truth of texture of
both drawing and light and shadow
such as has made the expression and
sentiment as perfect as it seems to me
the means for producing them in black
and white would allow.'

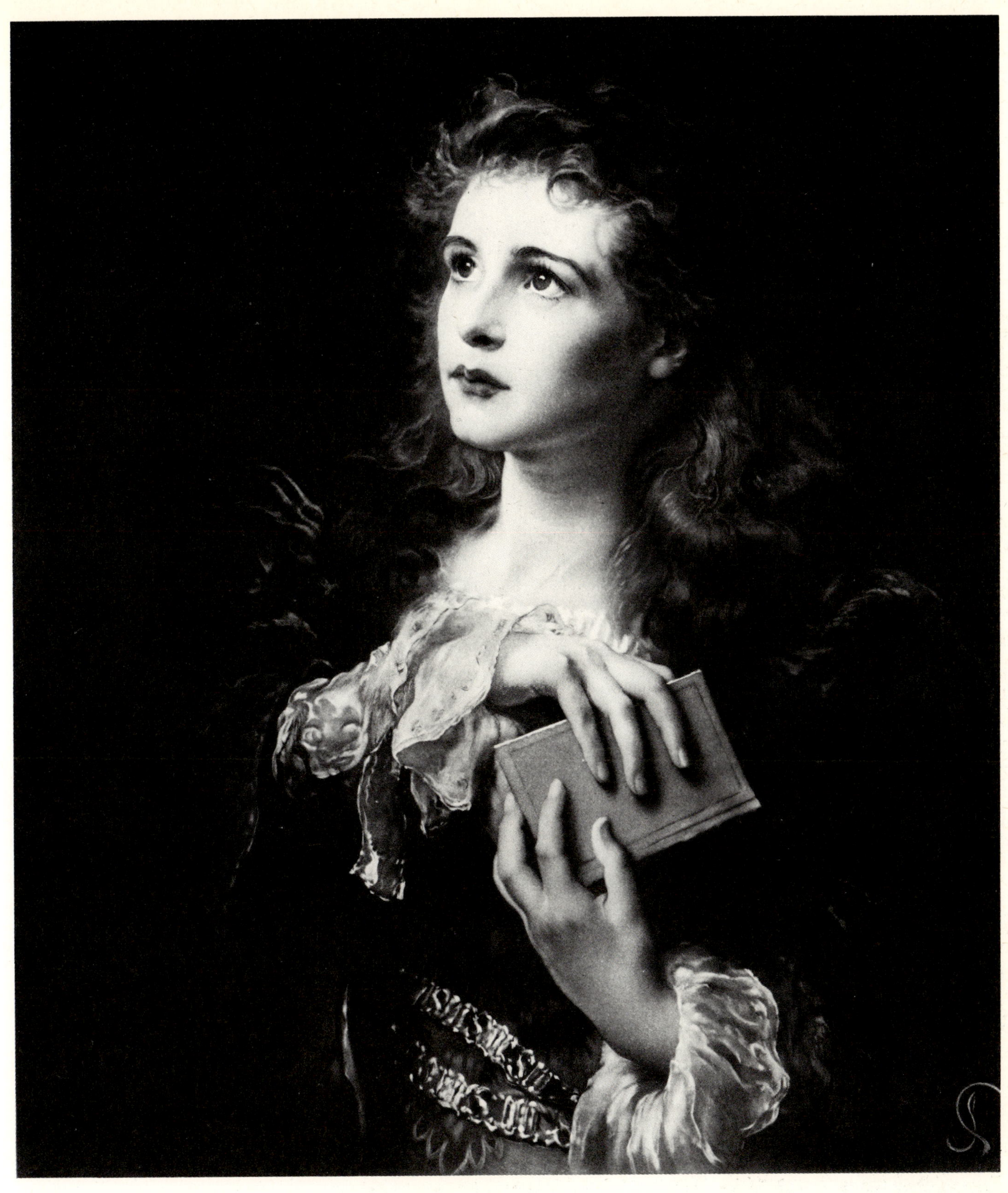

Henry Scott Bridgwater (1864–c.1893) *The Soul's Awakening* mezzotint printed in brown
After the painting (R.A. 1888) by James Sant R.A. (1820–1916). Published in 1890. The print, a companion to *Lead Kindly Light*, was exhibited at the Academy in 1890. Engravers were often commissioned by religious tract societies and missionary groups to illustrate their work and teachings. George Baxter (1804–1867), a colour printer who worked for religious societies in the later part of his life, engraved *Portrait of the Rev. John Williams* which was advertised in 1843 as 'a splendid full length portrait . . . represented in the picture at his reception by the natives of Tanna the day before he was massacred, and acknowledged by the friends of missions as a faithful likeness of this lamented missionary.'

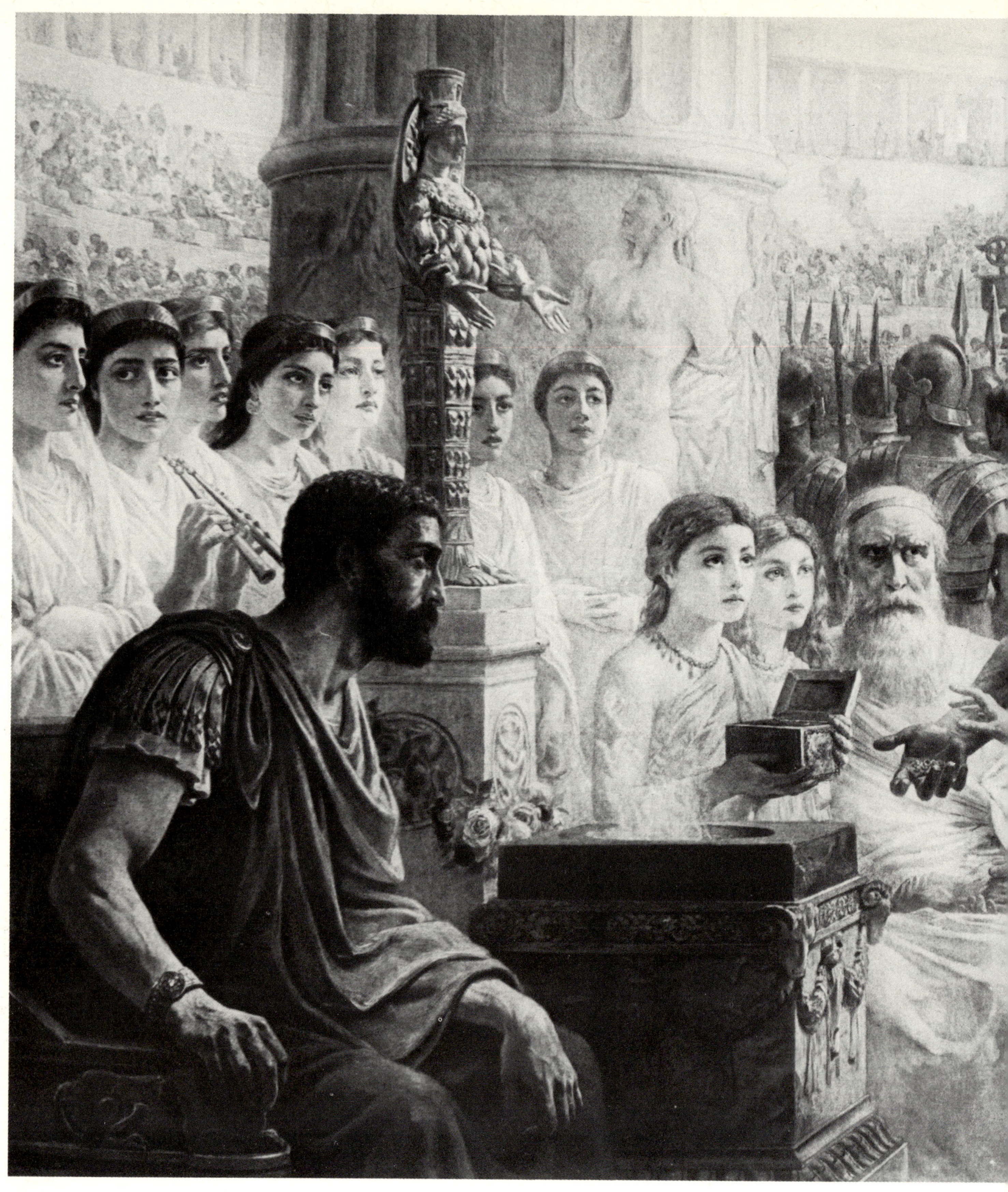

Diana or Christ? Let her cast the incense – But one grain – and she is free photogravure
After the painting (R.A. 1881) by Edwin Long R.A. (1829–1891). Published by Thos. Agnew and Sons in 1889, in a declared edition of 675, although subsequent editions made it the firm's largest selling print. The scene depicted is Ephesus at the end of the stadium, which may have been used as an amphitheatre at one time. Long was a popular painter of historical and biblical subjects, and especially Egyptian themes. His style resembles that of Alma-Tadema. His paintings fetched large amounts: *Babylonian Marriage Market* of 1875 was sold for £6,300, then a record price for the work of a living artist.

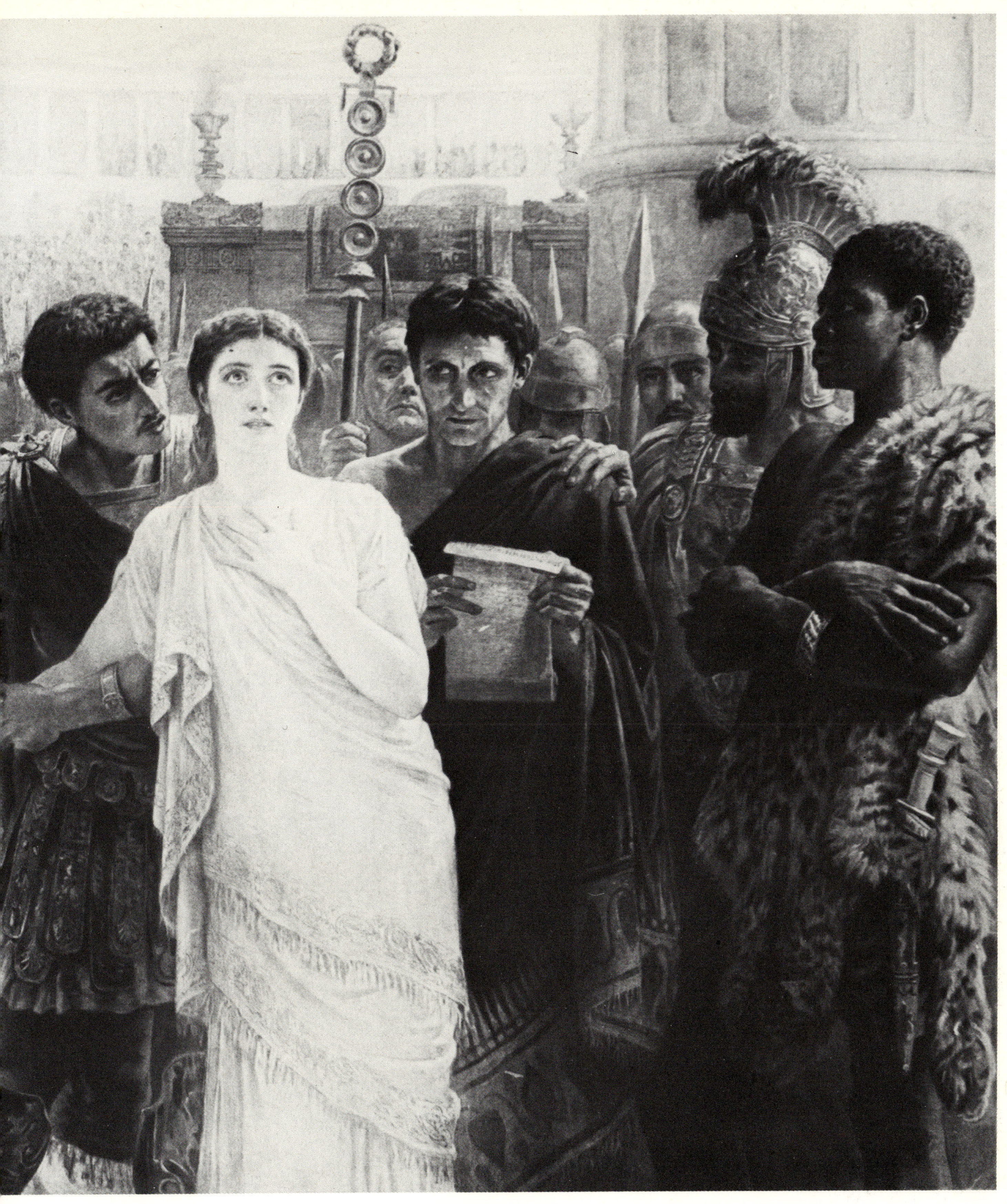

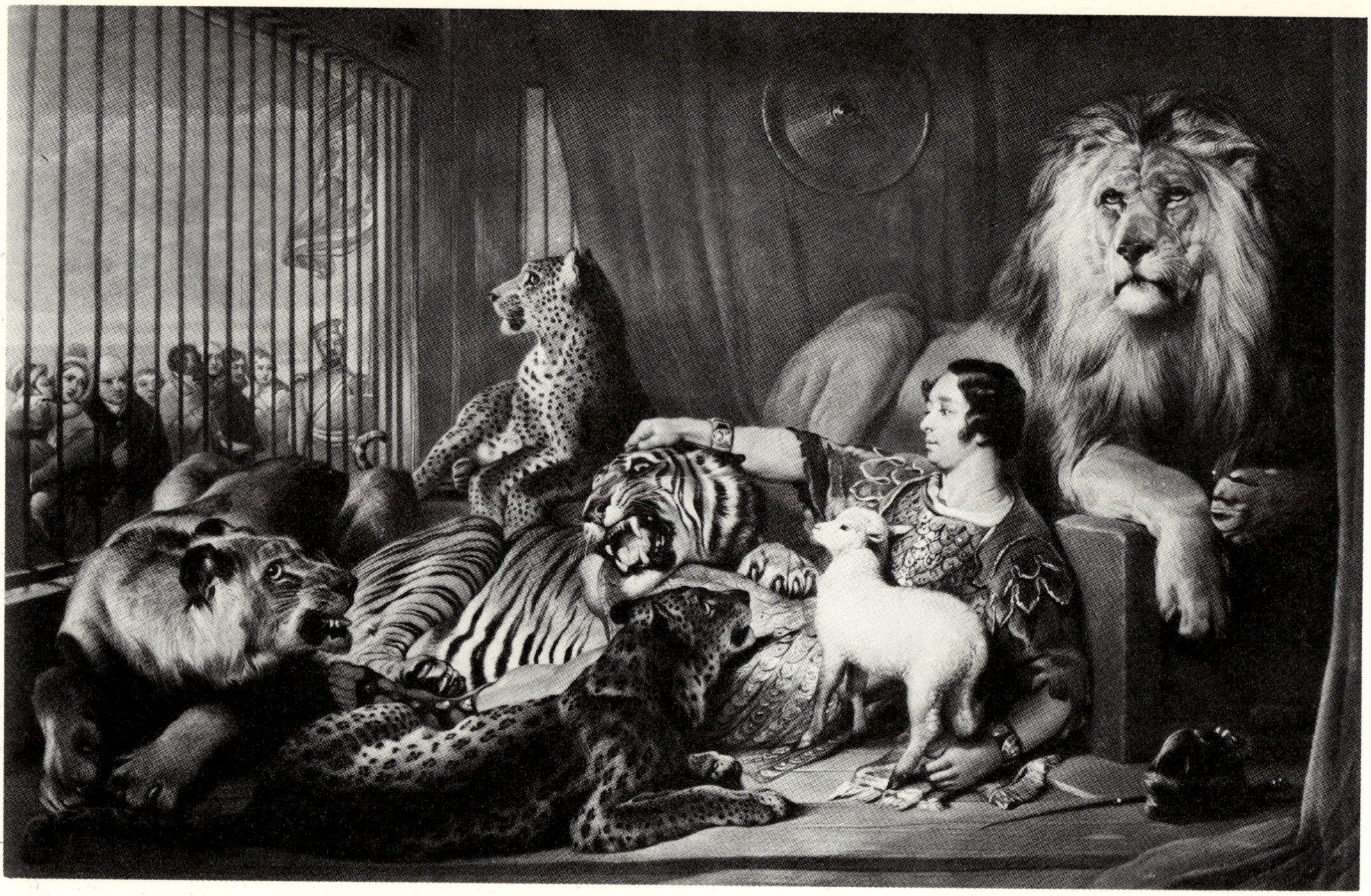

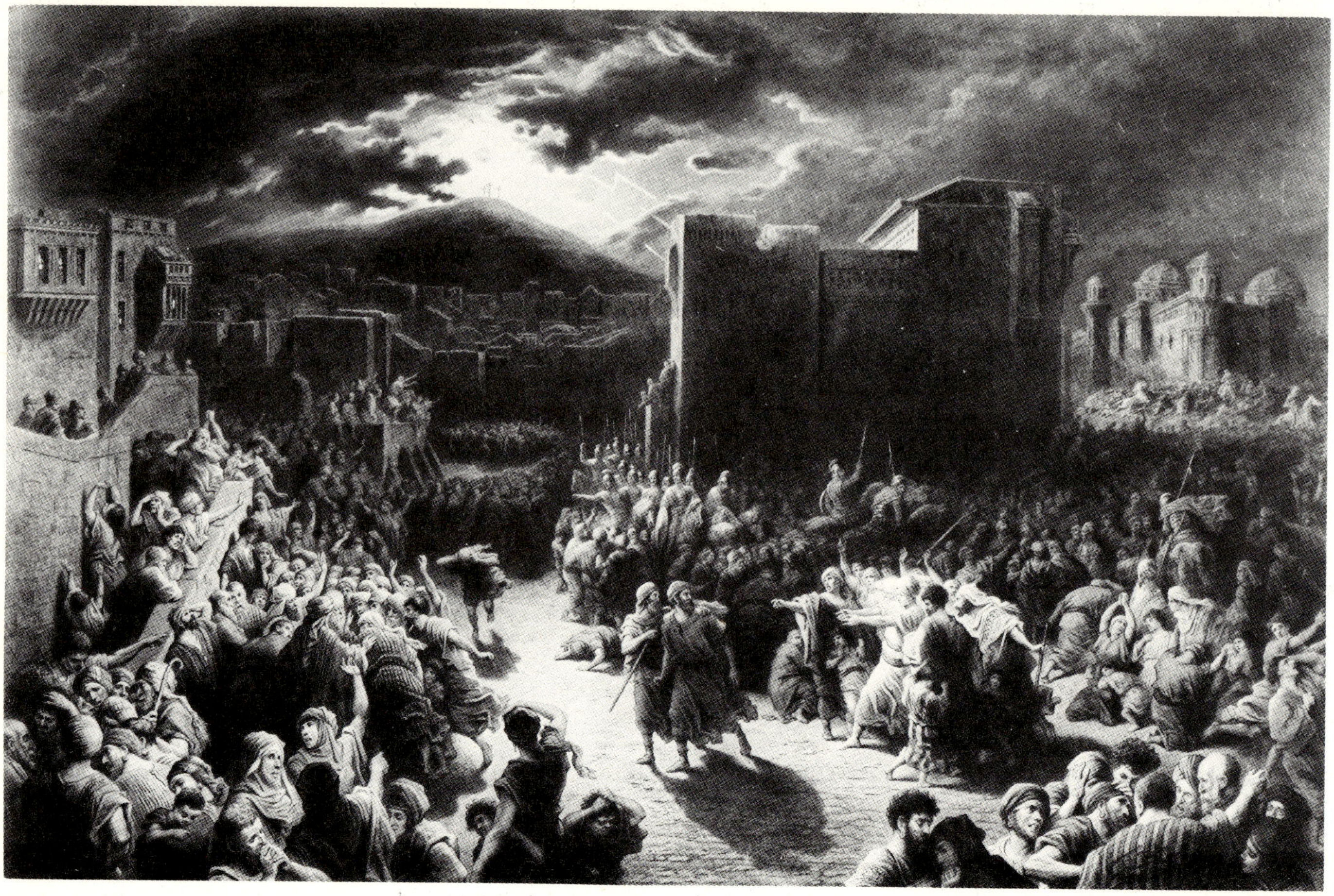

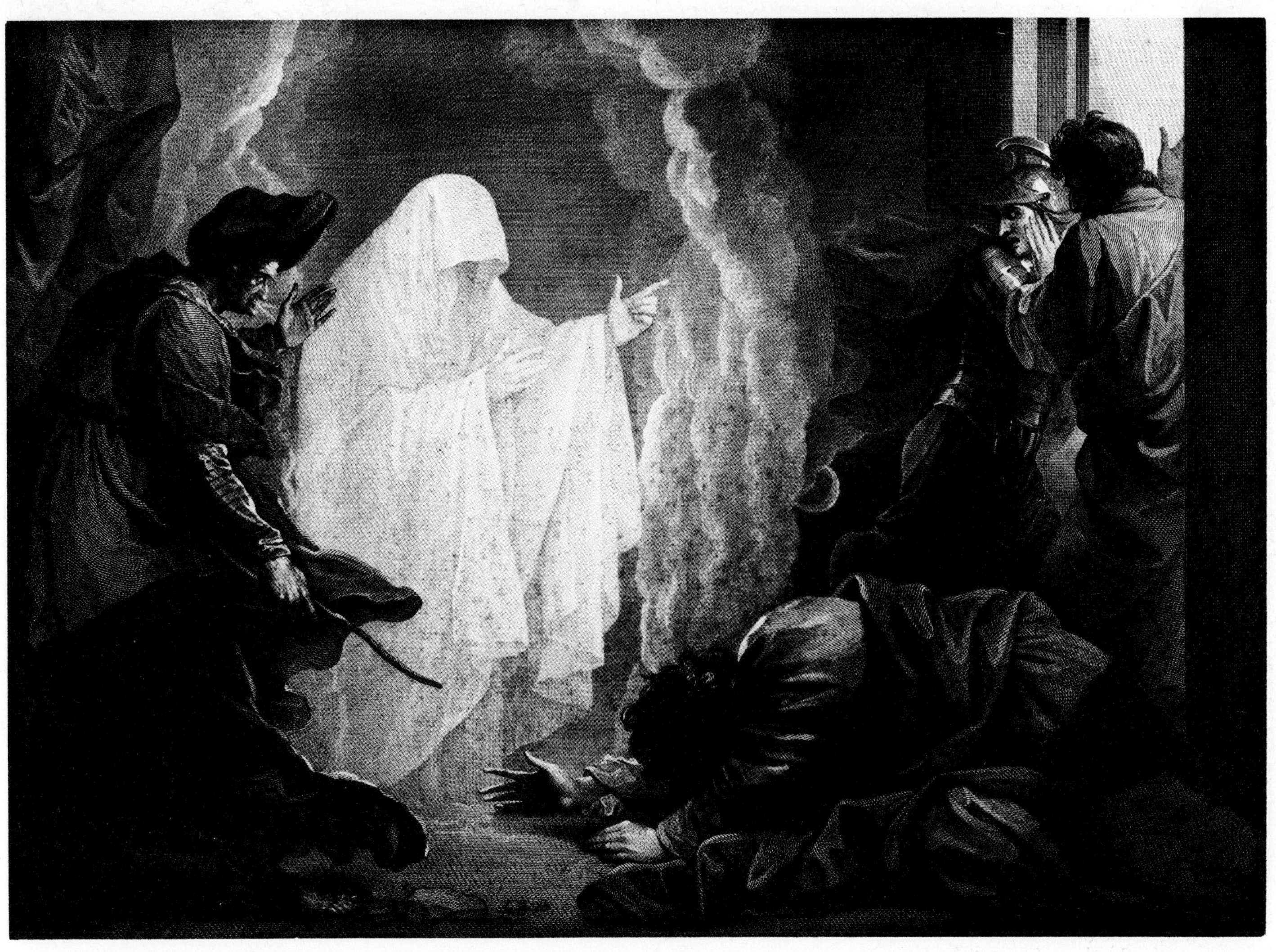

William Sharpe (1749–1824) *Saul and the Witch of Endor* line engraving
After a painting by Benjamin West (1738–1820). Sharpe was one of the most celebrated English engravers who developed his own style of blending landscape and figures within each plate. He became known more as 'an artist and less a mechanic' during his lifetime, and thus helped to dispel the prejudice surrounding the engraver as a true artist.

William Henry Simmons (1811–1882) *Dominion* mezzotint (TOP LEFT)
After the painting by Sir Edwin Landseer R.A. (1802–1873). Published in 1878 with the full title *Dominion . . . And God said have dominion over every living thing that moveth upon the earth. (Gen. I:28)*

Herbert Bourne (1820–1885) and William Ridgway (c.1860–1880) *The Ninth Hour* line engraving (BOTTOM LEFT)
After the painting by Gustave Doré (1832–1882). Engraved in 1880 for Fairless and Beeforth and the Doré Gallery.

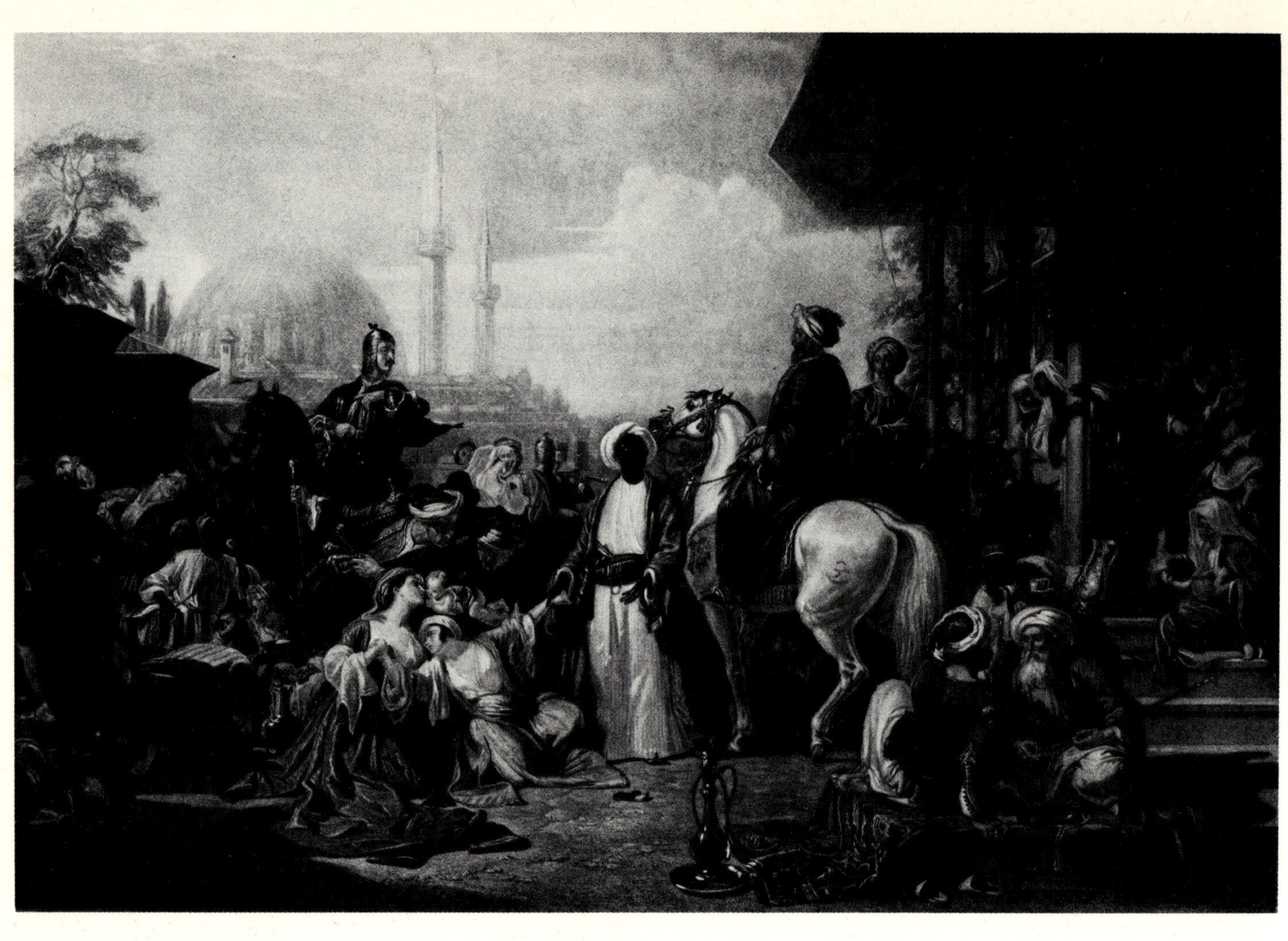

Charles George Lewis (1808–1880) and William Giller (1805–1858) *The Slave Market (Constantinople)* mezzotint and etching
After the painting by Sir William Allan R.A., P.R.S.A. (1782–1850). Published by F. G. Moon in 1842.

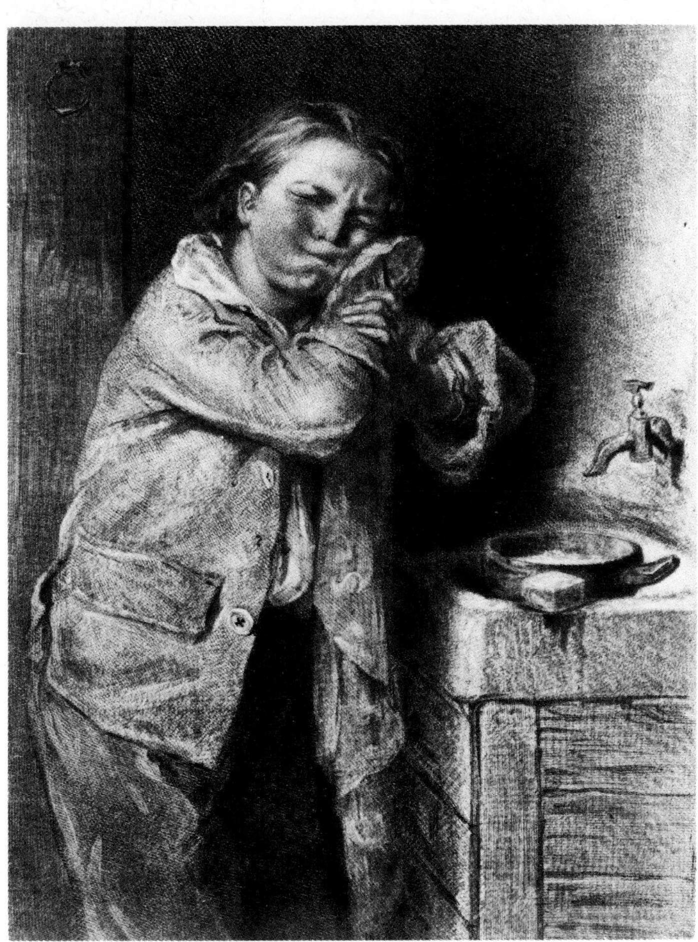

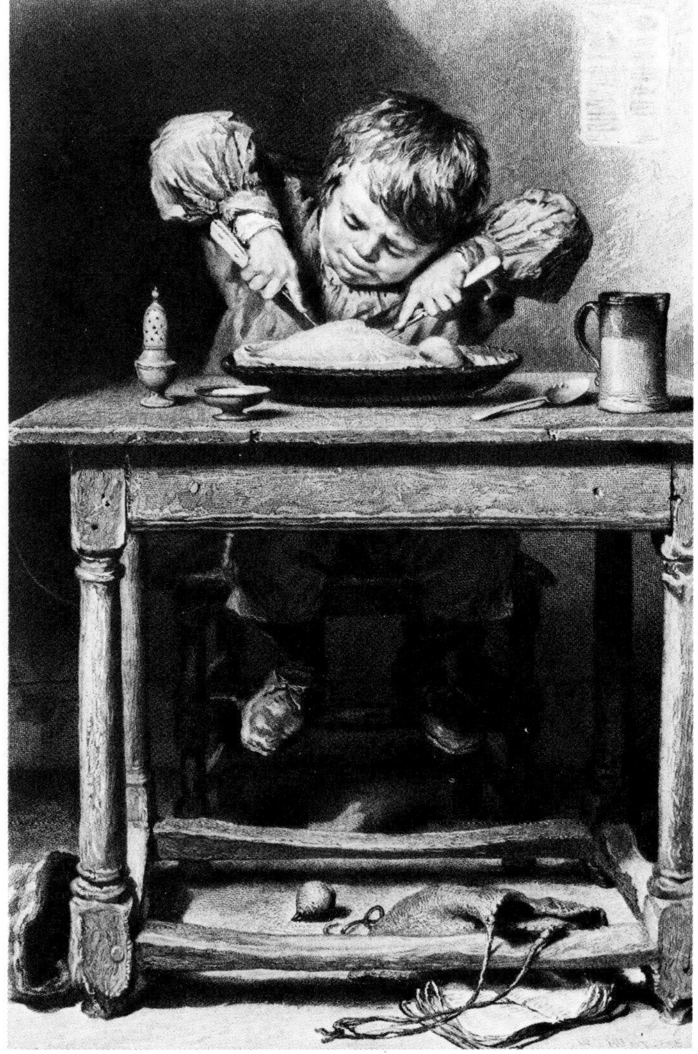

Charles Fox (1794–1849) *The Attack* mezzotint and etching
After the painting of 1835 by William Henry Hunt, an influential painter and water-colourist of rustic genre and still life. He developed an individual method, of hatching and stippling over a white ground, which was admired by Ruskin and imitated in paintings and engravings.

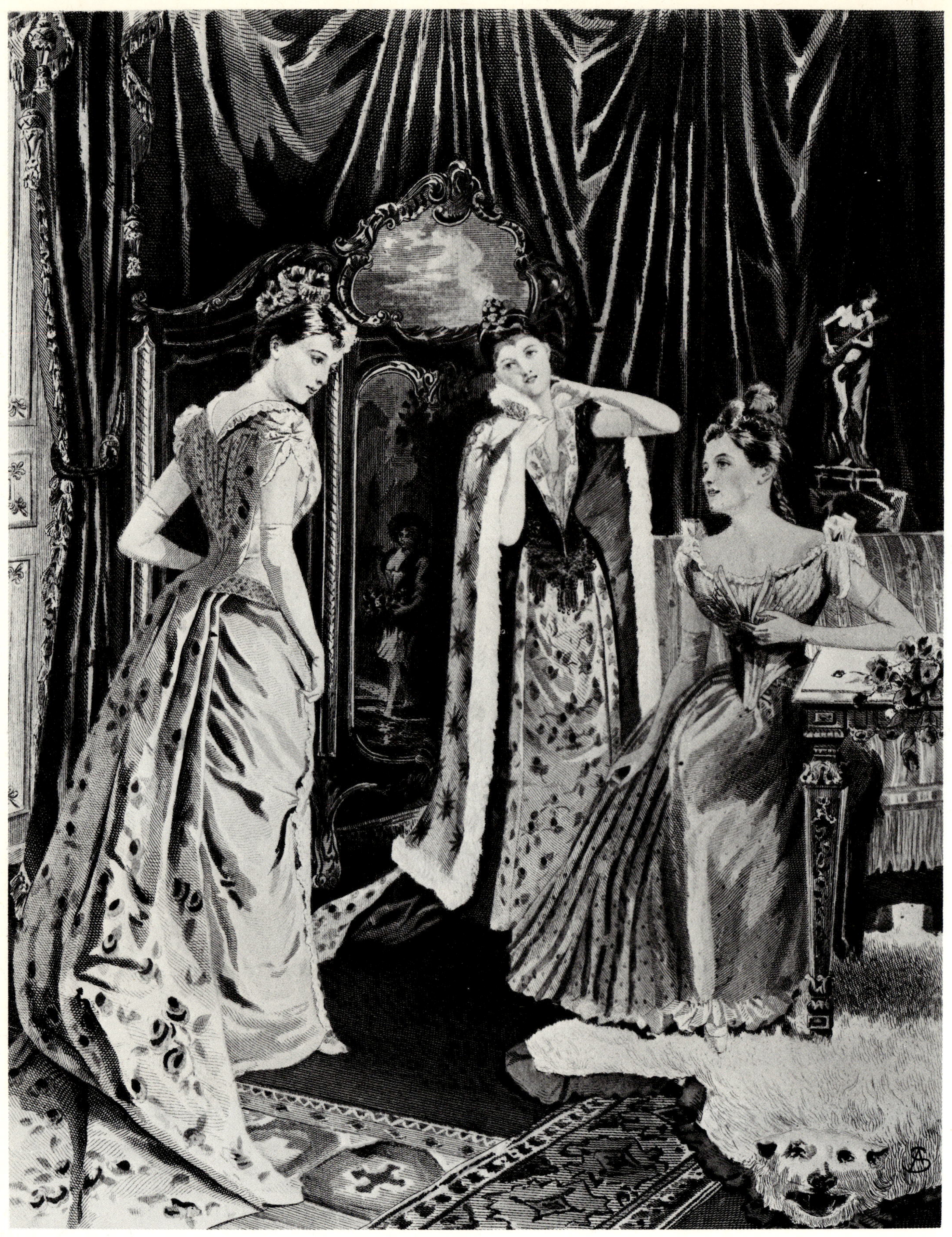

A. Sandoz *Fashion Plate* hand-coloured line engraving from *The Queen*
The Queen, first published in 1861, was the oldest fashion magazine in the world, and began to publish the mysterious Sandoz's works in 1888. These elegant line drawings successfully competed with the ubiquitous French engraved plates of Jules David, Anais and Toudouze.

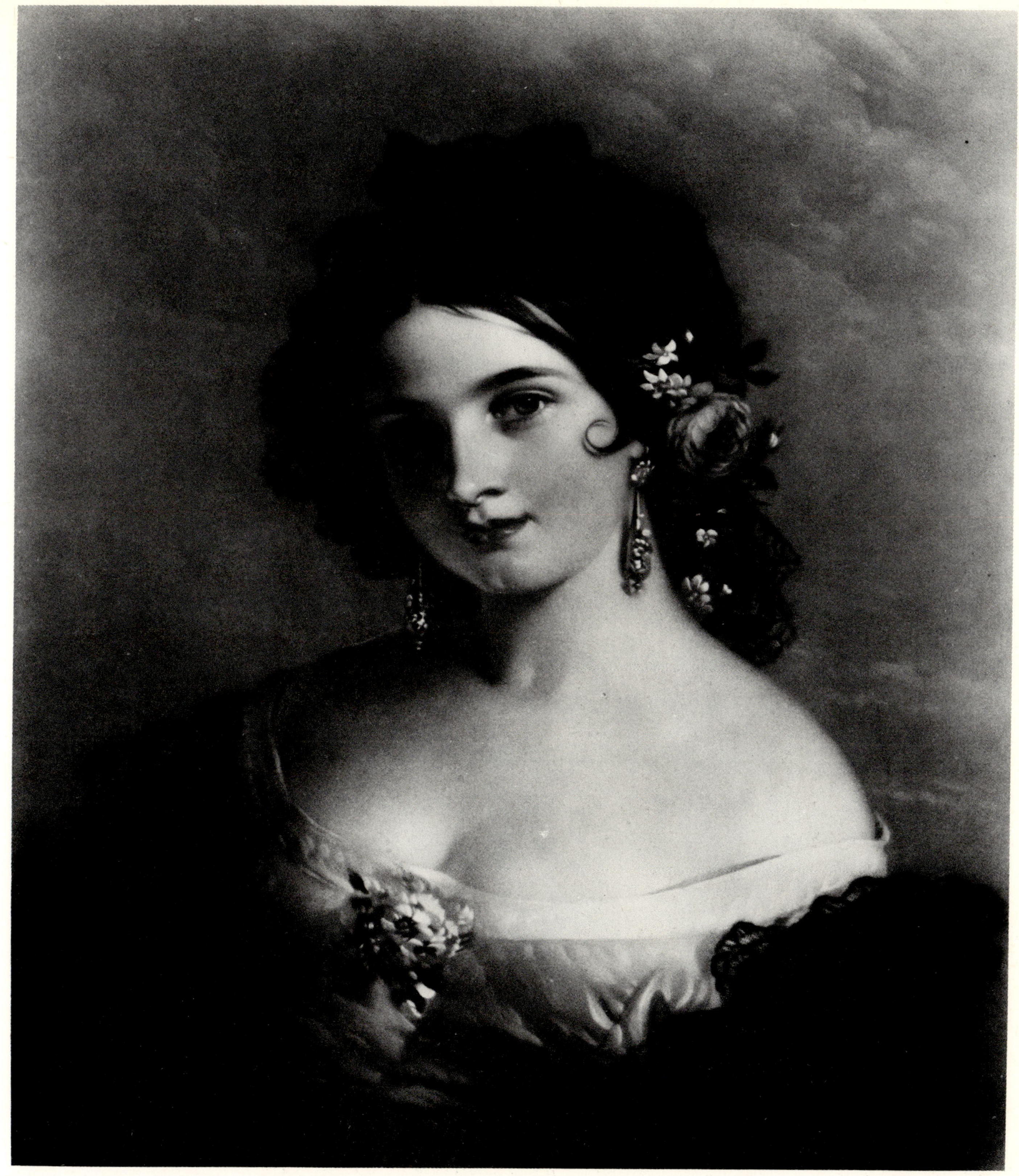

Henry Cousins (1809–1864) *Beaming Eyes* mezzotint
After the painting by Charles Baxter (1809–1879), published in 1856. *The Printseller* magazine (vol. 1, no. 1, 1903) discussed the current popularity of the mezzotint portraits of women:

. . . though mezzotints of men are as equal and better than women now. They include men who have won fame in politics, the navy, army and literature, men who have built up the Empire, the fruits of whose energies we at present enjoy. Surely they have some claim on our attention! The time will come when mezzotint portraits of men will be popular and command as high a price as women (although now they are almost despised).

Artist's proofs of mezzotint portraits of women after Romney, Raeburn, Gainsborough and Reynolds sold for five to ten pounds in 1905.

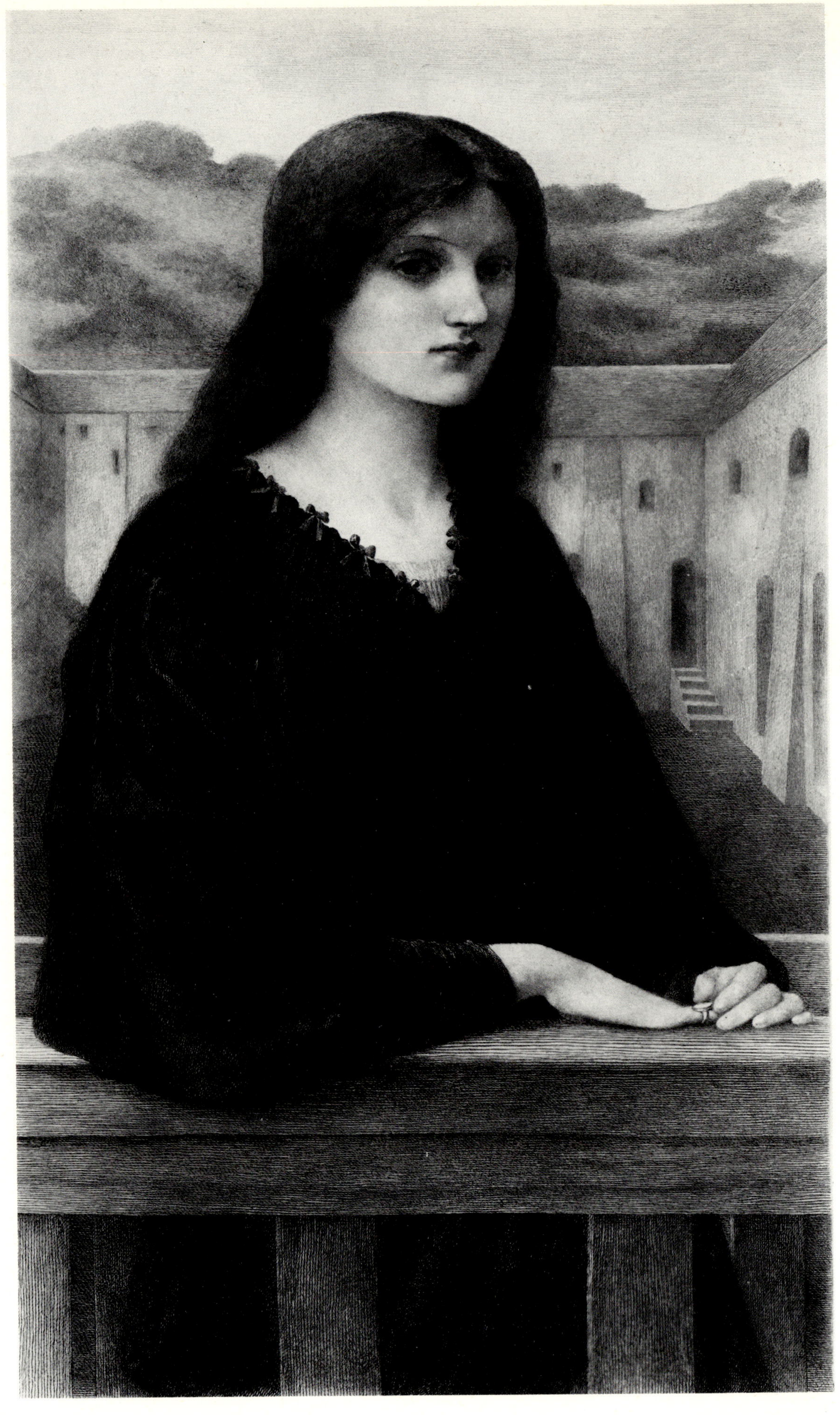

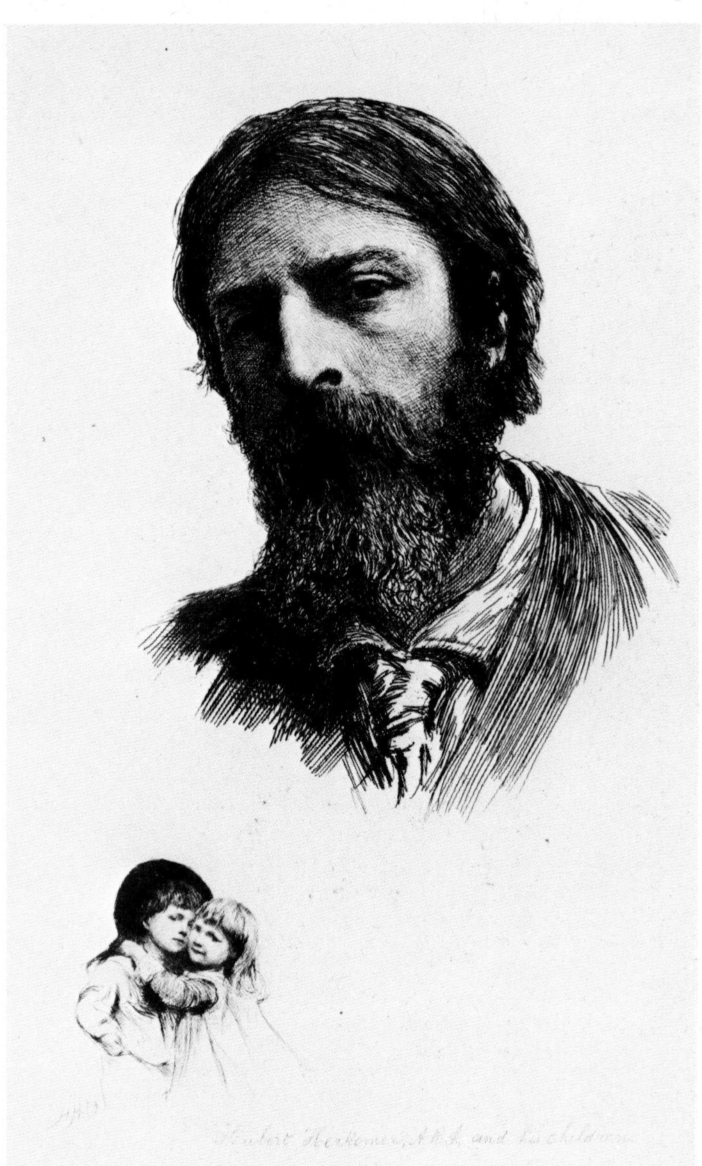

Published for the British and Foreign Artists' Association in a
declared edition of 1,475. Herkomer was a popular painter of
social realism and portraits of Victorian life, and an engraver
for *The Graphic*. He was also the founder of the School of Art
at Bushey, composer of operas, actor, designer of stage and
cinema settings, and writer on the techniques of etching.

Francis Holl A.R.A. (1815–1885) *A Siesta* line engraving
After the painting by Charles Edward Perugini (1839–1918),
an Italian genre and portrait painter whose style resembled
that of Lord Leighton, and who exhibited at the Academy
from 1863 onwards. Holl was the engraver of the Queen's
picture collection for twenty-five years, and engraved works
after Frith, J. Sant and A. Solomon. He exhibited prints at
the Academy from 1856 to 1879.

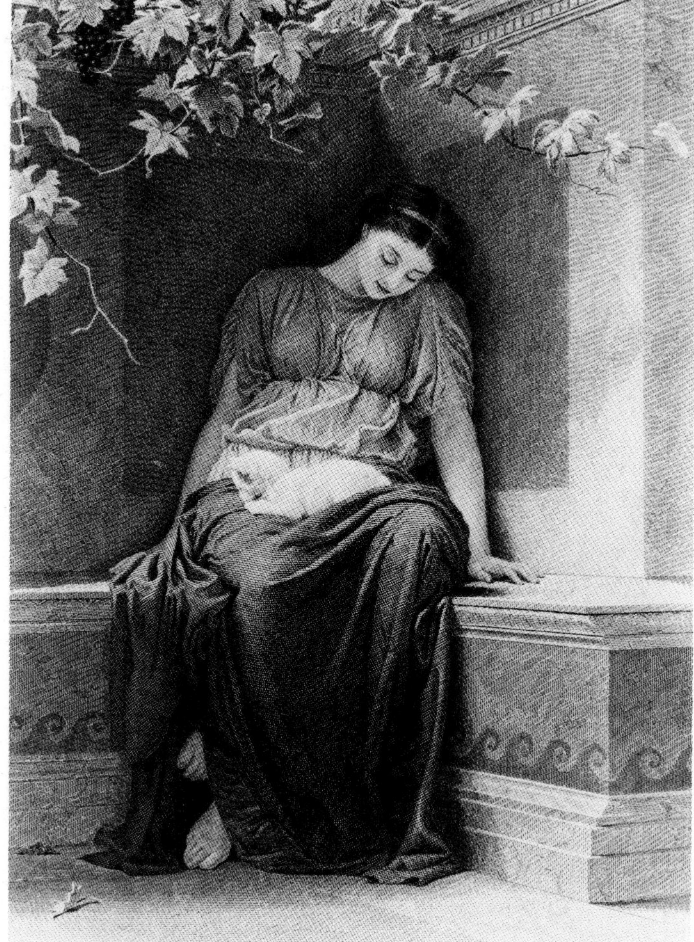

Emile Boilvin (1845–1899) *Vespertina Quies* etching (LEFT)
After the painting of 1893 by Sir Edward Coley Burne-Jones
(1833–1898). Published by A. Tooth and Sons (copyright
1897) in a limited edition of 300. Boilvin was a French
engraver who was highly honoured for his ability to accurately reproduce a painting while adding his own personal
touch. His works include etchings after Franz Hals, Rubens
and Meissonier.

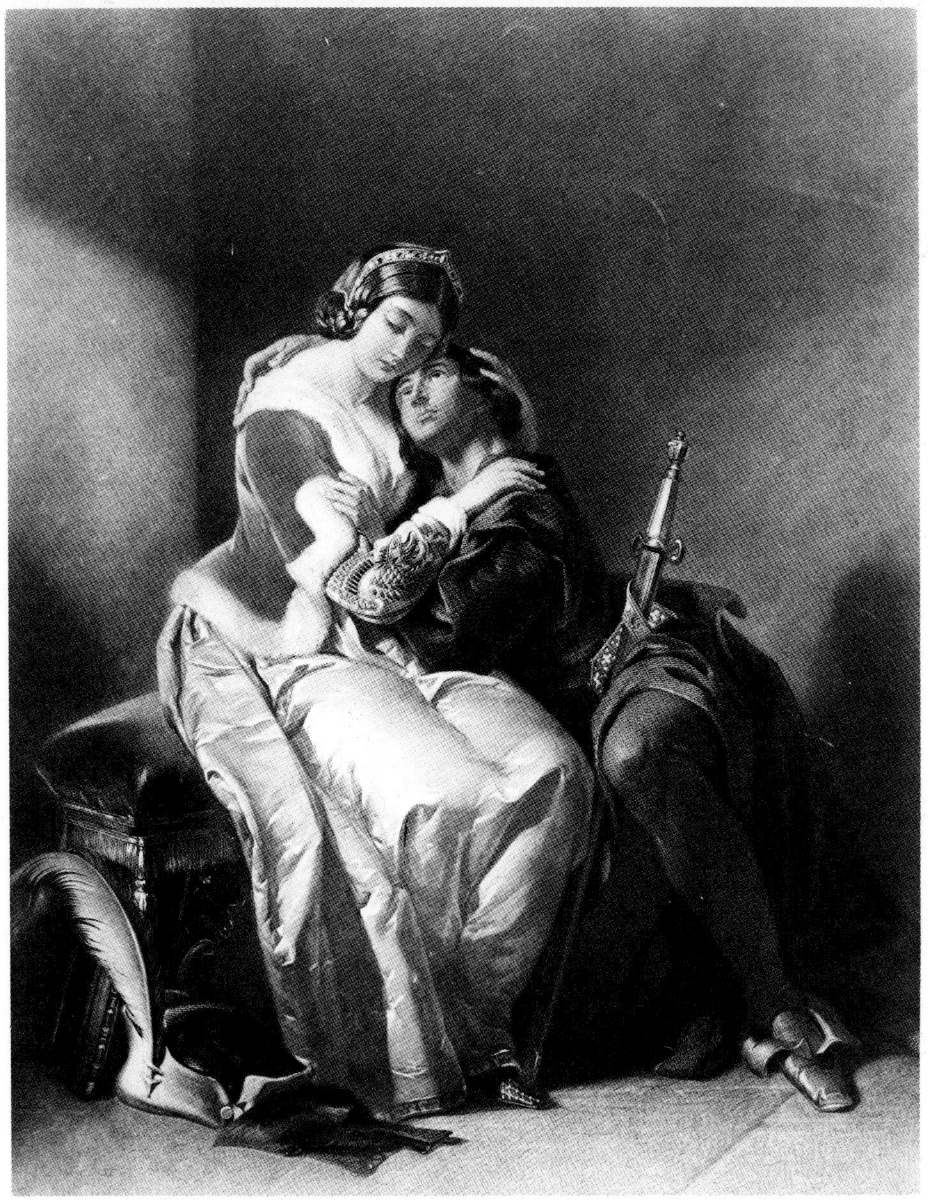

George H. Every (1837–1910) *Thine Own* mezzotint
After the painting by Daniel Maclise R.A. (1806–1870). Published and declared
in 1859 in an edition of fifty, and accompanied by the verse:

> Come, rest in this bosom, my own stricken deer,
> Though the herd have fled from thee, thy home is still here;
> Here still is the smile, that no cloud can o'ercast,
> And a heart and a hand all thy own to the last.
> Oh! what was love made for, if 'tis not the same
> Thro joy and thro torment, thro glory and shame?
> I know not, I ask not if guilt's in that heart,
> I but know that I love thee, whatever thou art.
>
> Thou hast call'd me thy angel in moments of bliss –
> And thy angel I'll be, mid the honours of this –
> Thro the furnace, unshrinking, thy steps to pursue,
> And shield thee, and save thee, – or perish there too!

Thomas Lewis Atkinson (1817–c.1889) *Flora* mezzotint (RIGHT)
After the painting by Valentine Walter Bromley (1848–1877), published and declared in 1876 in an edition of 1,125.
Atkinson was taught by Samuel Cousins and was one of the best mezzotinters of the period, with over sixty plates registered
by the Printsellers' Association (1894).

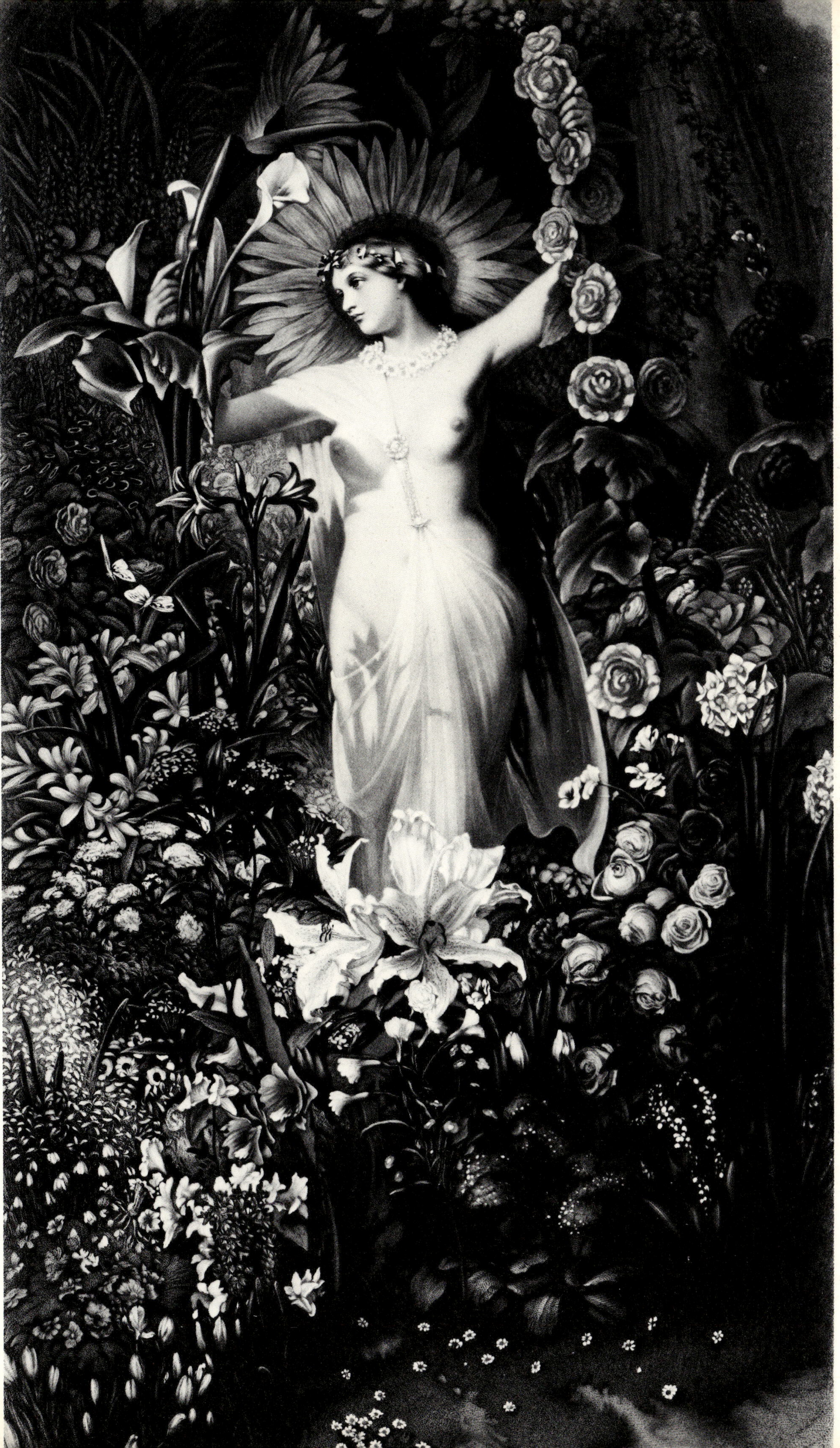

After the painting by Sir Augustus Callcott R.A. (1779–1844)
known as the 'English Claude' for his romantic English
landscapes. Stocks engraved this print in 1843, as well as
others after T. Faed, T. Webster, F. Leighton and Frith.

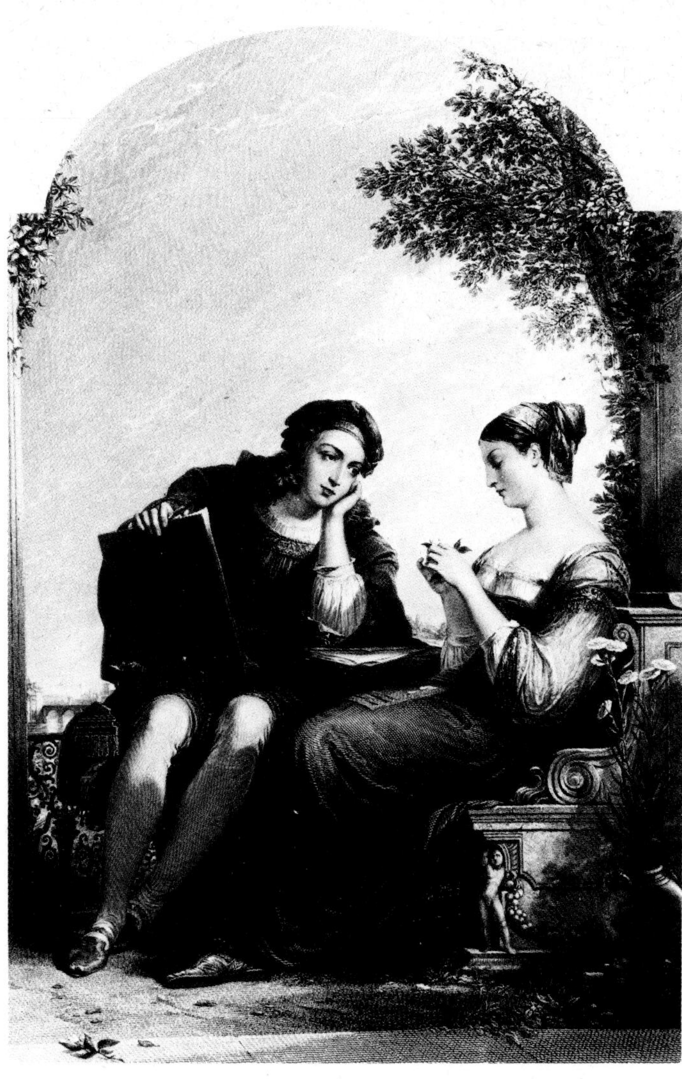

An Al Fresco Toilet goupilgravure
After the painting (R.A. 1889) by Sir Luke Fildes R.A.
(1843–1927). Fildes's popularity rose with the publication of
his works by Boussod, Valadon and Co., London and Paris,
who perfected the goupilgravure (photographic reproduction)
process considered to be the ultimate in accuracy of reproduction (later surpassed by their colour facsimile process).

Messrs. Boussod, Valadon and Co. undertake the reproduction of Paintings, Drawings of all kinds by their process of
Goupilgravure, by which an engraved metal surface is
obtained capable of yielding impressions which show every
detail of an artist's work, with the softness and texture of a
mezzotint. The copies are as permanent as etchings or
engravings. This method of reproduction is not only suitable
for the large plates, of which so many are now before the
public, but is admirably adopted for the production of
small plates for book-illustration, and for the preservation
of Historical or family portraits, and other works of art.
(Boussod, Valadon and Co., *Catalogue*, 1894).

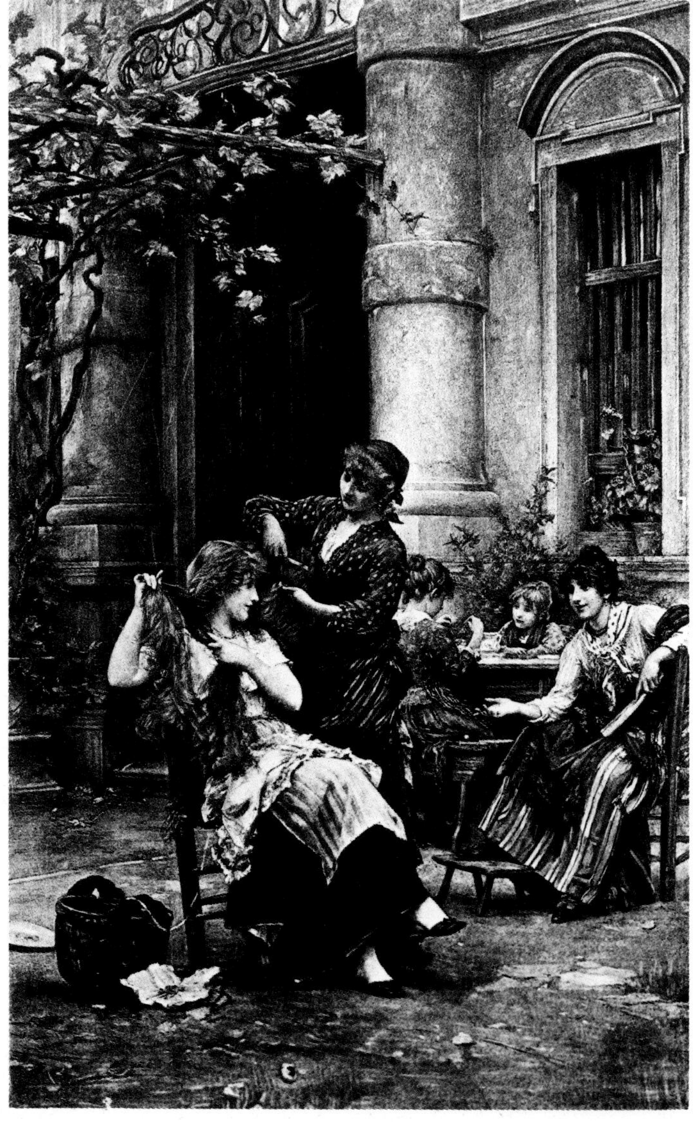

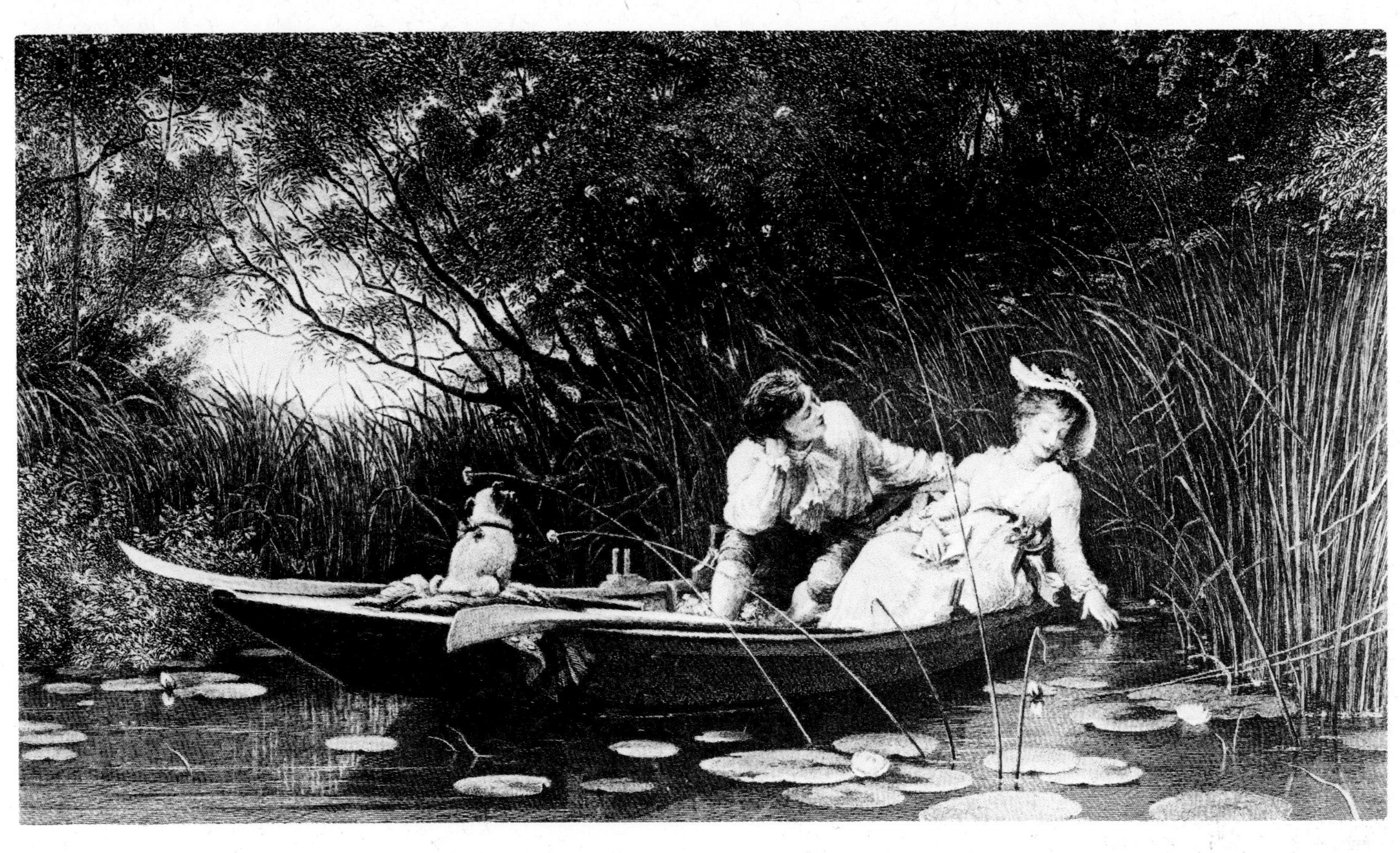

The Sweet River photogravure
After the painting by Sir Luke Fildes R.A. (1843–1927), published in the *Art Journal*.

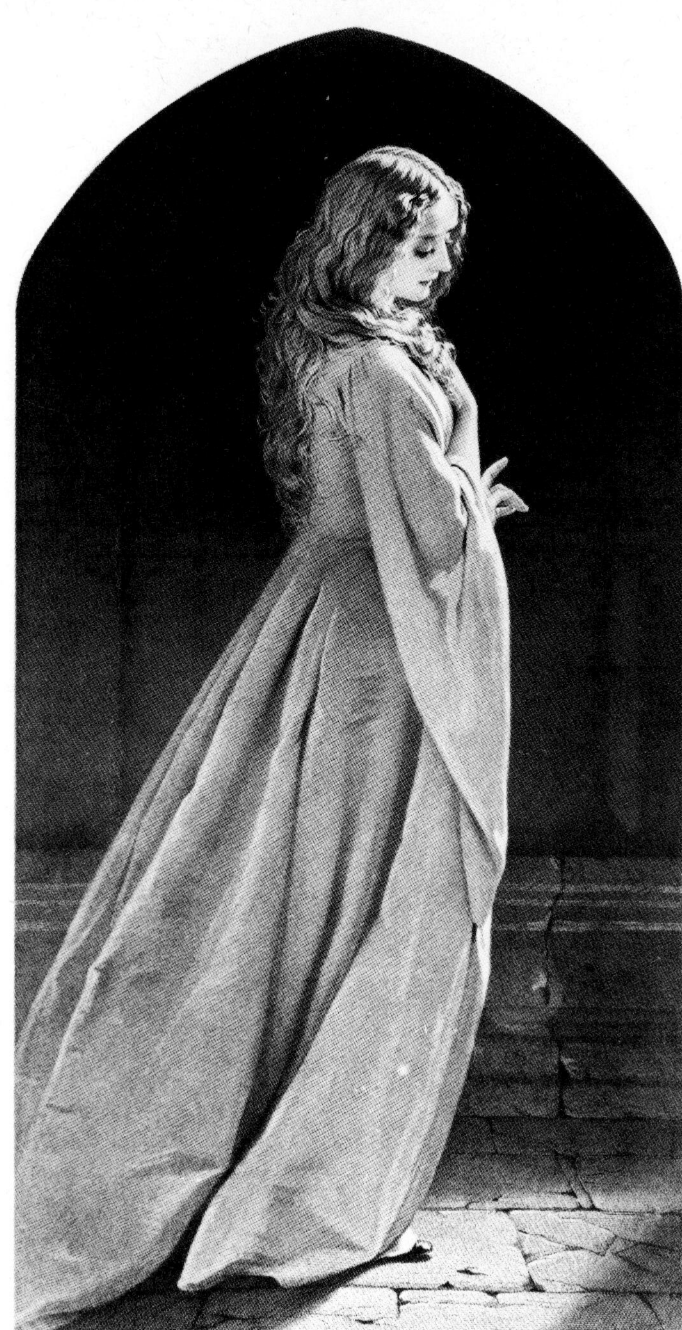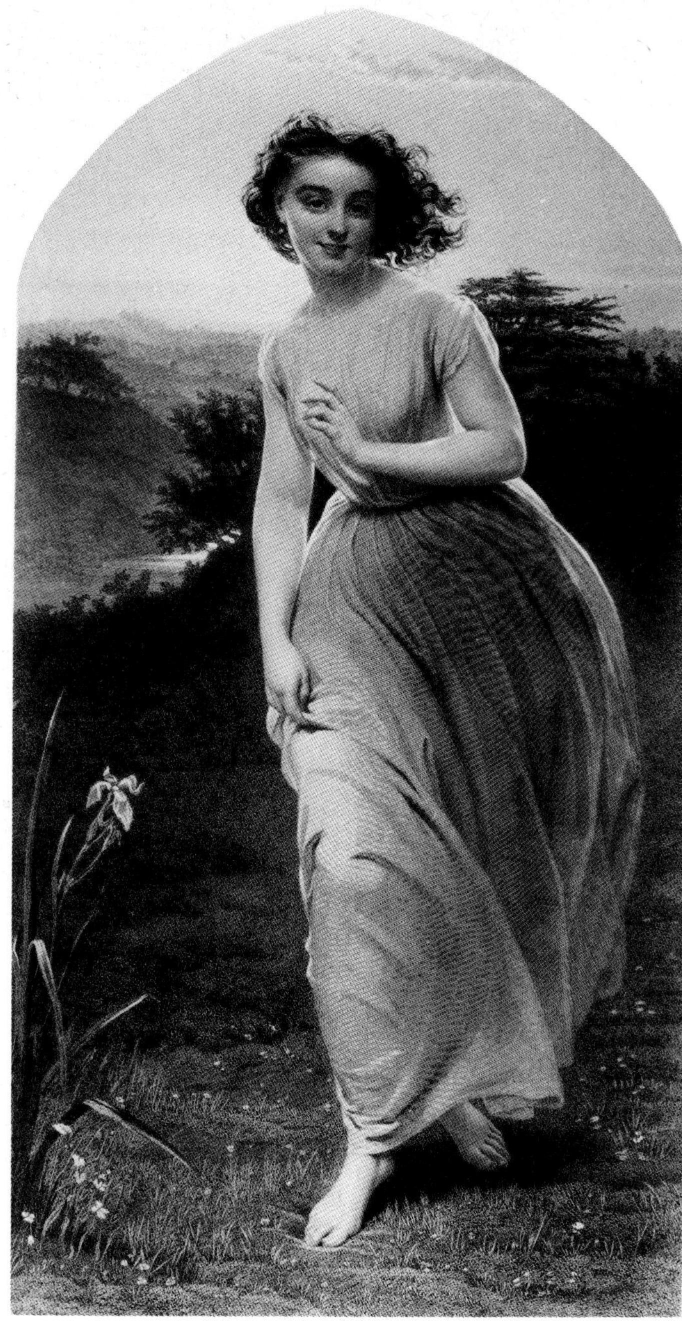

Francis Holl A.R.A. (1815–1884) *Il Penseroso* and *L'Allegro* mixed style
After the paintings by George Elgar Hicks R.B.A. (1824–1914) published as companion prints in 1868.

E. Gilbert *Girl in the Garden* mezzotint (RIGHT)
After the painting by Marcus Stone R.A. (1840–1921) published in 1899. Stone was described by *The Times* as 'a lover of arts and crafts, a devotee of fashionable attire and of his own elegance and refinement'. He wished to be known as Marcus Apollo Belvedere Stone, and dismissed the sentimentality and popularity of his paintings with a resigned, 'one sells one's birthright'. Such paintings were called 'Dorothy pictures'; girls, presumably named Dorothy, were depicted in innocent poses, dressed in vaguely period costumes.

Dorothy was just a day-dream of what love ought to be, a pretty girl sitting in a garden until an honourable proposal drops from the sky, which would be a perfect arrangement from the point of view of parents and men who wanted to settle down, and for the girls themselves at least one way of escaping from home. (M. Clive, *The Day of Reckoning*, 1964.)

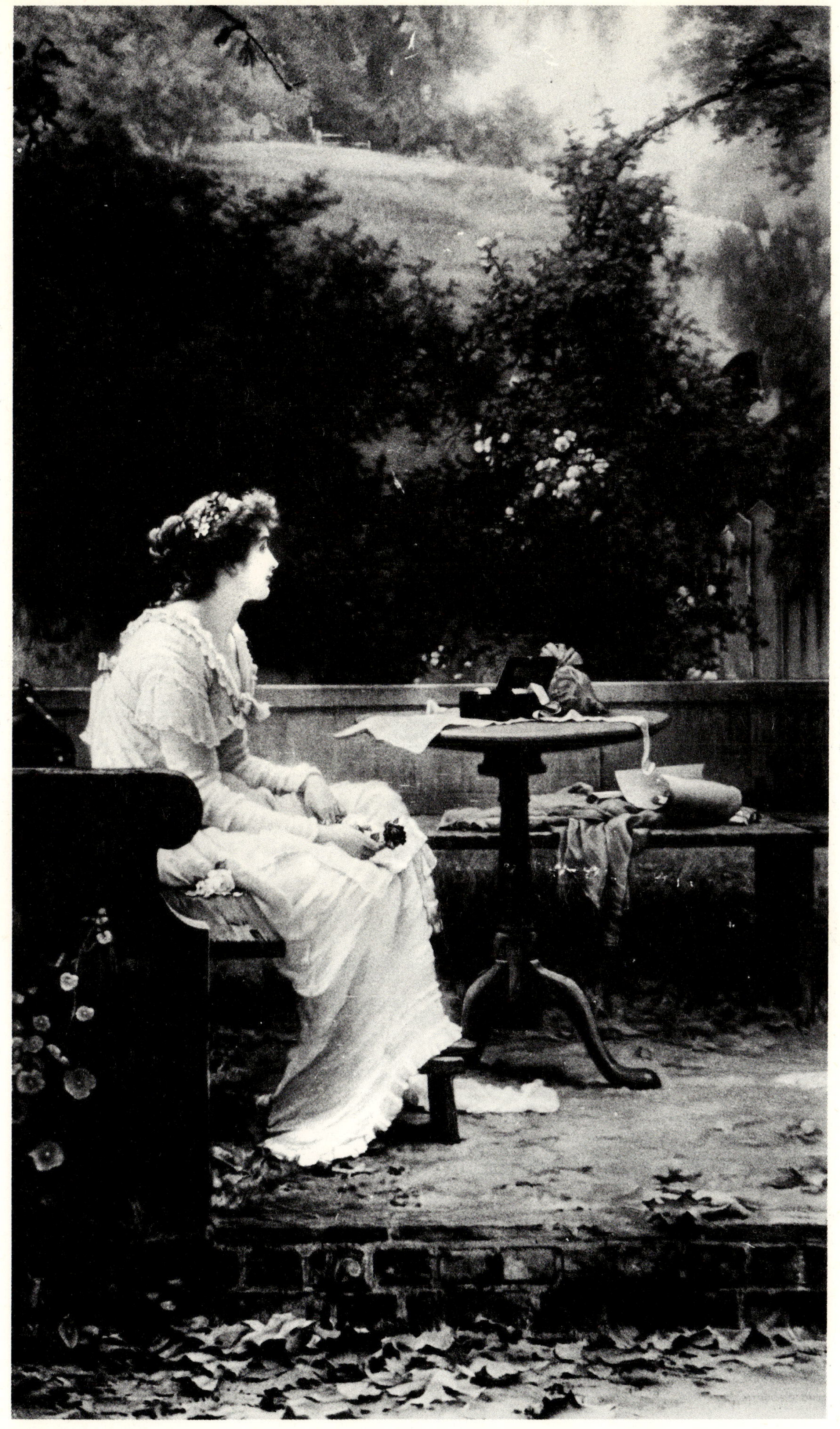

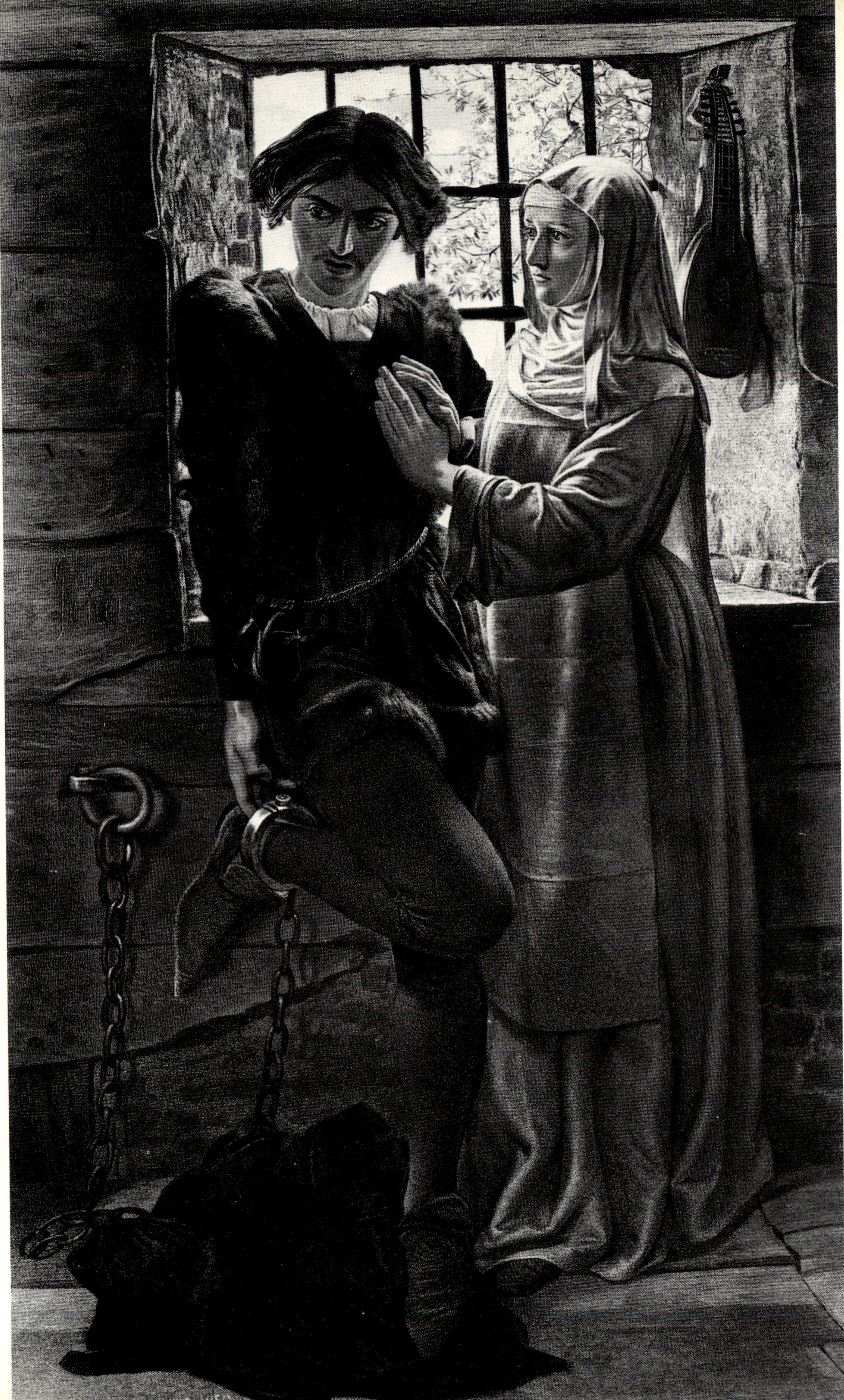

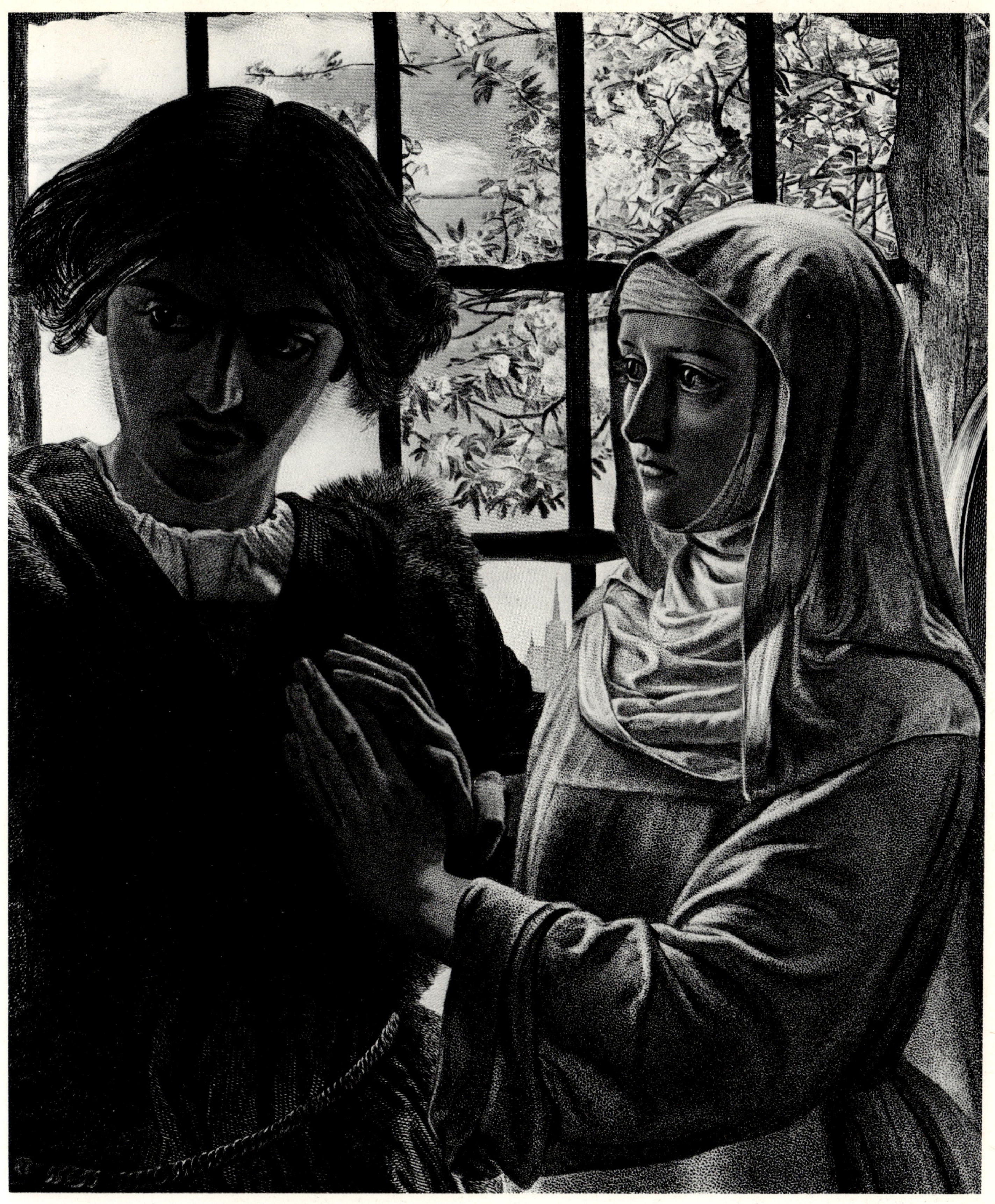

William Henry Simmons (1811–1882) *Claudio and Isabella* (with detail) line and stipple engraving
After the painting of 1850 by William Holman Hunt O.M. (1827–1919), published by Gambart and Co. in 1864. The subject is a scene from *Measure for Measure*, Act III, scene I. Claudio is asking his chaste sister Isabella to yield to Angelo in order to save him from execution. Hunt was commissioned by Augustus Egg R.A. (1816–1863) to paint this, the first of his 'problem' pictures. It was engraved in a declared edition of 225. Simmons also engraved after the Pre-Raphaelite works of Millais, J. Collinson and N. Paton.

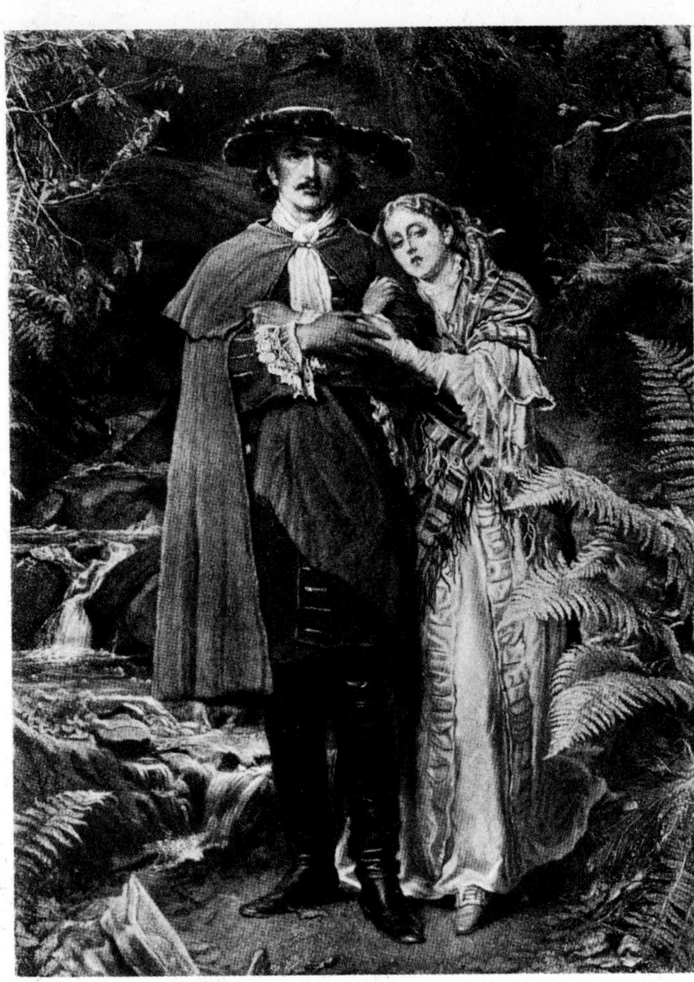

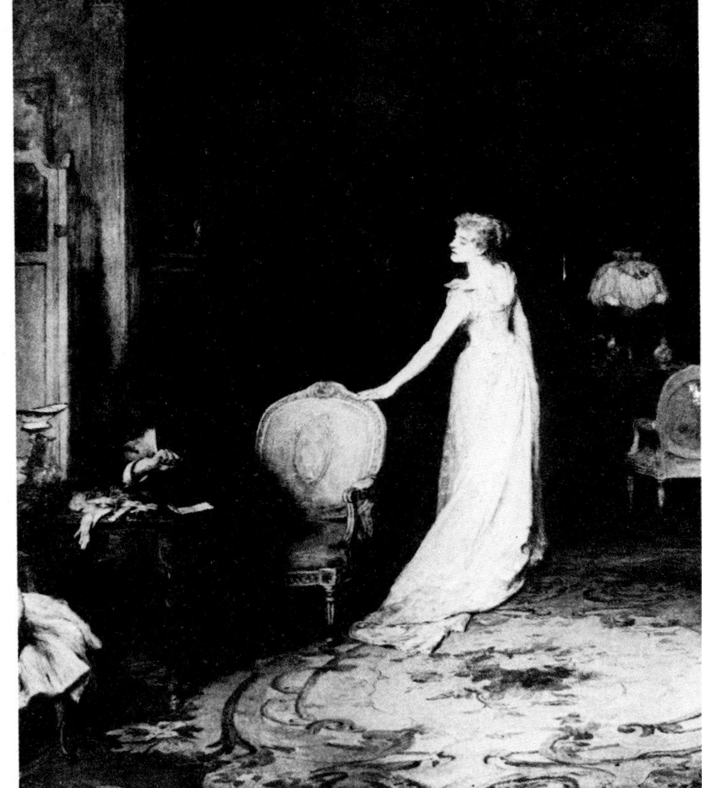

Thomas Oldham Barlow R.A. (1824–1889) *The Bride of Lammermoor (The Parting of Edgar and Lucy of Lammermoor)* mixed style
After the painting by Sir John Everett Millais P.R.A. (1829–1896). Published in 1881 in a declared edition of 1,000. The print was exhibited at the Academy in 1882. Engravings of themes of love and sorrow were popular as morality lessons.

Trouble mezzotint
After the paintings by Sir William Quiller Orchardson R.A. (1832–1910) published in the *Art Journal*. Orchardson was a Scottish genre painter noted for his psychological dramas of upperclass life, such as *Le Mariage de Convenance* (R.A. 1883) in which he used deliberately muted colours quite suitable for mezzotint reproduction. (*Art Journal*)

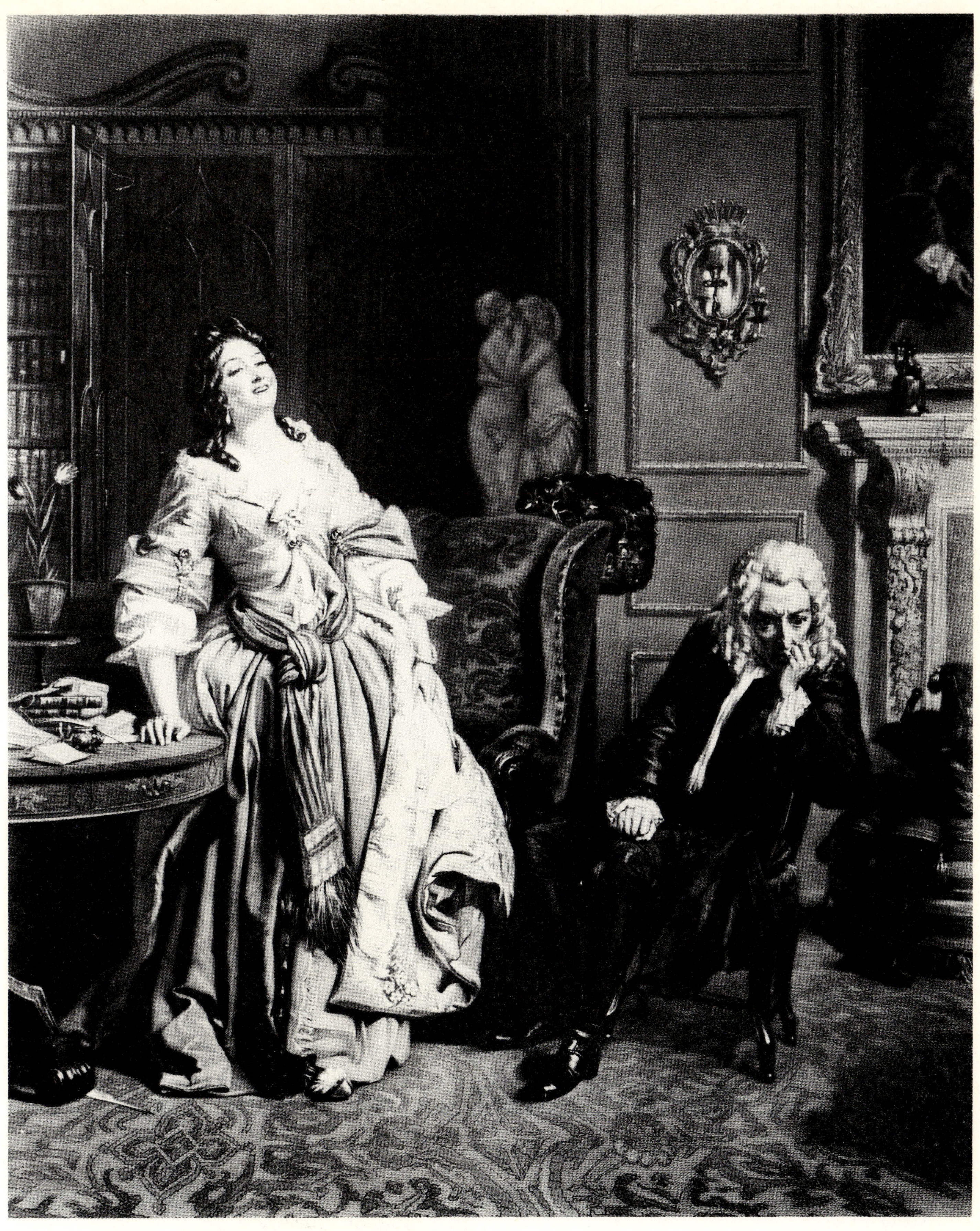

Ferdinand Jean Joubert F.S.A. (1810–1884) *The Rejected Poet* mezzotint
After the painting by William Powell Frith R.A. (1819–1909), published in 1861. The work was also engraved by
C. W. Sharpe (1819–1899) in the *Art Journal*, 1867.

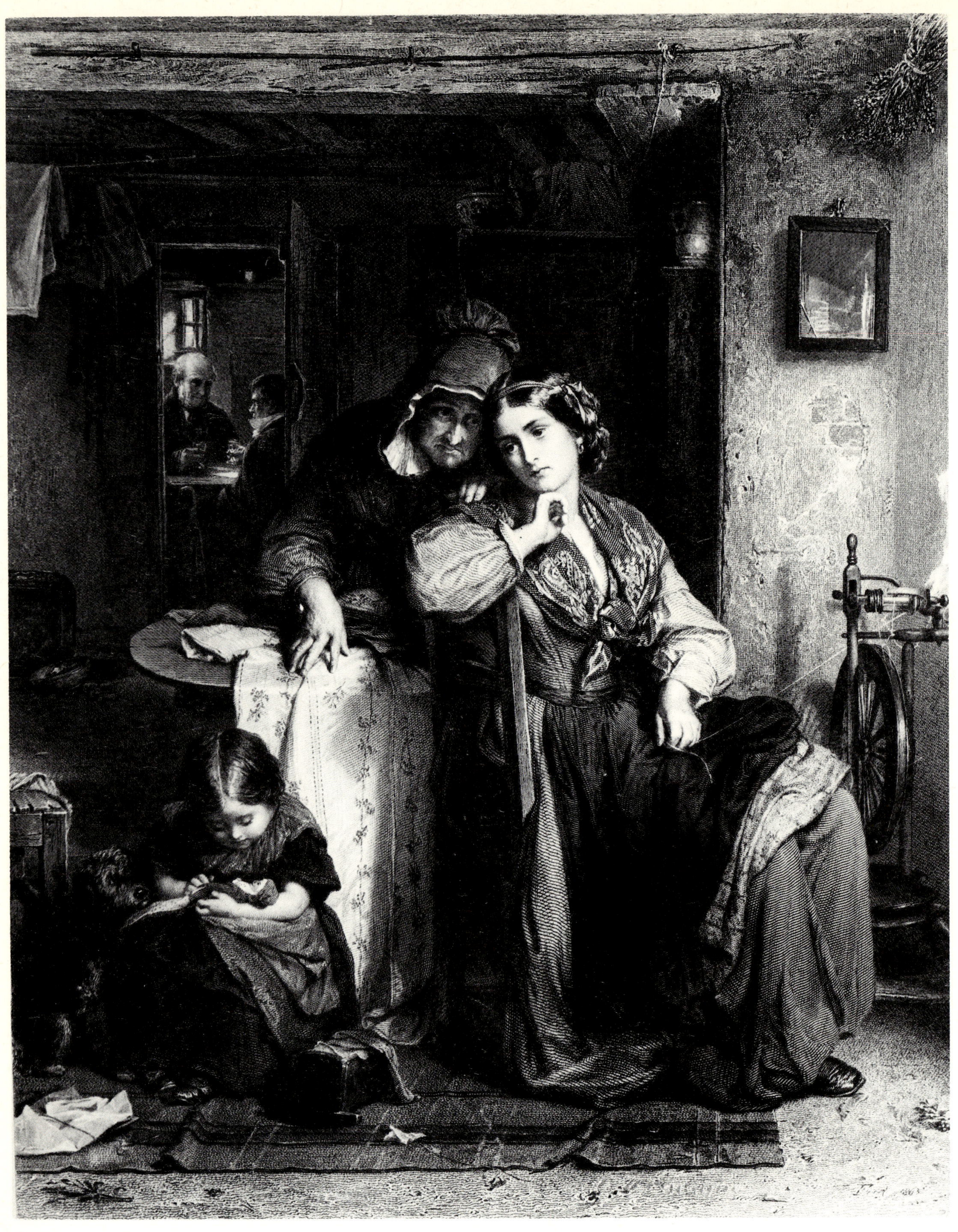

Lumb Stocks R.A. (1812–1892) *Ye Shall Walk in Silk Attire* mixed style
After the painting by Thomas Faed R.A. (1826–1900). Published as a companion print with *The Momentous Question* after Miss Sarah Setchel (1813–1894), engraved by Samuel Bellin (1799–1893) in 1874.

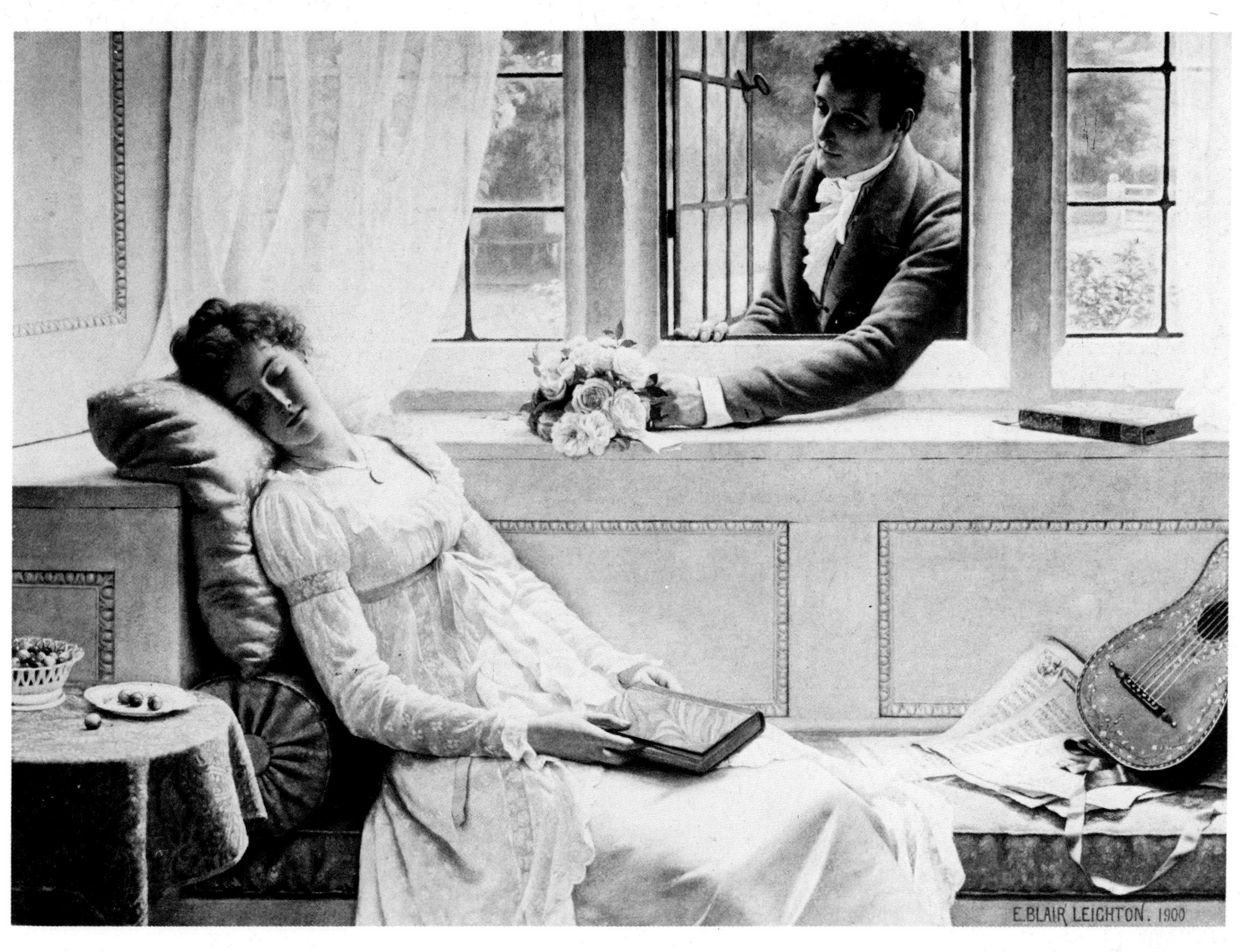

Sweets to the Sweet photogravure
After the painting (1900) by Edmund Blair Leighton (1853–1922). Published by Arthur Tooth and Sons in 1901.

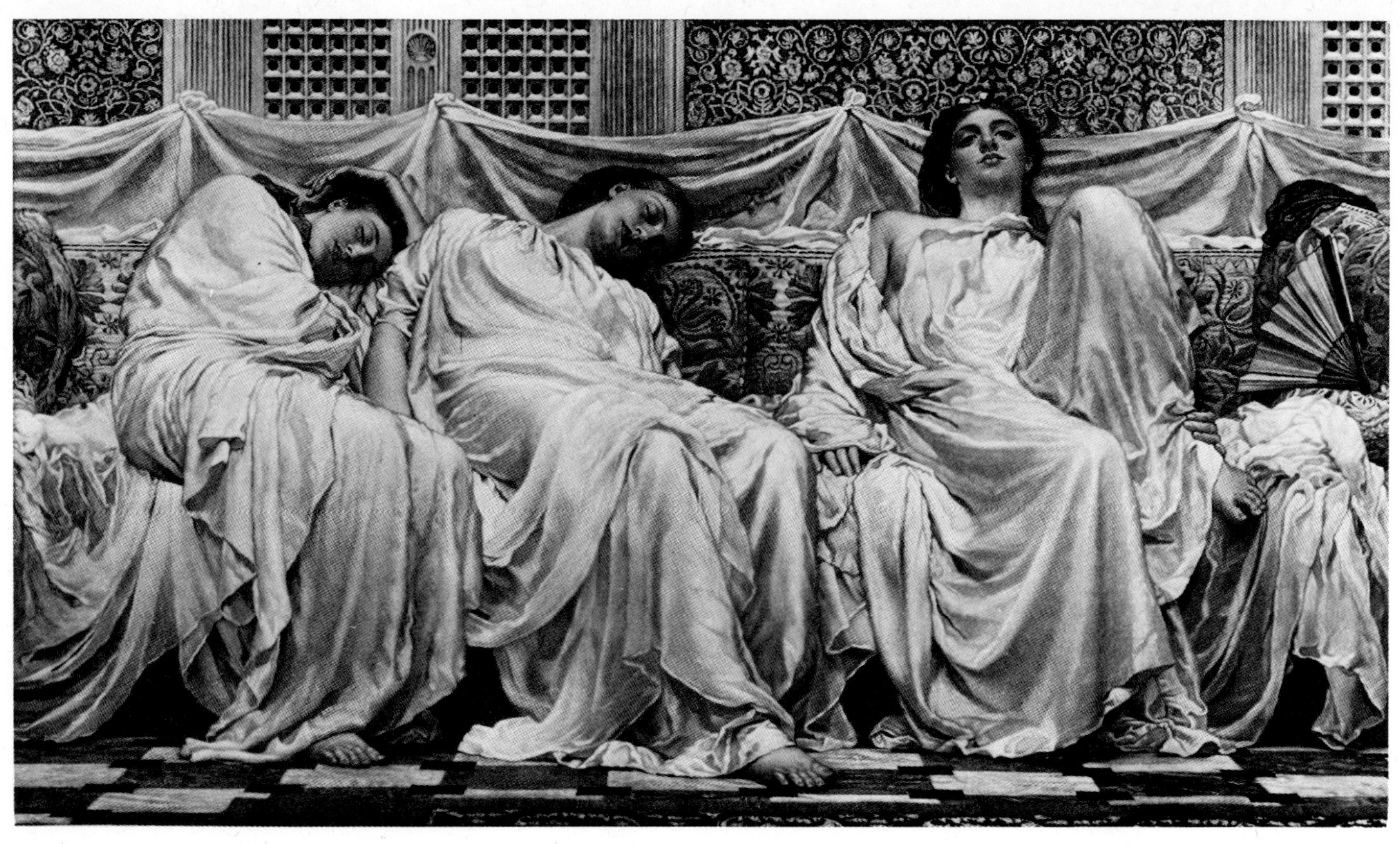

Thomas Gooch Appleton (1854–1924) *Dreamers* mezzotint printed in sepia tone
After the painting (R.A. 1882) by Albert Joseph Moore (1841–1893), published in 1898 in a declared edition of 525. The rich decorative backgrounds and drapery of Moore's paintings were especially suitable for the soft ground mezzotint. Appleton was a prominent mezzotinter of portraits, with over thirty registered prints in 1894 after Fildes, N. Paton, F. Dicksee, Leighton and J. Hoppner.

James (Jacques Joseph) Tissot (1836–1902) *Le Matin* mezzotint (RIGHT)
Tissot was a French painter-etcher and mezzotinter who studied in the studio of Sir Seymour Haydon. He was one of the many French artists who emigrated to England during the Paris Commune of 1870–71. His pictures of elegant women in social settings were reasonably popular, although *The Spectator*, 1879, attacked him for depicting a lady pouring tea for 'a couple of Hyde Park swells'. It commented: 'To have the power of painting almost perfectly anything in the world and to choose to paint a five-o'clock tea table?'

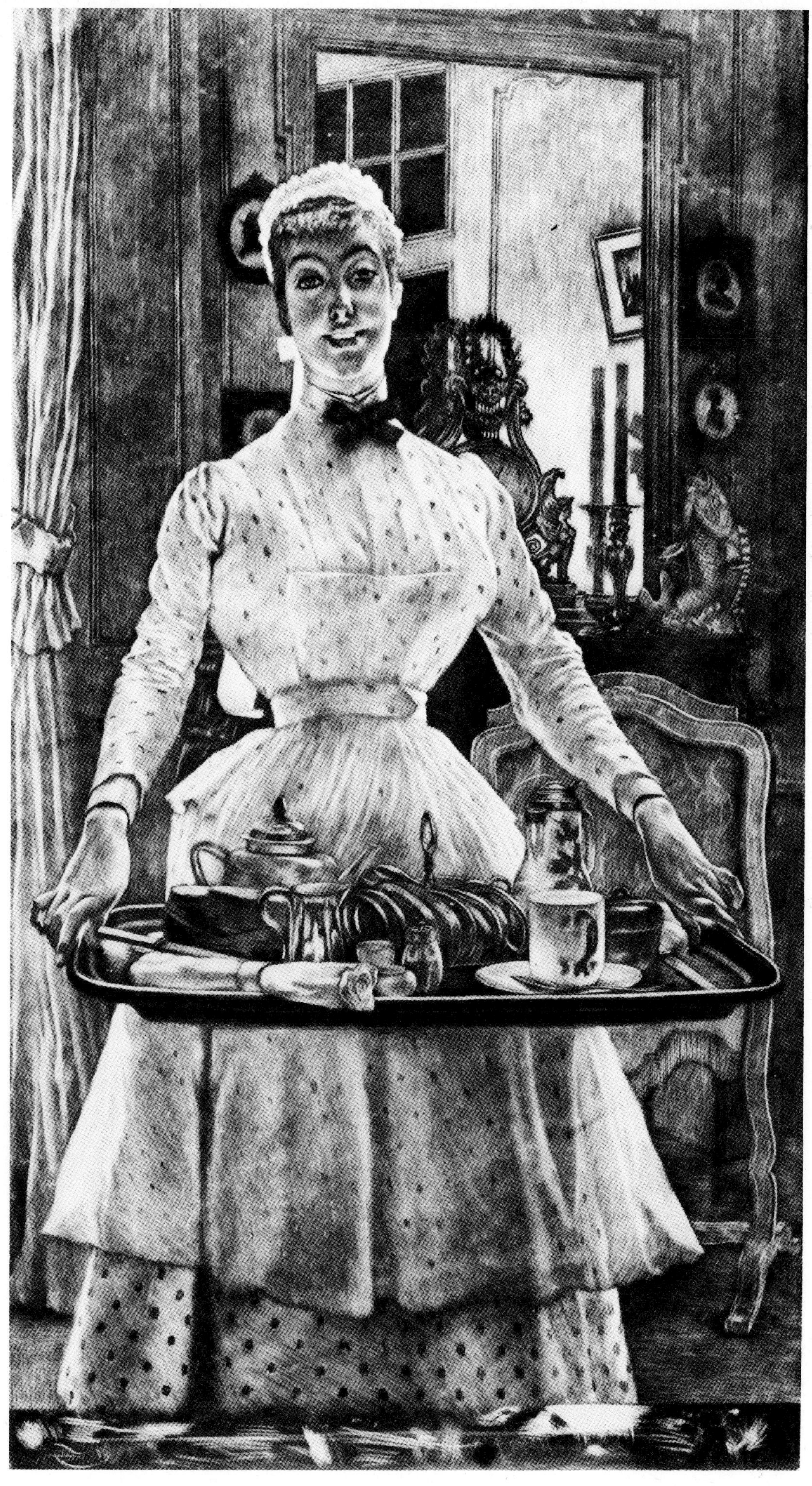

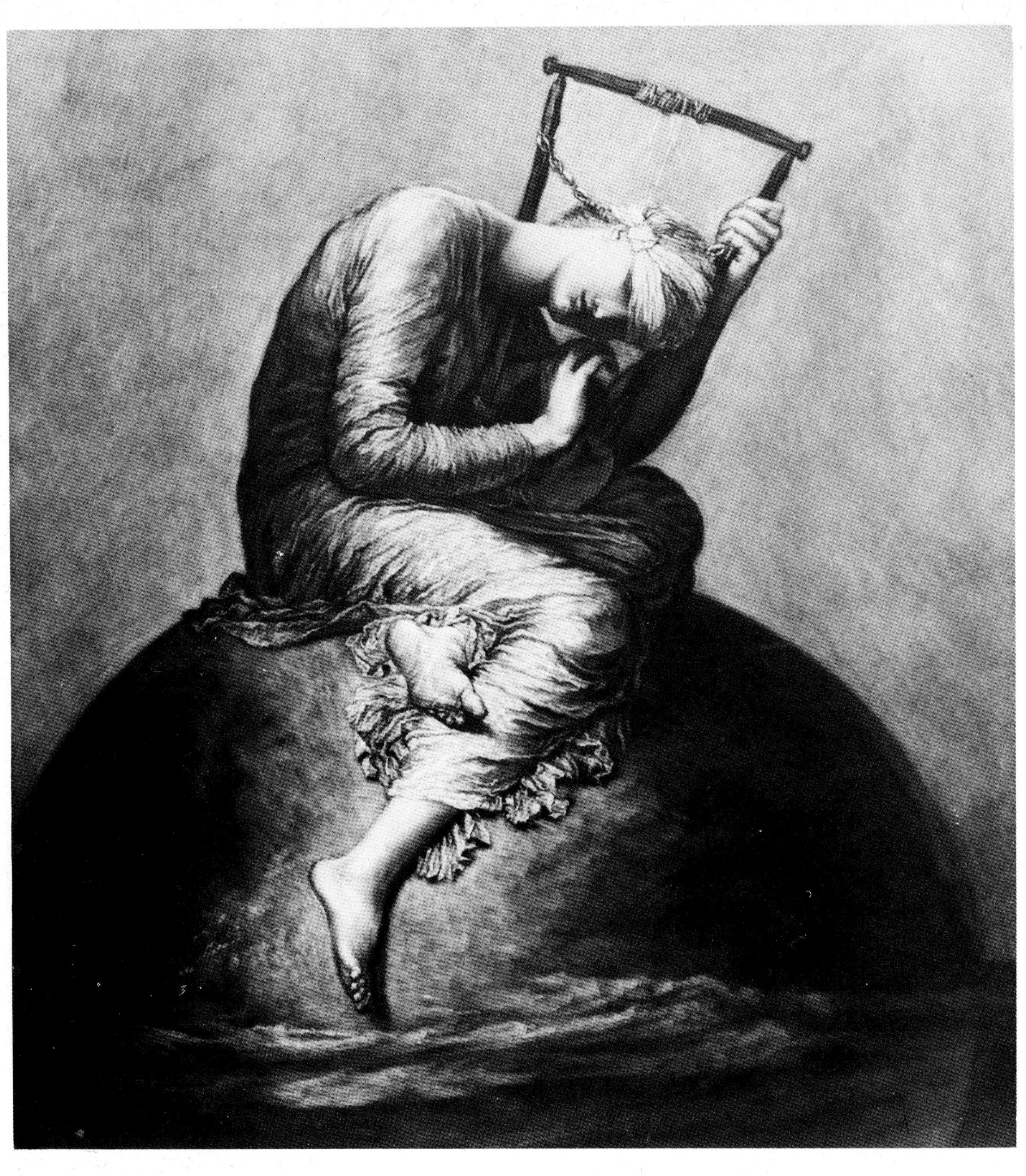

Sir Frank Short R.A. (1857–c.1906) *Hope* mezzotint
After the painting of 1886 by George Frederick Watts O.M., R.A. (1817–1904) which was widely reproduced. Short was a prominent engraver who worked after Watts, Constable, and Turner's *Liber Studiorum*, and was Director of Engraving at South Kensington School of Art. Reproductions of *Hope* were even given to the Egyptian troops after their defeat in the 1967 war.

86

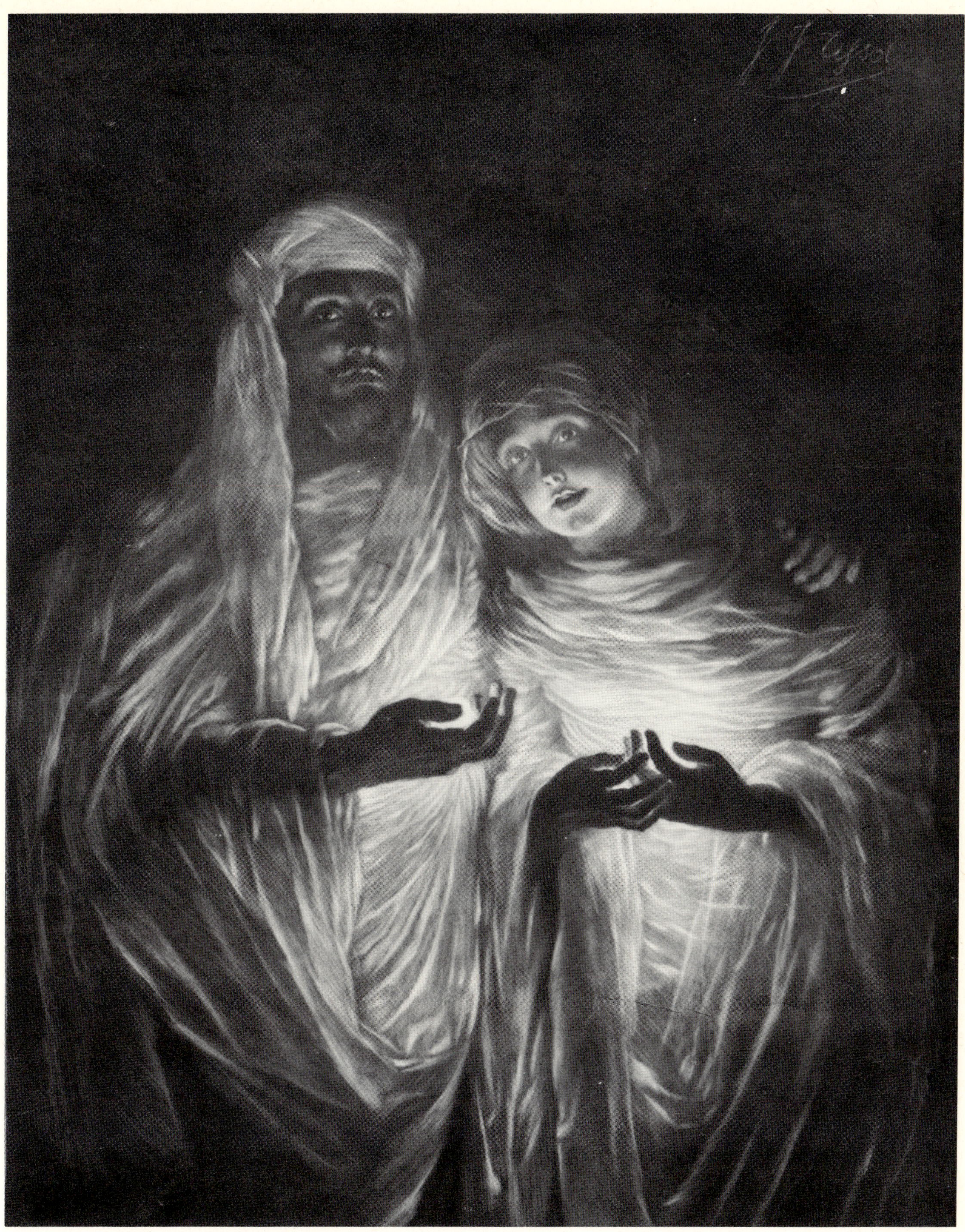

James Tissot (1836–1902) *Apparition Mediumque* mezzotint
Inscribed 'Dark Seance d'Eglinton du 20 Mai 1885 Londres', the picture may depict a seance held in the home of Tissot's mistress, Miss Kathleen Irene Newton. In addition to mezzotint, Tissot was an accomplished member of the new School of Painter-Etchers. He etched works such as *The Trafalgar Tavern* 1878, a work similar to Whistler's etchings.

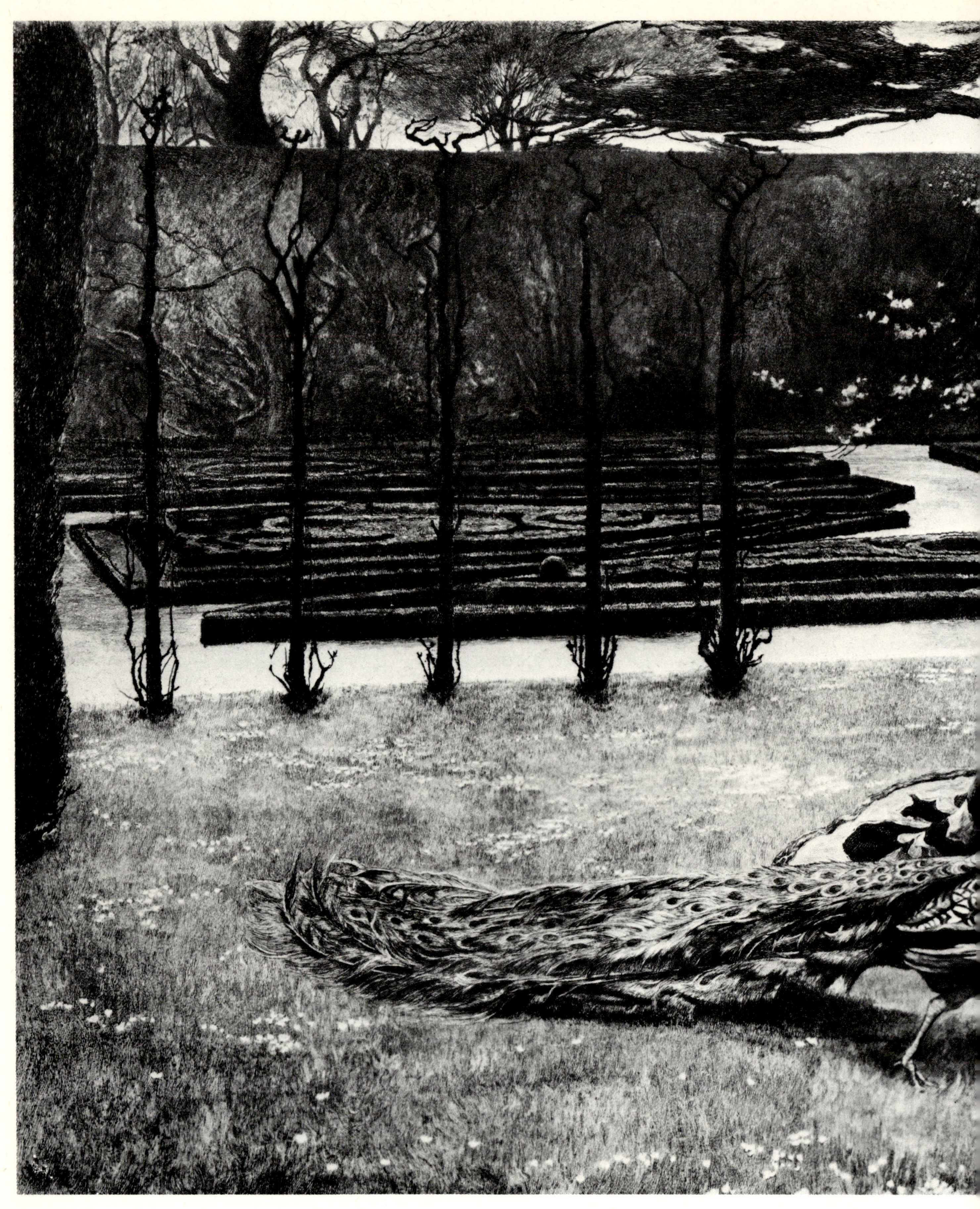

Charles Oliver Murray, R.A. (1842–1923) *My Lady's Garden* etching in brown tone
After the painting (R.A. 1899) by John Young Hunter (born 1874). Published in 1904. The etching was exhibited at the Academy in 1901. It is an example of the aestheticism of Oscar Wilde and Whistler, with Renaissance-inspired costume popularized by the Pre-Raphaelites.

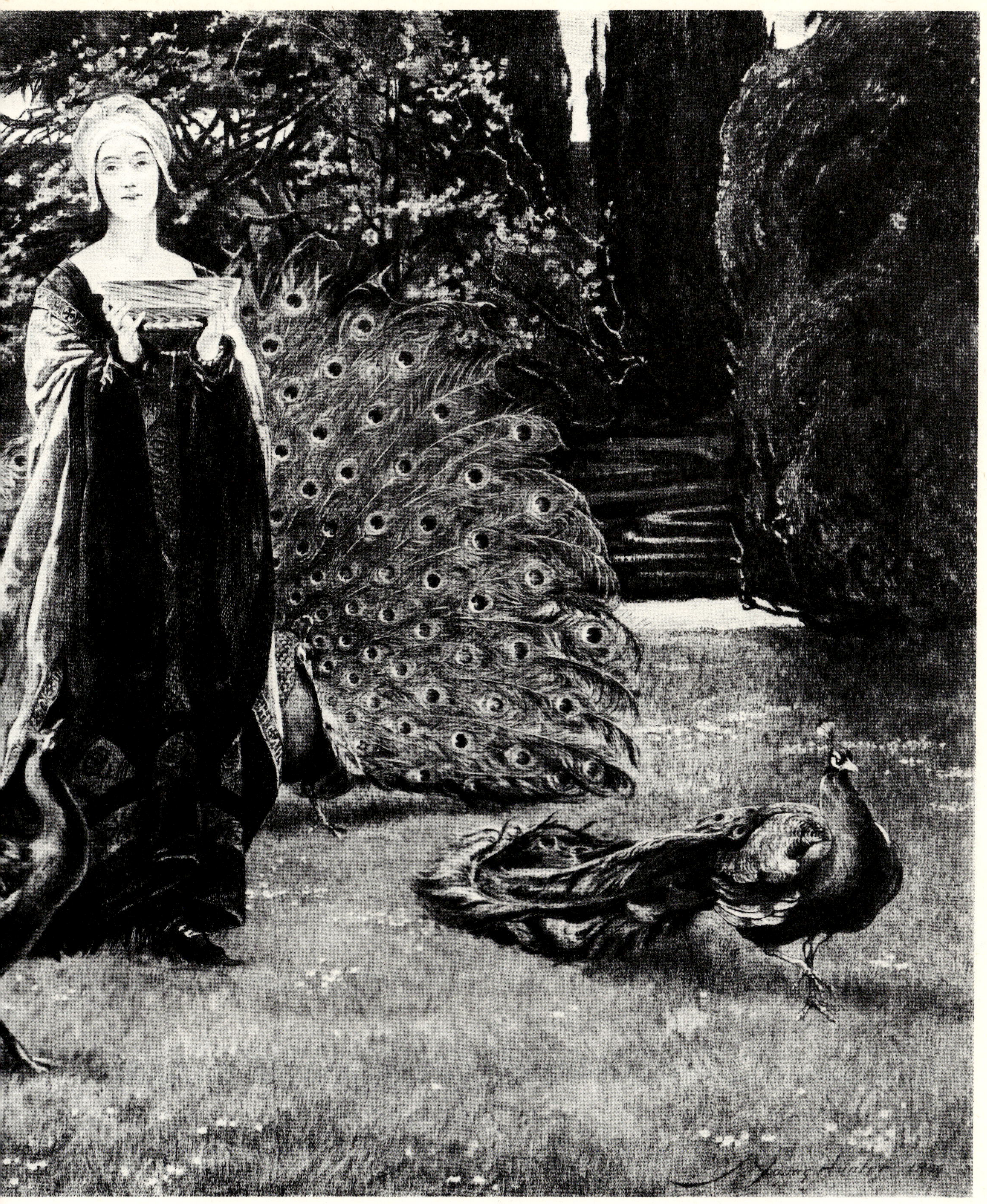

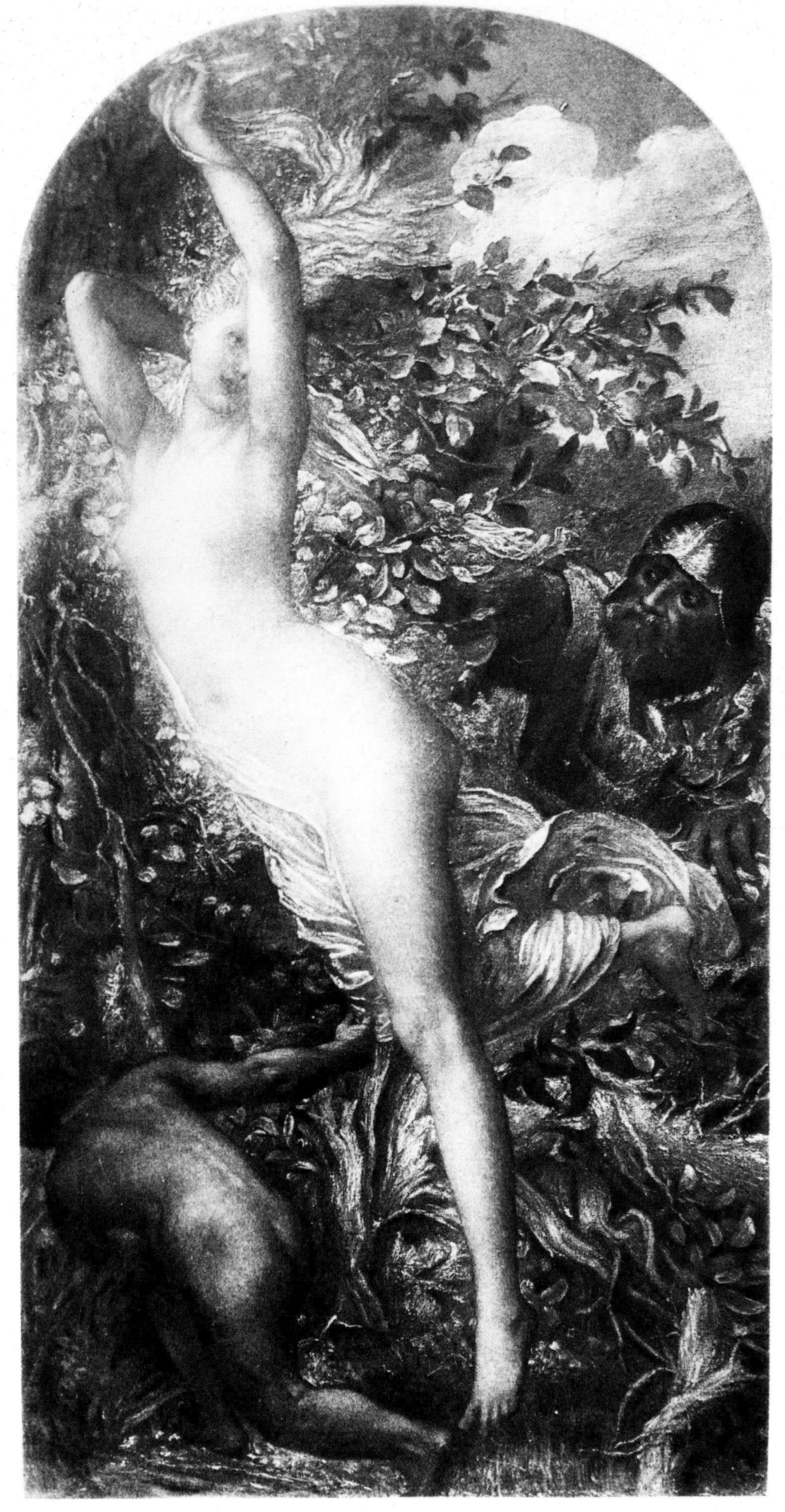

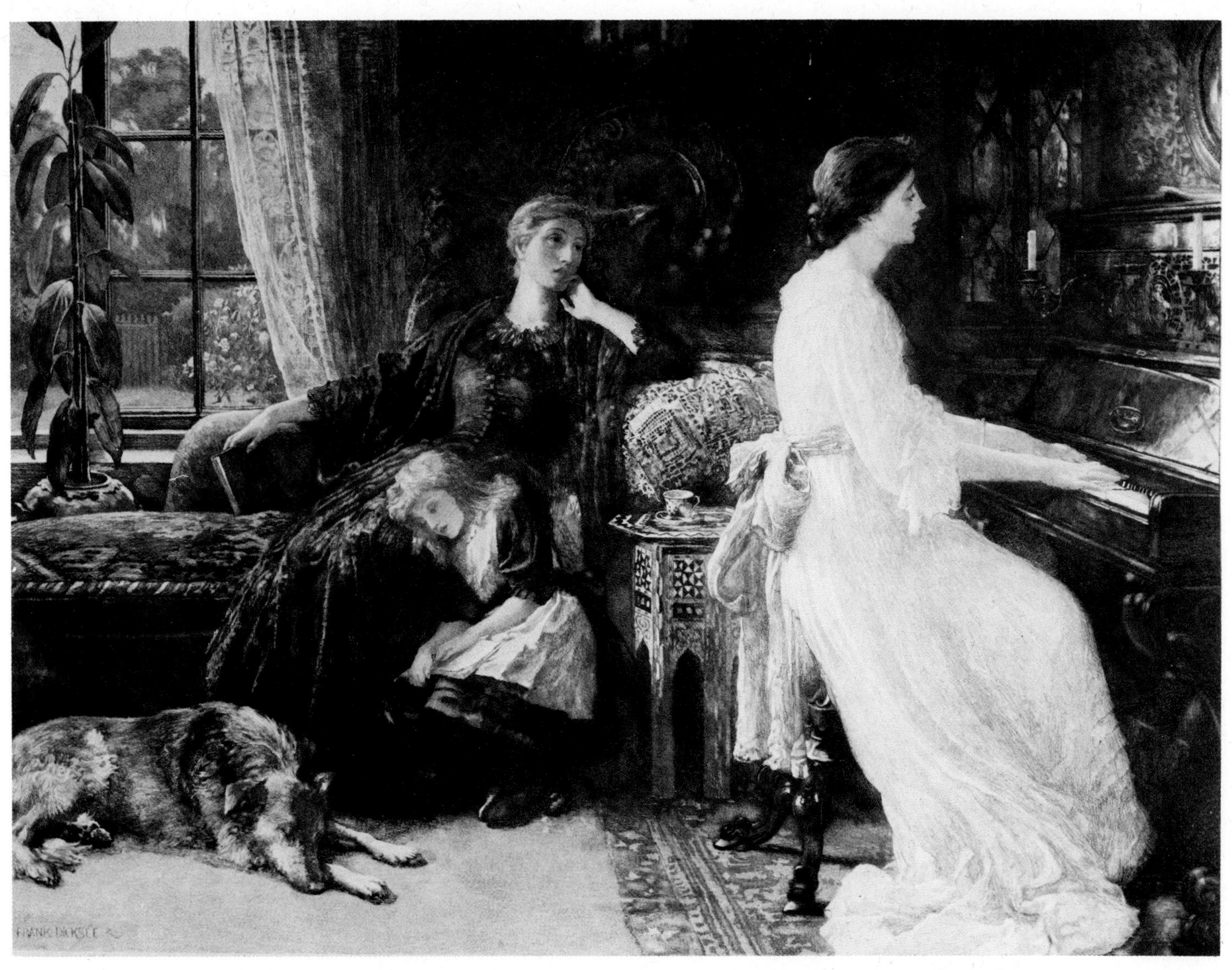

Herbert Dicksee (1862–1942) *Memories* etching
After the painting by Sir Frank Dicksee P.R.A. (1853–1928), published in 1892. Dicksee etched several other works besides the paintings of his brother Frank. Most of these were highly sentimental animal subjects, published by Frost and Reed Ltd. of Bristol.

Fata Morgana photogravure (Also etched by James Dobie, and exhibited at the R.A. 1893) (LEFT)
After the paintings by G. F. Watts O.M., R.A. (1817–1904). Most of Watts's paintings depicted classical-style figures which were covered with a thick veil of pigment. This was thought to add an extra dimension, 'a certain sense of celestial perfume'. Consequently they were difficult to accurately reproduce except by etching and photogravure. The subject here is Orlando's pursuit of the fairy Morgana (symbolizing Fortune or Opportunity) to secure a key with which he can release a group of imprisoned knights (symbolizing Servitude). (*Art Journal*)

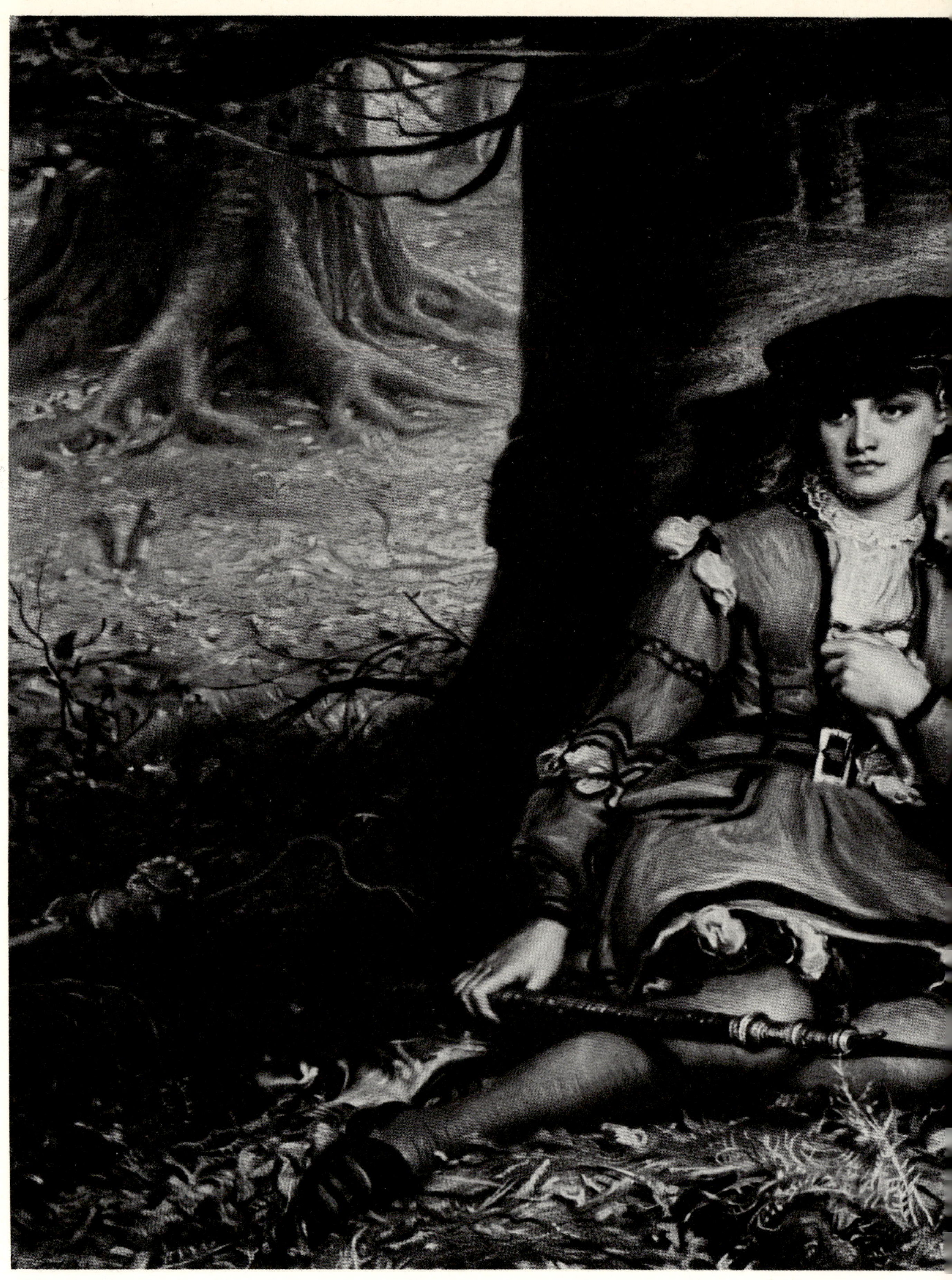

William Henry Simmons (1811–1882) *Rosalind and Celia – a scene from Shakespeare's 'As You Like It'* mezzotint
After the painting (R.A. 1868) by John Everett Millais, published by Henry Graves in 1870 and declared to the
Printsellers' Association

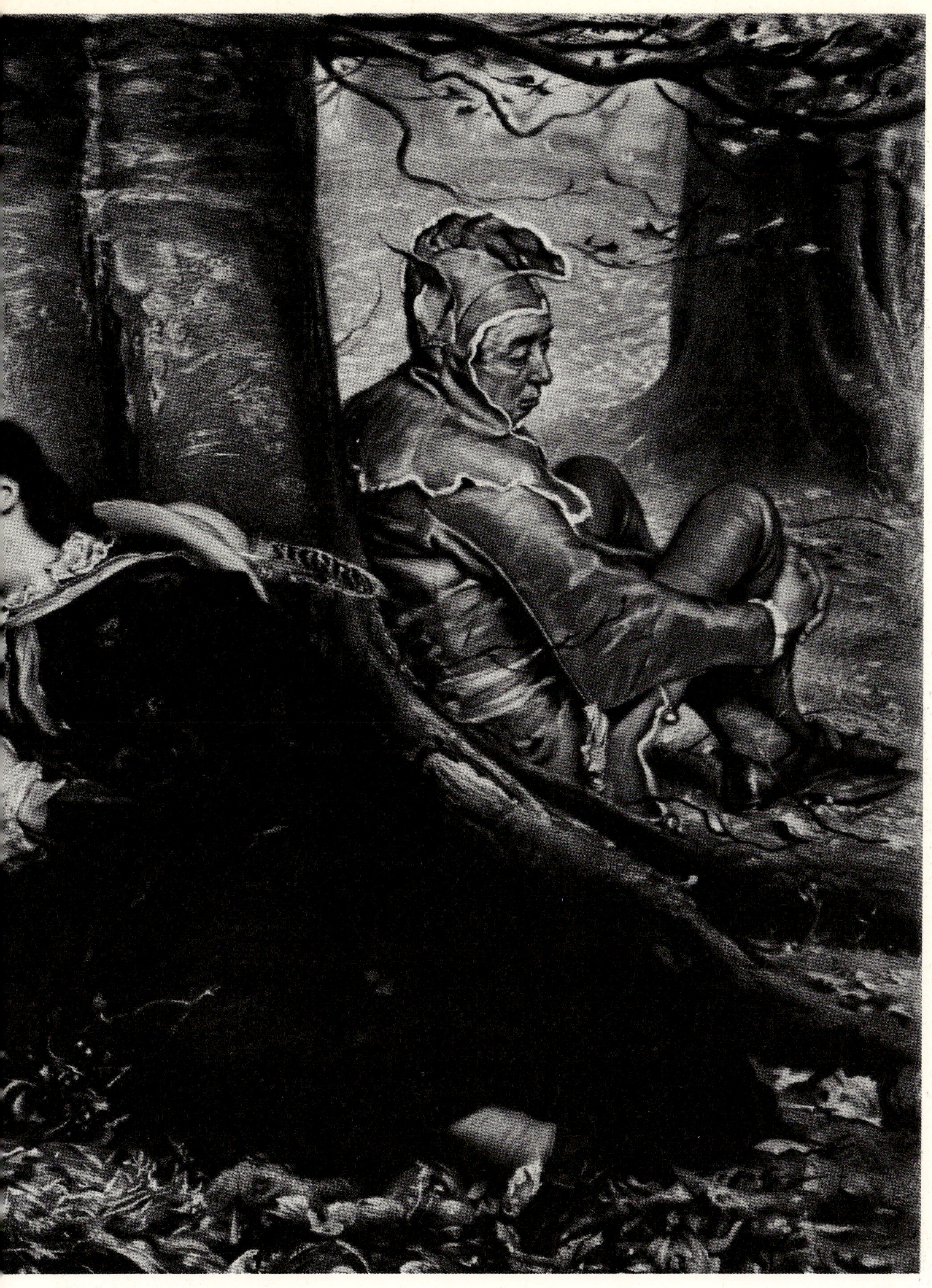

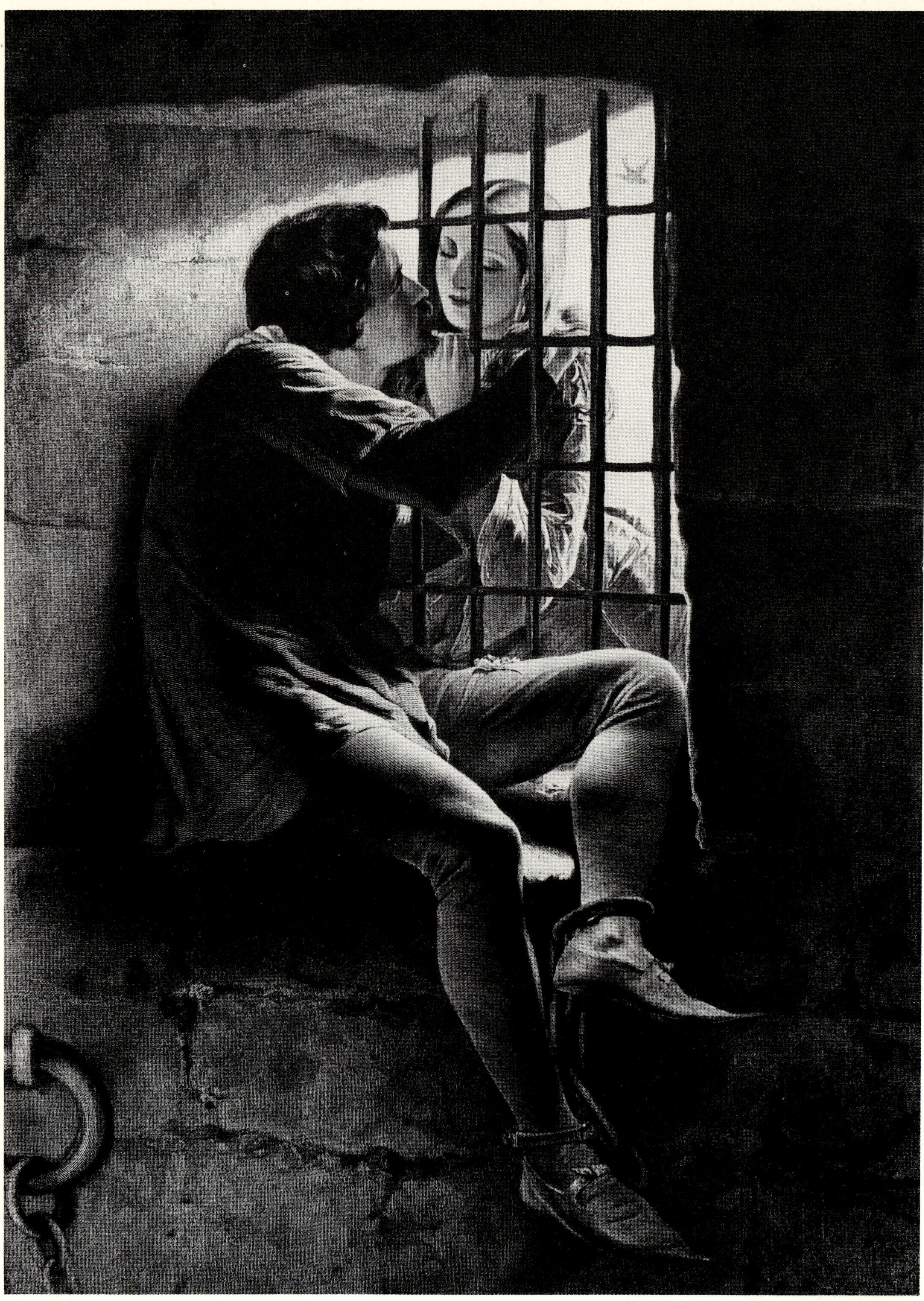

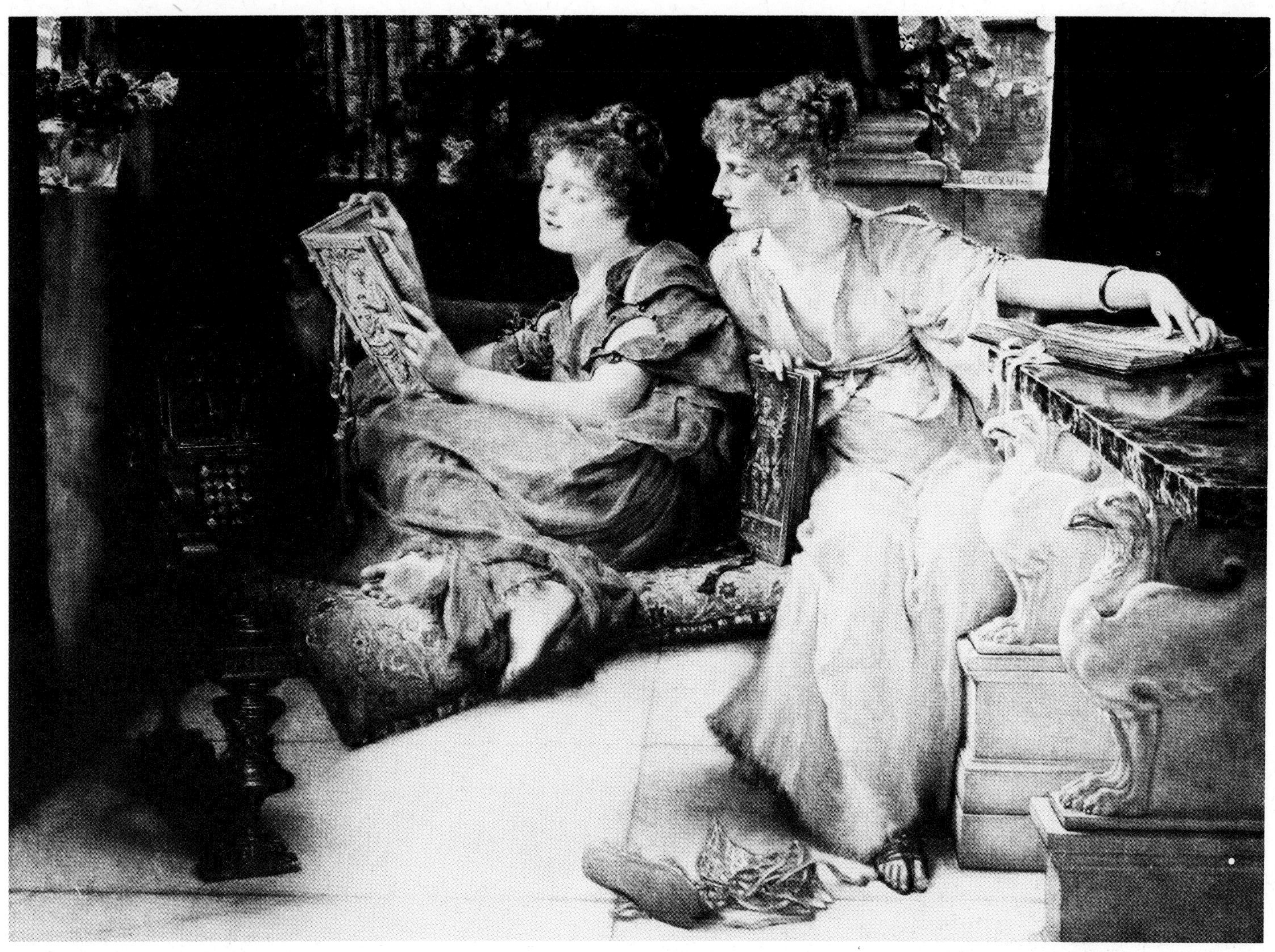

Two girls reading photogravure
After the painting by Alma-Tadema, published by Stephen T. Gooden in 1893 and declared to the Printsellers' Association

William Holl *Prison's Solace: 'When love with unconfined wings'* stipple engraving (LEFT)
After the painting (R.A. 1859) by Robert Carrick, published by Moore, McQueen and Company in 1863 and declared to the Printsellers' Association

BIBLIOGRAPHY

Agnew, Thos. and Sons, *Catalogue of Engravings and Etchings*, London 1907.
Aslin, E., 'The Rise and Progress of the Art Union of London', *Apollo*, London 1967, vol. 85, no. 1 (p. 12f).
Beck, H., *Victorian Engravings*, Victoria and Albert Museum Catalogue, London 1973.
Beraldi, H., *Les gravures du XIX siècle; guide de l'amateur de l'estampe moderne*, Paris 1885–92.
Bryan, M., *Dictionary of Painters and Engravers*, London 1903.
Chaloner-Smith, J., *British Mezzotint Portraits*, 4 vols., London 1878–83.
Clark, K., *Ruskin Today*, London 1964.
Cleaver, J., *A History of Graphic Art*, London 1963.
Clive, M., *The Day of Reckoning*, London 1964.
Davenport, C., *Mezzotints*, London 1904.
Engen, R., *Dictionary of Victorian Engravers and their work*, in preparation.
Fagan, L., *Engraving in England*, 3 vols., London 1893.
Farleigh, J., *The Graven Image: An Autobiographical Textbook*, London 1940.
Frost and Reed Ltd., *Catalogue of Etchings and Engravings*, Bristol 1925.
Gilbey, W., 'The Royal Academy and Engravers', *The Times*, 15 April 1903.
Grant, Col. M. H., *A Dictionary of British Etchers*, London 1952.
The Graphic Portfolio, London 1877.
Graves, A., *Catalogue of the works of the late Edwin Landseer, R.A.*, London 1874.
 Royal Academy of Arts 1769–1904, London 1905.
Hardie, M., *Catalogue of Modern Wood Engravings*, Victoria and Albert Museum, London 1906.
Harris, E. M., *Experimental Printing Processes in England 1800–1859*, Reading 1965.
Herkomer, H., *Etching and Mezzotint Engraving*, London 1892.
 'Drawing and Engraving on Wood', *Art Journal*, 1882 (p. 136f).
Hind, A. M., *A History of Engraving and Etching*, London 1908.
Hubbard, H., *Some Victorian Draughtsmen*, Cambridge 1944.
Hughes, T., *Prints for the Collector*, London 1970.
Ivins, W. M., *How Prints Look*, New York 1943.
Lewis, C. T., *The Story of Picture Printing in England during the Nineteenth Century*, London n.d.
Lilien, O. M., *History of Industrial Gravure Printing to 1920*, London 1972.
Linton, W. J., *Masters of Wood-Engraving*, London 1895.
Martindale, P. H., *Engraving Old and Modern*, London 1928.
McLean, R., *Victorian Book Design and Colour Printing*, London 1963.
 Reminiscences of Edmund Evans, Engraver, Oxford 1967.
The Printseller, London 1903–
Printsellers' Association, *List of Engravings*, London 1847–75, 1892, 1894, 1912.
Redgrave, S., *Dictionary of Artists of the English School*, London 1874.
Reid, F., *Illustrators of the Sixties*, London 1928.
Reitlinger, H., *From Hogarth to Keene*, London 1938.
Sitwell, S., *Narrative Pictures*, London 1969.
Slater, J. H., *Engravings and their Value*, London 1929.
Smith, Dr. F. B., *Radical Artisan: James Linton 1812–97*, Manchester 1974.
Wedmore, F., *Etching in England*, London 1895.
White, G., *English Illustrators of the Sixties*, London 1928.
Whitman, A., *Masters of Mezzotint*, London 1898.
Wood, C., *Dictionary of Victorian Painters*, London 1971.